Books are to be returned on or before
the last date below.

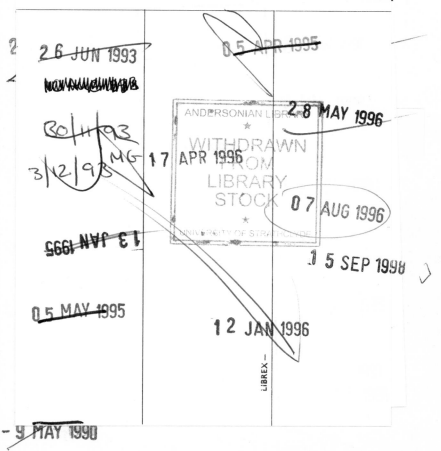

2 6 JUN 1993

30/11/93

3/12/93 MG 17 APR 1996

ANDERSONIAN LIBRARY
★
WITHDRAWN
FROM
LIBRARY
STOCK 07 AUG 1996
★
UNIVERSITY OF STRATHCLYDE

2 8 MAY 1996

0 5 APR 1995

13 JAN 1995

1 5 SEP 1998

0 5 MAY 1995

1 2 JAN 1996

- 9 MAY 1990

LIBREX —

Tools and Techniques
for
Strategic Management

A Related Journal

LONG RANGE PLANNING*

The Journal of the Society for Strategic and Long Range Planning and of the European Planning Federation

Editor: Professor Bernard Taylor, The Administrative Staff College, Greenlands, Henley-on-Thames, Oxon RG9 3AU, England

The leading international journal in the field of long-range planning, which aims to focus the attention of senior managers, administrators, and academics on the concepts and techniques involved in the development and implementation of strategy and plans.

Free specimen copy gladly sent on request.

Tools and Techniques
for
Strategic Management

by

Patrick B. McNamee

University of Ulster, U.K.

PERGAMON PRESS

OXFORD · NEW YORK · TORONTO · SYDNEY · PARIS · FRANKFURT

U.K.	Pergamon Press Ltd., Headington Hill Hall, Oxford OX3 0BW, England
U.S.A.	Pergamon Press Inc., Maxwell House, Fairview Park, Elmsford, New York 10523, U.S.A.
CANADA	Pergamon Press Canada Ltd., Suite 104, 150 Consumers Rd, Willowdale, Ontario M2J 1P9, Canada
AUSTRALIA	Pergamon Press (Aust.) Pty. Ltd., P.O. Box 544, Potts Point, N.S.W. 2011, Australia
FRANCE	Pergamon Press SARL, 24 rue des Ecoles, 75240 Paris, Cedex 05, France
FEDERAL REPUBLIC OF GERMANY	Pergamon Press GmbH, Hammerweg 6, D-6242 Kronberg-Taunus, Federal Republic of Germany

First edition 1985

Library of Congress Cataloging in Publication Data
McNamee, Patrick B.
Tools & techniques for strategic management.
Includes bibliographies.
1. Corporate planning. 2. Industrial management.
I. Title. II. Title: Tools and techniques for strategic management.
HD30.28.M3855   1985   658.4'012   84-25363

British Library Cataloguing in Publication Data
McNamee, Patrick B.
Tools & techniques for strategic management.
1. Corporate planning
I. Title
658.4'012   HD30.28
ISBN 0-08-031810-X (Hardcover)
ISBN 0-08-031809-6 (Flexicover)

658·40101 '84
MACN

*Printed and bound in Great Britain by
Biddles Ltd, Guildford and King's Lynn*

For Brid

Preface

THIS book aims to show how some of the best-known contemporary approaches to strategic management can be linked together and applied. The book tries to achieve a balance between the theoretical and the practical aspects of the subject, i.e. although it should contain enough research and theoretical material to satisfy advanced undergraduate business policy students and MBA students, it also has the practical orientation necessary for practising managers. Other distinctive features are:

The extensive and up-to-date bibliographies which are given at the end of each chapter. These bibliographies should help readers focus on contemporary publications relevant to their particular interests or circumstances.

The inclusion of small computer programs written in BASIC. As the price of microcomputers continues to fall and they become more widely available to students and business planners at all levels, it seem appropriate to include programs which will help readers use certain of the tools and techniques covered in the book. Consequently, it will be assumed, throughout the book, that readers will be able to generate easily, on a computer, the quantitative elements necessary for certain sections.

The highlighting of strategic issues through extensive references to the current strategies and behaviour of well-publicised international companies.

A schematic representation of how the various tools and techniques are linked together in this book is shown in Fig. 1.

The fundamental concepts and terms in strategic management, which will be employed in subsequent chapters, and the overall competitive context in which businesses operate are considered in Chapter 1. This chapter is really concerned with acquainting the reader with certain fundamentals — specific terminology and concepts which are frequently used in strategic management plus an appreciation of the importance of the competitive environment for business. Building upon this, the book

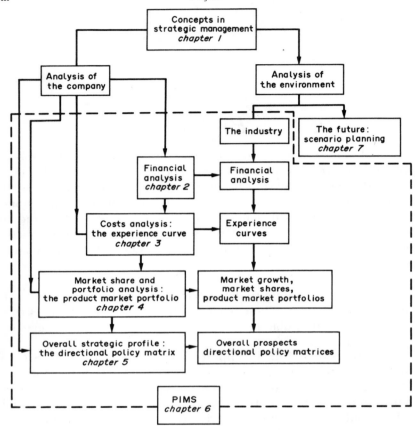

FIG. 1. *Overview showing how the tools and techniques for strategic management are integrated*

then proceeds, by means of a series of linked and largely incremental steps.

The first of these steps is taken in Chapter 2, where financial analysis for strategic management is considered. It is the philosophy of this book that it is very difficult to make a strategic judgement about a firm itself, its position or performance within its industry, and its future potential without using the only common and universal unit of performance measurement — money. Hence a knowledge of financial analysis is assumed to be a prerequisite to a sound understanding of strategic management. Finance is considered from a strategic rather than an accounting point of view and makes two major linked contributions. Firstly, the strategic control contribution, i.e. how finance can be used to implement, monitor and evaluate business strategy. Secondly, the creative strategic contribution, i.e. how a knowledge of finance can be used to power a firm towards its objectives and to give it advantage over its competitors. Additionally, as with all the tools and techniques considered, financial analysis is considered from two perspectives. From the perspective of the firm itself, i.e. the quality of its current financial performance measured against its historical performance, and secondly from an industry or competitive perspective, i.e. how does the firm's financial performance compare with other competitors and potential competitors in the same or adjacent industries?

Chapter 3 abstracts from the multidimensional strategic context in which all firms exist and concentrates on analysing just one fundamental component of a company's strategic position — its costs. Costs are of crucial importance because, in any industry, that company with the lowest costs, all other things being equal, should enjoy the highest profits. Although there are many ways of effecting cost reductions, this chapter examines in detail just one approach which seems to be of particular importance in today's global market place — experience curve analysis. A knowledge of experience curve effects, for certain industries at least, appears to be essential either for the success of one's own firm or for its defence.

Experience curve analysis has, primarily, a production orientation and, as portrayed in Chapter 3, is concerned exclusively with single-product situations. This somewhat narrow perspective is expanded in Chapter 4, through the Product Market Portfolio model, to consider two other crucial determinants of strategic position:

> Management of the overall portfolio of businesses that a multi-business company will have, i.e. how to achieve overall corporate objectives while simultaneously accommodating the inevitable diversity of behaviour and results inherent in a multibusiness company.

> Market appraisal, i.e. appraising the market prospects for each market sector in which the company is competing and also appraising the strategic position of each business in its particular market.

Chapter 5 builds upon Chapter 4 by expanding the criteria upon which a business's strategic position is based from the somewhat narrow marketing oriented criteria to include a large variety of other complementary criteria. This is achieved principally through the use of the Directional Policy Matrix model. As with the Product Market Portfolio model, this is an excellent device for succinctly displaying a company's internal strategic balance and also its strategic position relative to its competitors.

Chapter 6 is an exposition of selected findings of the PIMS program.

It therefore differs philosophically from the other chapters in that it relies for its strategic currency upon the analysis of a large pool of data provided by a very large number of diverse businesses. In this respect it is a unique chapter in that it asserts that past experience is a good guide to the future. This chapter is included because, in the view of the author, as the PIMS program is the largest and most comprehensive business data base ever developed, a textbook concerned with contemporary tools and techniques of strategic management must examine this most significant contribution.

Chapter 7 is concerned with scenario planning and considers how this approach can help managers set up scenarios which will turn out to be realistic contexts in which the tools and techniques of strategic management can be applied.

The final chapter — Chapter 8 — examines, briefly, some of the implications that microcomputers have had and will have for strategic management. Its major function is to explain the use of the computer programs which are on the disk which can be purchased with this book. Listings of the programs are also provided, in this chapter, for readers who wish to tailor the programs to run on computers other than the Apple II Europlus and the Apple IIe.

Included at the end of this Preface is a spreadsheet which summarises the type of problem that the subject matter of each chapter attempts to solve and also summarises the advantages and disadvantages of each technique. This spreadsheet is meant to give the reader a quick indication as to which technique might be most appropriate for the issues that he is considering.

At a more personal level now that this book is completed, I would like to thank the many people whose influence, ideas, assistance and patience have made it possible. First of all, and most importantly, my family — Brid, David and Stephen — for their forbearance and encouragement; the University of Ulster for its support; Professor Krish Bhaskar of the University of East Anglia for encouraging my writing and research aspirations; my fellow participants on the ITP Program held in Manchester 1980; my summer colleagues at Northeastern University, Boston, especially Professor Dan McCarthy; Professor Bernard Taylor of the Administrative Staff College, Henley, for his many ideas and suggestions; David Hussey of Harbridge House Europe for his constructive criticisms, his guidance and all the efforts he made on my behalf. Finally, it is most important that I thank a large group of people who have been a constant source of inspiration and encouragement to me — the students at the University of Ulster.

PATRICK B. McNAMEE

Spreadsheet Showing How the Tools and Techniques for Strategic Management are Used

Problem to be solved	Chapter	Advantages and disadvantages
Unfamiliarity with selected concepts of strategic management. Ascertaining the nature of the industry in which the business competes in terms of the five competitive forces. Defining the business in the context of its competitive environment. Determining the internal capabilities and potential of the business.	Chapter 1 Concepts in Strategic Management	Essential for readers who are new to strategic management. Enables a business to be perceived in terms of its industry location. Enables a business's internal configuration to be ascertained.
Determining the financial performance in the industry. Ascertaining the financial performance of a single firm. Comparing the firm's performance with that of competitors. Using a knowledge of finance to gain strategic advantage over competitors.	Chapter 2 Finance for Strategic Management	Essential to ascertain the "bottom line" for the business. A crucial reality in formulating strategy. Major advantage: enables a quick diagnosis to be carried out. Major disadvantage: the figures may not reflect reality: they may reflect "creative accounting".
Is the nature of the industry such that having a low cost–high volume strategy can confer advantage? If this is so then: What is the cost of position of the business *vis-à-vis* others in the industry? Does the firm have the resources to compete against those firms with the lowest costs? Can the feasibility and risk of embarking upon a low cost strategy for the business be appraised?	Chapter 3 Experience Curve Analysis	Major advantages: in certain industries the use of experience strategies can provide significant competitive advantages. Major disadvantages: too narrow a perspective; can be a risky strategy when the environment changes. May be more suited to an era of growth. Can be very expensive to implement.

Chapter 4 — Product Market Portfolio Analysis

Does the firm have a portfolio of products or a portfolio of SBUs? If so then:
Is it difficult to strategically manage the diversity of the portfolio in order to achieve corporate goals?
Is the nature of the industries in which the firm competes such that having high relative market share strategies can confer advantage?
What are the relative market shares of the various businesses in the portfolio?
Is the firm's portfolio balanced?
What are the risks of following a product market portfolio strategy?

Major advantages: can provide very quickly a strategic picture of a diverse firm.
Good for businesses where market growth and relative market share are fundamental determinants of success.
Major disadvantages: too narrow a perspective — strategic position may depend upon more than just two parameters. The link between profitability and relative market share may be weak. More suited to an era of growth.

Chapter 5 — The Directional Policy Matrix and Other Matrix Displays

Does the firm have a portfolio of products or a portfolio of SBUs? If so then:
Is it difficult to strategically manage the diversity of the portfolio in order to achieve corporate goals?
Is the nature of the industries in which the firm competes such that strategic position is determined by factors other than, or in addition to, relative market share and market growth rate?
Is the portfolio balanced?

Major advantage: enables a multi-attribute strategic position of a diverse firm to be graphically and clearly displayed.
Major disadvantages: May be excessive subjectivity in determining strategic position. Strategic position can be determined by just two nebulous figures.

Chapter 6 — The PIMS Findings

Are there any "laws of the market place" that govern business strategy?
Is there empirical evidence which suggests what these laws are?
Is there a "normal" ROI, cash flow, profit level, etc., for a particular business?
What are the major factors that determine the particular levels of ROI, cash flow, etc., for various industries and businesses?
What will be the effects of changes of strategy upon a particular business?

Major advantage: a unique contribution, the largest business data base ever assembled.
Major disadvantages: may be lack of independence in the "independent" variables. Ignores behavioural realities. Assumes that the past is a good guide to the future.
Does not allow for the variety of goals found in business. Too slanted towards large American firms.

Is the future of the industry likely to be difficult to predict? Has the firm, historically, been disadvantaged through assuming that the past would be a good guide to the future? How can a scenario which will help solve this problem be constructed?	Chapter 7 Scenario Planning	Major advantage: allows non-extrapolative forecasts to be made with provision for handling sudden environmental shocks through contingency planning. Requires managerial creativity. Major disadvantages: not built upon past experiences. Not neatly structured. Requires managerial creativity!
Tedious calculations which are frequently necessary for strategic management.	Chapter 8 Microcomputer Programs for Strategic Management	Major advantage: frees managers from tedious calculations. Major disadvantages: requires some commitment to learning a little about operating computers. Can lead to addiction to using microcomputers.

Contents

List of Tables

List of Figures

CHAPTER 1

Concepts in Strategic Management

Introduction

How a challenge is perceived will determine how the challenge is met. In some aspects of management limited perceptions are relatively unimportant. In strategic management the quality of perception is crucial. If challenges are not perceived through high-quality multi-dimensional filters, then the consequences can be disastrous. Hussey has illustrated this well in terms of Europe's motor cycle manufacturers' strategic reaction to the challenge posed by Japanese manufacturers.

> ". . . But if you misdefine the market you probably miss opportunities, and underestimate the competition, which means that strategic decisions at the level of the business may be wrong. If the Japanese have started to penetrate your market, based on factories designed to serve the world, your intention to build a modern plant to serve the UK only is likely to be wrong, and to be a waste of resources in the long term. For example, in its dying moments the British Motor Cycle industry achieved production rates of 18 cycles per man year. Doubling productivity would have seemed a worthwhile achievement, until one realises that the Japanese factories produced 200–350 motor cycles per man year." (Ref. (11), p. 12.)

A similar example of the importance of having high-quality strategic perception is afforded by the consequences of subscribing, unquestioningly, to "orthodox" wisdom. Thus, it is a commonly held view that a major problem with Europe in general, and the United Kingdom in particular, has been the failure of business to invest in capacity increases and automation on a scale sufficiently large to compete effectively with U.S. and Japanese competitors. Implicit in this view is the sentiment that it is somehow a "good thing" for business to do this. After all, if the investment is carried out successfully, then costs will be reduced and so the business will be more competitive at home and abroad. Yet, when individual companies implement this, frequently costly and irreversible strategy, it is not unknown for them to find that, far from their profits increasing as a result of this action, they may actually decrease.*

The miscalculation is caused by strategic myopia. When the decision is appraised on financial grounds alone — on the basis of the reduced costs that will accrue through the increased investment — the exercise does indeed seem worthwhile. However, when a strategic perspective is applied, then several complicating elements enter the equation, namely:

Those industries that appear to require, and benefit most from, increased investment to increase the scale of their operations — for example, automobiles and oil refining — are frequently industries which have, already, a very high level of capital investment. As a consequence, these industries require that their plants must be loaded as fully as possible. This requirement has three major effects:

— it causes "volume at all costs", rather than say profitability, or return on investment, to become the core of all strategies;
— it increases the bargaining power of the employees, as it is imperative that the plant be kept as fully loaded as possible and it is less costly to accede to employee demands than to risk closing the plant;
— competitors develop a similar predisposition towards keeping their plants as fully loaded as possible.

Thus the nature of the competition in the industry becomes one of volume grabbing at all costs, and this may lead to price wars and increased promotional costs. Consequently, due to the erosion of the gap between costs and revenues, the hoped-for benefits of the increased investment do not accrue to the company. But two major groups do benefit — the public, through reduced prices, and employees, through increased bargaining power.

In summary, and at a more general level, this strategic myopia is caused by a lack of understanding of the overall competitive context of the industry in which the business operates.

The above examples illustrate the importance of having an informed strategic perspective and presage what this book is about. It is concerned with ways of thinking about strategic challenges and formulating effective strategies.

Ways of Thinking About Strategic Challenges

This book is concerned about extending managers' mental horizons. This extension will be pursued, principally, along the following axes:

This illustration is taken from Ref (16) and is considered in greater detail in Chapter 6 page 192.

competitive, geographical, informational, quantitative, spatial, environmental and behavioural.

Competitive

Managerial awareness of, and sensitivity to, the locus of a business's competitive context is a fundamental determinant of the future success of a business.

Traditionally, this context has tended to be viewed from a single business discipline perspective. The perspective applied has tended to be a function of the backgrounds of the leaders or planners in the business and the nature of the industry in question. Table 1 illustrates typical patterns of perception.

However, Porter[15]* has shown very clearly that the competitive location of a firm in its industry cannot be inferred from such

Table 1. Patterns of Strategic Bias

Background of leaders	Principal areas of strategic interest and bias	Typical type of business/industry
Finance/ Accounting	Control of costs, efficiency; results measured by financial yardsticks, e.g. return on equity, earnings per share, return on investment, etc.	Mature, established industries, e.g. leather, textiles, also conglomerates
Marketing/ Sales	Market share, growth of market, developing new markets, results measured by marketing indices plus the above financial indices	Standard product industries, e.g. beer, soft drinks, standard electronics
Production/ R & D	Innovation in products and processes, technical superiority. Results measured by new product introductions plus the above financial indices	New industries, e.g. high-tech. industries such as information technology
Personnel/ Human relations	Motivation and happiness of workforce, results measured by productivity, strike record, absenteeism, etc., plus the above financial indices	Service industries where good atmosphere is important. Also new industries where creativity counts

Superscript numbers are to references at ends of chapters.

unidimensional perspectives, but rather it depends (as shown in Fig. 2) upon five economic and technical competitive forces that shape the industry. He further suggests that to compete effectively a firm should strive to find a position where it is best able to defend itself against these competitive forces or can influence them in its favour.

In order to do this a firm must know where it is located on the competitive map of its industry. Therefore, the starting point in strategic management is an industry structure analysis which will determine where a firm is located in relation to each of the five competitive forces. Each of these forces is now considered in greater detail.

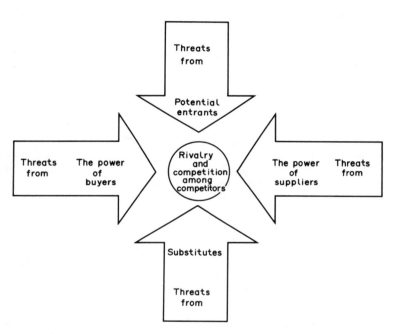

FIG. 2. *The five forces that shape the competitive environment (Ref. (15), p. 4)*

Threats from Potential Entrants

New entrants to an industry tend to make it more competitive. The additional competitiveness may be due to a number of factors including: the additional capacity which they bring with them, their attempts to build market share, or increased costs due to the building up of the costs of the factors of production.

However the effects of new entrants materialise, it is frequently in the interests of existing competitors to deter potential new entrants by making their prospects look as unattractive as possible. This can be done in two major ways — through the erection of barriers to entry and or through the threat of severe retaliation.

Clearly, it is in the interests of existing firms to have as high entry barriers as possible. Porter[15] lists six major barriers to entry which are:

economies of scale,
product differentiation,
capital requirements,
switching costs,
access to distribution channels,
cost disadvantages independent of scale, for example: proprietary knowledge,
government policy.

Two contrasting examples illustrate the importance of entry barriers to strategic planning. The U.K. aircraft engine manufacturer Rolls Royce has erected around it substantial entry barriers in the form of economies of scale, product differentiation, capital requirements, switching costs, proprietary knowledge, experience advantages and government support. It seems extremely unlikely that the threat of new entrants pose a threat to this company. The competitive threats which Rolls Royce faces come from other quarters.

By way of contrast, an "industry" that has grown rapidly in the early 1980s and which faces continuous threats from new entrants, because of the extremely low entry barriers, is retail domestic video rental libraries. In this industry many small independent entrepreneurs with limited resources have opened such businesses. They have been able to do so because of the low entry barriers: low capital requirements, low switching costs, immediate distribution and no major economies of scale being possible.*

Threats from Substitutes

Substitutes, or alternative products that can perform the same function, limit the price that an industry can charge for its products. Substitutes are not always perceived by an industry to be present, and indeed may only be noticed when it is too late to arrest their dominance. One topical example, which illustrates the rise of a substitute product, is the current increasing proliferation of low cost microcomputers plus low cost easy to use business packages in such areas as accounting, data base

---

Industries with low entry barriers tend to have many small independent firms. If the Yellow Pages of a telephone directory are consulted, it will be seen that those industries that have the largest number of independents tend to be those with the lowest entry barriers.

management and word processing. This "product" has adversely affected the "industry" of specialist programmers and specialist computer bureaux. It seems likely that this trend will continue.

Threats from the Power of Buyers

The more powerful the buyers from an industry are, the greater will be the presence on industry profits. Porter[15] suggests that buyers are particularly powerful when:

purchasers are large relative to sellers,
purchases represent a significant proportion of the buyers' costs,
purchases are undifferentiated,
there are few switching costs,
buyers earn low profits,
buyers have the potential for backward integration,
the buyers' product is not strongly affected by the quality of the suppliers' product,
the buyer has full information.

Again two contrasting U.K. examples are used to illustrate how buyer power influences two industries. In the U.K. retail clothing industry, chains such as Marks and Spencer and Burton are dominant. The power of such chains, relative to that of their clothing suppliers, is very great. Consequently, the major competitive, and of course, profit pressures which clothing suppliers face is that of the power of the buyers. In contrast, the domestic consumers (buyers) of electricity in the United Kingdom are very weak *vis-à-vis* the sole supplier of this product — the state monopoly.

Threats from the Bargaining Power of Suppliers

Powerful suppliers can have the same adverse effects upon profitability as powerful buyers. The big difference is the sources of their power — it is really the opposite of the sources of buyer power. Thus suppliers tend to be powerful when the following conditions obtain:

there are few of them,
there are few substitutes,
the industry supplied is not an important customer,
the suppliers' product is an important component to the buyer's business,
the supplier's product is differentiated,
suppliers can integrate forward.

The two industries which were used to illustrate the threat from the power of buyers are again used to illustrate the threat from the power of suppliers. Thus the retail clothing chains do not face serious competitive threats from the clothing supply industry while consumers of electricity are, more or less, at the mercy of the state monopoly.

Rivalry and Competition Among Competitors

Industries do not, in general, have the same competitive temperature. Some industries are much more inclined to severe competition than others: for example, the level of competition that obtains in the petrol retailing industry is much greater than that which obtains in the private health care industry. Rivalry or competition can take many forms, from simple price competition to competition in such areas as product quality, after sales service, warranty periods, etc. Some of the major determinants of strong competition are listed below:

many equally balanced competitors,
slow rate of industry growth,
high fixed or storage costs,
lack of differentiation,
capacity can only be increased by large amounts,
there are many diverse competitors,
there are higher strategic stakes,
there are high exit barriers.

It is in the context of the above five dimensional competitive environment that strategic decisions should be made. The context for each firm and industry, as illustrated above, tends to be different and therefore the types of strategic action necessary for success will be shaped by the overall industry structure. Therefore, one of the first steps in strategic analysis should be an industry structure analysis, with the objective of locating the firm in its competitive environment. Henderson[9] made a similar point about the importance of the competitive environment when he talked about Competitive Mapping. He has suggested that companies will only be able to evolve effective strategies after they have plotted their own and their competitors' locations on a competitive map. Once an individual company has done this, then its strategy should be to move against the weakest sectors in its competitive map.

Geographical

The complementary trends of the "shrinking of the world" — in terms of transport and communication — and the expansion of international trade have determined that, today, strategic management is, for almost all businesses, a global rather than a national or regional discipline. Businesses which fail to recognise and respond to this additional dimension will ultimately perish. The trend towards international business strategies with marketing, production, finance, personnel, etc., planned on a global basis has been, and will continue to be, inexorable. Expertise in this global strategic perception is evinced perhaps most clearly by Japanese manufacturers:

> "Implementation in a Global Marketplace . . .
>
> One of the key reasons that the Japanese have made such inroads into American and European markets is often cited: their ability to look at the entire world as a potential marketplace, while Americans, especially, think primarily in terms of their domestic market. This global marketing view held by the Japanese provides the framework for a five-step implementation cycle of their strategy. . .". (Ref. (17), p. 40.)

This concept of a global competitive environment is important not just for what are conventionally considered to be global industries such as, for example, automobiles, but also for industries which have traditionally had "parishes" of advantage and consequently, protection. An industry's parish can be regarded as that area in which it has substantial protection against globally prevailing competitive forces. These parishes are frequently delineated by geographical and cultural boundaries, and sustained by geographical distance. For example, it has, until recently anyway, been assumed that, normally, a country which is self-sufficient in an agricultural commodity will purchase its requirements from its domestic industry. This is no longer completely true, and is likely to be less true in the future — witness the "parochial disruption" caused by the efforts of U.K. producers to supply the French market with U.K. lamb and by the efforts of French producers to supply the U.K. market with U.H.T. milk in the early 1980s.

To borrow from Marshall McLuhan, the global village has revealed the global market.

Informational

It is likely, in the opinion of many strategies, that the decade of the eighties will be regarded as the decade which began the information revolution. This book emphasises the importance to strategic planners of having good information, or access to it, and encourages managers to become harvesters and beachcombers of information. With advances in computer technology and the reduction in the costs of obtaining and storing information it is now possible for managers to store, at minimal cost, and as a matter of routine, a much greater harvest of strategic and operating information than ever before. Additionally, strategic planners should be able to scan their organisation, and the environments in which it operates, for random information which may contain weak signals of forthcoming strategic challenges or opportunities. Once again, the Japanese show the way in this activity.

"In other words, a firm's ability to gather vital economic and technological information abroad must also be regarded as the factor that determines the competitive advantage in international trade and investment. A firm's knowledge of various overseas territories can also be accumulated, improved and updated by its conscious investment in information-gathering activities. Japanese trading firms have performed the useful function of monitoring foreign markets and technologies for many manufacturing firms, both large and small. For since the 1850s, Japan has been consciously investing time, manpower, and money in worldwide information-getting activities." (Ref. (17), p. 33.)

To borrow from an old saying, a little knowledge is a very dangerous thing.

Quantitative

A sound quantitative base is frequently essential to develop a robust strategy, and, in this age of information, vast amounts of quantitative data are available, or can be acquired easily. Today, computer technology has made available, to even the smallest businesses, sophisticated packages which can contribute signficantly to the effectiveness of a company's strategic and operational management. An attempt to integrate some aspects of this quantitative revolution into the fabric of strategic management is provided by a number of simple strategic management packages which are listed in Chapter 8. All of these packages can be run on an Apple II computer. It is hoped that the inclusion of these packages will help free planners from the drudgery of tedious, but necessary, calculation and thus facilitate them in concentrating on what should be their major task — strategic management.

Spatial

It can be the case that even when managers do have the relevant strategic information they do not perceive its significance or do not perceive the appropriate strategic actions which the information ought to trigger. An aim of this book is to encourage managers to consider, constantly, alternative ways of presenting information, in the belief that the new methods of presentation can yield new insights. This can be particularly true when numeric information is displayed graphically in two, or even three, dimensions. Indeed, many of the techniques presented in this book are not really original in the content of their information, but rather the originality lies in the graphic way in which the information is presented. For example, the portfolio approaches considered in Chapters 4 and 5 attempt to show spatially, in two dimensions, the following quantitative data: the power of the business itself (this can be measured in a number of ways — relative market share, sales, return on investment, etc.), the position of the business in question *vis-à-vis* other businesses owned by the corporation itself and rival businesses owned by other corporations and, finally, the prospects for the business in the particular industry sector in which it operates. This method of displaying strategic positions helps simplify large amounts of complex data and helps strategists to quickly gain insights that might otherwise be elusive.

It is further suggested that readers should not confine their graphical displays to those that are included in this book. Rather, the displays in this book should serve as merely a starting point and planners should strive to develop their own approaches tailored to their own needs.

Environmental

Although the competitive environment considered on pages 3 to 7 above is the part of the total environment which most affects the operation of businesses, it is also necessary for managers to take cognisance of some broader aspects of the environment. Today, especially, it is vital for managers to realise how increasingly uncertain and complex is the nature of the environment in which strategic decisions must be taken. That is, strategic management has, as this century has progressed, become increasingly difficult because of the increasing uncertainty about forecasting the future. This uncertainty, following Ansoff,[4] can be attributed to two major factors:

A general decrease in predictability: this has been caused, largely, by a decrease in the time remaining until the full impact of a strategic change is felt. For example, it took approximately 112 years (from the 1820s to the 1840s) for photography to change from a laboratory concept to a commercial reality. In contrast to this, the "gestation" period for the solar battery was approximately 2 years in the 1950s. Thus, the time *available* for a business to make a strategic response to an environmental change has been shrinking. Compounding this complexity has been the increase in the time *required* for a business to make an effective response to a major environmental change, i.e. with the increasing technological complexity of business and its products and services, adequate responses to challenges require much more time and resources.

A general increase in the novelty of change: because of the speed and extensiveness of change, firms are no longer appropriately structured to deal with it effectively.

An implication of the above is that the extrapolative forecasts of yesterday are no longer sufficient, i.e. the past is not a good guide to the future. Therefore, a forecasting approach which is somewhat more discontinuous, better able to handle unexpected contingencies and capable of detecting weak signals which may presage forthcoming strategic change is required. Scenario planning is advocated as a method of achieving this and is considered in Chapter 7.

Behavioural

It is not unusual for texts on strategic management to suggest that effective strategic management can be effected by marshalling the relevant "facts", analysing them within a "logical framework" and then, based on the analysis, advocate a "logical" strategy which will ensure, assuming that the "facts" were correct, success. Such a view of strategic management is as arid as Mr Thomas Gradgrind's dry, incorrect and idiosyncratic views on the "factual nature of life", one aspect of which is quoted briefly below.

"... In this life, we want nothing but Facts, sir, nothing but Facts!"
. . .

"Blitzer," said Thomas Gradgrind. "Your definition of a horse."

"Quadruped. Graminivorous. Forty teeth, namely twenty-four grinders, four eye-teeth, and twelve incisive. Sheds coat in the spring; in marshy countries, sheds hoofs too. Hoofs hard, but requiring to be shod with iron. Age known by marks in mouth."

"Thus (and much more) Blitzer." (Ref. (8), pp. 47, 50.)

Similarly a strategy based upon facts plus logic alone, no matter how important the challenge is, or how persuasively the strategy is pursued, will degenerate into mere words unless it fits with and is sustained by the behavioural fabric of the business and the society in which the business operates. Four major aspects of this behavioural fabric are of crucial importance. These are:

Power. Power — who has it, how strong it is and how it is used — has a major influence on the strategic behaviour of firms. The power of a firm *vis-à-vis* the other constituent groups in society at large and just where power resides within the firm are of crucial importance in strategic management.

The distribution of power, both inside the firm and in terms of the firm's power over other groups in society, has, during the course of history, changed considerably and is still changing today. This can be seen clearly if the power of the nineteenth-century American "Robber Barons" such as Rockefeller, Pierpoint Morgan and Carnegie is compared with the power of the leaders of large corporations today. This shift in the power relation of the firm to society has been accompanied by shifts of power within the firms themselves. Thus the power which was, in the early part of the twentieth century, vested in the owners of firms has, over time, been dispersed to stockholders, managers and blue collar workers. A current manifestation of the transfer of power and its effects upon the strategic management of companies is provided by high technology companies. In these types of companies real power is possessed by those technocrats whose skills and knowledge are essential for the firm's success. A feature of these industries is the speed with which new companies are developed and then splinter into other companies as the technocrats leave to develop their own companies. In such industries, because of their power, technocrats may have a veto on strategy.

The final observation on power is that, irrespective of which group is the dominant power group in a firm, any strategy which does not appeal to the group which has the power will have little prospect of success.

Leadership. Leadership has a fundamental influence on the success of a business. The influence of leadership can be assessed in three major areas: Does the leadership have vision?, i.e. are the leaders of the business able to perceive quickly and accurately major strategic trends? Does the leadership have power?, i.e. are the leaders of the business, through whatever devices they choose to use, able to translate strategic aspirations into operating reality? Does the leadership have the political astuteness necessary to neutralise the negative effects of conflicting internal interests and transform these sectional interests into a vector of coordinated policies and activities which support overall company goals. The influence of Sir Arnold Weinstock on the U.K. company G.E.C. is a visible example of the importance of leadership.

Culture. By culture is meant the powerful and complex net of values, traditions and behaviour patterns that somehow bonds together the people who comprise the business. The culture of a business can have profound effects, for as Ackoff[2] points out, behaviour is not value free, i.e. individuals and organisation exhibit preferences for certain types of behaviour and may persist in a certain type of behaviour even if it leads to sub-optimal (or even disastrous) results. Expressing this slightly differently: firms do not strive just for results, they also strive for a certain mode of behaviour.

An example of sub-optimal behaviour which is persisted in, in order to conform with the culture of the organisation, is provided by poorly managed family businesses. In such businesses a frequent cause of failure is that, even when the controlling family does not have the professional and technological skills to run the business in an effective way, it fails to bring in "outside" non-family expertise until it is too late. This may be so because the primary cultural bond of the company is that it must be controlled by the family and this bond is so strong that failure is preferable to dilution or loss of control.

Finally, it is important to realise that it is unusual for a firm to have a catholic universal culture. Different cultural climates may well exist in different divisions and in different functions within a single division. For example, it is not unusual for personnel in an accounting function to have different cultural values from personnel in a marketing department.

Clearly the cultural acceptance of strategic plans is crucial to effective strategic management.

Risk. The attitude towards risk in a business, which is, of course, really part of its culture, will have fundamental affects upon the strategic perspectives of the managers of the business. Thus businesses which are extremely conservative towards risk will, even if necessity requires a bold and risky strategy, tend to eschew such a strategy because it offends their value systems.

It is within the context delineated by the above influences — Competitive, Geographical, Informational, Quantitative, Spatial, Environmental and Behavioural — that the tools and techniques of strategic management will be considered.

Selected concepts which are important in understanding strategic management are now considered.

Selected Concepts in Strategic Management

This section defines and illustrates selected concepts in strategic management which will be subsequently employed.

The Influence of Structure and the Concept of the SBU

Although the fundamental objective of strategic management — obtaining a good fit with the environment — should always be the same (see page 27 below), the tools and techniques of strategic management employed in order to achieve this, and the organisational framework within which it is effected, will be influenced by the size, complexity and nature of the organisation. The main standard types of organisational structure and the implications that these structures have for strategic management are now considered briefly.

The Small Business Structure

The simplest type of organisation structure is that which is frequently referred to as a "Small Business", or "Entrepreneurial". This type of structure is shown schematically in Fig. 3. Here it is assumed that there is simply an owner of the business (or, if the business is owned by shareholders, a manager) who has a relatively small number of employees who produce a relatively small range of products.* Examples of such businesses could be: a locally owned small food processing plant, a local construction company, a local boat builder, etc.

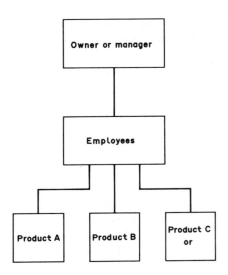

Fig. 3. *Small business structure*

Although, throughout, the term "product" is used to describe the output of a business, all the descriptions in this section could apply equally well to companies that produce only "services".

This type of business is considered to produce a distinct product (or group of products) for distinct groups of customers and the owner (or manager) is responsible for the business's strategic and operational management. In other words, this is a discrete, self-contained and largely self-controlled business unit. Henceforth, any business structure which, in general, meets these conditions will be called a Strategic Business Unit or SBU. In passing, it should be noted that a SBU is not restricted to producing and selling a single product. Indeed, it will be the case that most SBUs will have more than one product and more than one market. For example, the small boat builder mentioned earlier may build a variety of boats for a variety of markets.

In the small business structure strategic management takes place at two levels. Firstly, at the corporate level: this is planned and executed by the owner (or manager) and is primarily concerned with issues such as the overall mission of the business and what could be called the "master strategy for the whole business". Secondly, at the functional or operational level: this is planned by the owner or manager and is executed mainly by the employees. This level of planning is mainly concerned with the detailed implementation of the master strategy. For businesses with this type of structure, portfolio analysis (see page 23) takes place exclusively at the "product" level, i.e. when portfolio analysis is used the objective is to have a balanced portfolio of products.

The Functional Business Structure

Frequently, as businesses grow — through the range of products and activities being expanded and consequently more employees joining — the structure of the business is changed. The structure is changed in order to accommodate the additional complexity that accrues with size and to maximise the contributions from the additional resources available. The structure that often evolves from the Small Business Structure is "The Functional Business Structure".

Figure 4 shows, schematically, a typical Functional Business Structure. Here the employees are grouped according to the work they perform (i.e. according to their function), and in this case they have been grouped according to the functions of Production, Accounting and Finance, Marketing, Personnel, Research and Development and Management Information Systems. It is furthermore assumed that each functional area has an overall manager (thus there is a Production Manager, a Marketing Manager, etc.) and that some, or all, of these managers will be members of the Board of Directors. The Board of Directors is assumed to be made up of Functional Managers and shareholders.

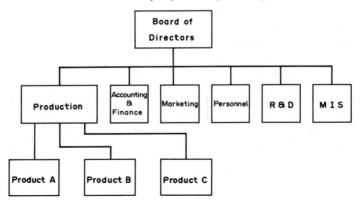

FIG. 4. *Functional business structure*

Once again the functional business structure is considered to produce a distinct product, or group of products, for distinct groups of customers, is responsible for its own strategic and operational management and is consequently a SBU.

In this type of business, strategic planning takes place at two levels: the corporate and the functional. The corporate strategy is planned and executed by the Board of Directors and is primarily concerned with designing the master strategy for the business. The functional aspects of the strategy are translated into operational terms and implemented by the functional managers.

In this type of structure portfolio analysis takes place at the product level.

The Divisional Business Structure

If a functionally structured business continues to grow by extending its activities into new and diverse fields, then a divisional structure may become appropriate. A typical divisional structure is shown in Fig. 5. Here it is assumed that the organisation portrayed by the functional structure in Fig. 4 has greatly expanded the range of products which it manufactures. In fact, the range has become so diverse that it is no longer organisationally or logically feasible to group the entire range of products together. Instead, the full range has been divided into three sub-ranges and the products within each sub-range are somehow related. Thus products A, B and C are related in some way and form the first sub-range; products L, M and N are related in some way and form the second sub-range; and, finally, products X, Y and Z are related in some way and form the third sub-range. In fact the functional structure

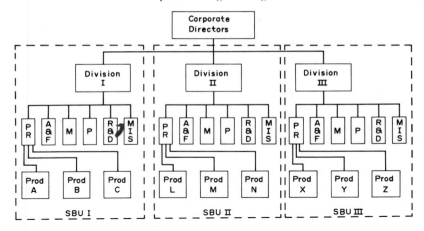

FIG. 5 *Divisional business structure*

of Fig. 4 now forms just one division — Division I — in the Divisional Business Structure of Fig. 5. As the dashed lines in Fig. 5 show, each division in the business produces distinct groupings of products for distinct groups of customers and is largely responsible for its own strategic and functional management. Consequently each division can be considered as a SBU. Thus Fig. 5 shows a multi-division and multi-SBU firm.* When companies are organised on a divisional structure, strategic planning gains an additional level of complexity. It takes place at three levels — the corporate, the divisional and the functional — and is carried out in a hierarchical fashion.

The highest level in the hierarchy of strategic planning is considered to be corporate strategic planning. At this level corporate strategic planners have the task of developing a corporate portfolio of divisions (or SBUs) which will meet the objectives of the company as a whole. Because of the size of the company and the diversity of its products, corporate strategic planners cannot be involved in the detailed implementation of strategic plans — this task is delegated to divisional heads. Corporate strategic planners have the conflicting tasks of controlling and guiding the divisions so that the competitive advantages *to the company as a whole* that accrue through having a diversity of businesses are maximised while simultaneously encouraging the divisions to make strategic plans which will bring the maximum advantage to each *division*. Thus, in this type of structure, portfolio analysis takes place firstly, at the division or SBU level.

Although here it is assumed that each division is a SBU, in practice, divisions are frequently set up without regard to SBUs.

The second level in the hierarchy of strategic planning is as described in strategic planning in the section "The Functional Business Structure" on pages 15 to 16. Here the objective is to develop a balanced portfolio of products which will meet the division's objectives and still fall within corporate guidelines.

Finally, the third and lowest level of planning is considered to be at the operational level and is as described in strategic planning in the section "The Small Business Structure" on pages 14 to 15. Here the objective is to operationalise the division's strategic plans.

In passing, it should be noted that the growth of large divisionalised corporations, especially in the United States, since the 1960s has been a major factor in developing portfolio approaches to strategic planning. In this book, depending upon the circumstances, portfolio analysis is carried out both at the level of the SBU, and also at the product level.

The Product Life Cycle

The product life cycle plays a fundamental role in strategic management. At its simplest, this concept asserts that all industries and products go through a series of stages called, collectively, a life cycle. The stage at which an industry or a product is at, in its life cycle, has major strategic implications. The various stages comprising the product life cycle — Development, Growth, Maturity and Decline — are illustrated in Fig. 6 and are described, briefly, below.

Development Stage

This stage is characterised by the development and introduction, usually by a limited number of firms, of a new product. Because initial sales tend to be small and expensive to achieve (customers must be "persuaded" to buy the new product), and also because development costs must be borne, prices tend to be high and profits tend to be negative or low. Additionally, this stage is characterised by high risk — the product is new, trends have not been established and the competitive rules for the new product have not yet evolved. Industries in the development stage in the early 1980s include fibre optics, teletext information transmission and biomass energy development.

Growth Stage

The second stage tends to be characterised by increased sales (customers' resistance has been overcome), increased profits and a reduction in prices. Prices tend to fall due to competition among firms:

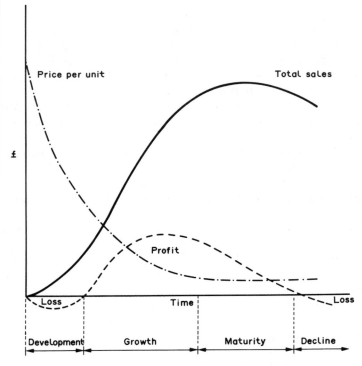

FIG. 6. *The product life cycle*

once the initial success of the pioneering firms has been observed, more firms enter the, initially, high price market. In order to achieve their desired sales, competition, based, among other things, on price, develops and there are overall price reductions. This price reduction is also due, in part, to cost reduction and so, because of the increase in volume, profits tend to increase. Industries in the growth stage in the early 1980s included personal computers and video games.

Maturity Stage

In this third stage, the days of really fast growth have passed and although sales continue to increase, they do so at a slower rate than in the growth stage. Additionally, profits and prices commence declining as the capacity build-up which has been effected in the growth stage continues to come on stream. Industries which could be considered to be at the mature stage in the early 1980s include the U.K. agricultural industry and the U.K. food retailing industry.

Decline

In this final stage the market demand for the product has been largely satisfied and industry overcapacity is likely. Consequently, prices tend to remain stable or fall. Frequently sales and profits both decline and the product becomes a loss maker. European shipbuilding is an example of an industry which is currently in this situation.

This is a summary of the product life cycle at its simplest. Although the product life cycle has had considerable strategic currency for many years, its specific usefulness is somewhat questionable. Probably its greatest shortcoming is the inherent assumption that all products will pass through a pattern similar to that shown in Fig. 6.

For many products this simply is not true. For example, many recreation and fashion products, for young people especially — for example, skate boards and their associated equipment — appear to have just two stages: growth and decline. Also, it is difficult for a firm to know exactly where its products are on the life cycle at a particular point in time. In short, the Product Life Cycle is a tool that is useful in analysing what has happened, but is of limited value in predicting what will happen.

In spite of the obvious limitations of the tool, three other aspects of the concept are deemed to be of particular importance to strategic planning and are now considered.

The International Product Life Cycle

As mentioned on page 7, it is no longer sufficient for strategic planners to consider strategic challenges within the context of national boundaries. The inadequacy of such a parochial view is demonstrated particularly well by the product life cycle. Today, companies which take a global view of their market frequently plan their products' life cycles to exploit the benefits which can be derived from geo-regional differences. Thus it may well be the case that a product which is at the maturity stage of its life cycle in a Developed Country may be at the growth stage in a Newly Industrialised Country and at the development stage in a Less Developed Country. Figure 7 illustrates the concept. In the figure at any single point in time, say time t, a single product, "product X", is at a different stage in its life cycle in each type of country. A simple, but nonetheless effective, example of the successful deployment of this strategy is provided by the American Crown Cork and Seal Company. This company has, since the 1960s, followed, under the direction of its President, John Connolly, a strategy based upon two geographic thrusts — the first was to expand its national distribution in the United States and the second was to invest heavily overseas; especially in

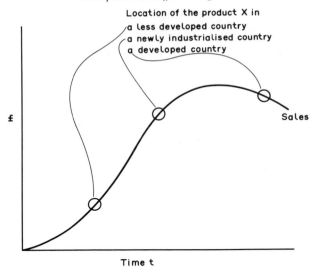

FIG. 7. *The international product life cycle showing the location of the product X in three types of country at time* t

underdeveloped nations. This overseas investment took the form of initially investing heavily in crown cork manufacture and then, as the countries developed, and packaged foods became more acceptable, to invest in can manufacture. The company was thus exploiting the international product life cycle.

So successful was this strategy that by 1976 Crown Cork and Seal was the largest U.S. overseas producer of metal cans and crowns, and, indeed, in that year its International Division contributed 36% of the total company sales and 44% of the total company profits. The overseas business was particularly good for Crown Cork and Seal, as in addition to the initial investment tax shelters that host countries gave

"... manufacturing costs were low as Crown used outmoded but fully depreciated equipment from its U.S. plants. For instance, when the company changed over to the drawn-and-ironed process, much of the three-piece equipment found its way into the foreign operations." (Ref. (7), pp. 130–1.)

The "Japanese" Perception of the Product Life Cycle

Particelli has suggested that one of the reasons for Japan's phenomenal industrial success is their different perception of the product life

*For a more detailed exposition of the product life cycle see Refs. (18) and (19).

cycle, particularly with regard to resource application. This difference is illustrated in Fig. 8 and its implications are described below.

"The Japanese support their emphasis on value in price, benefits and quality by applying resources in a way that differs dramatically from their U.S. and European competitors. . . .

"In general, the early emphasis in resource allocation by U.S. manufacturers is on innovation: the invention of new products and applications and product improvements. As a market begins to mature, emphasis is placed on market stimulation through marketing and sales. Only at the mature stage does the American manufacturer begin to focus a disproportionate share of his resources on cost takeout. Japanese firms take a different approach. Frequently, they don't invent the technology most important to success, but wait until someone else invents it, tests

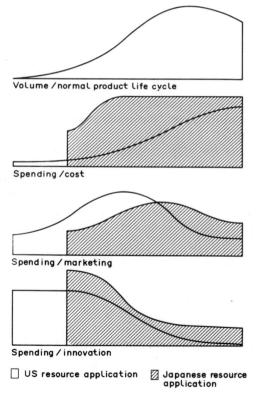

Volume / normal product life cycle

Spending / cost

Spending / marketing

Spending / innovation

☐ US resource application   ▨ Japanese resource application

FIG. 8 *Resource allocation — focused on product, cost (Ref. (14), p. 39.)*

and stimulates the market. At about the same time that U.S. manufacturers begin to diminish their product innovation, Japanese competitors enter the market with a significant emphasis on innovation, in order to differentiate product benefits and design for low cost. This heavy emphasis on innovation falls off rapidly; almost immediately the level of resources devoted to cost takeout escalates and remains high." (Ref. (14), p. 39.)

The "Wave of Products" Concept

Most companies have more than one product, and for such companies it is strategically important to sequence the introduction of and the maintenance of their products so that the company as a whole derives the maximum benefit from the life cycles of the products. It is suggested that, ideally, a company should sequence the introduction of products so that a dynasty of products which produces undulating "waves" of sales and associated profits (as shown in Fig. 9) develops. Such a sequencing can ensure a successful, smooth and continuing existence for the firm. This concept is closely linked to the portfolio concept which is examined below.

The Portfolio Concept

Capital investment (in the form of deciding which product, business or SBU to support), because it can be significant in size and because it is largely irreversible, is, perhaps, the most crucial business decision. The traditional criteria (i.e. net cash flow, present value, return on investment, payback, etc.) which, traditionally, have been used to assess the

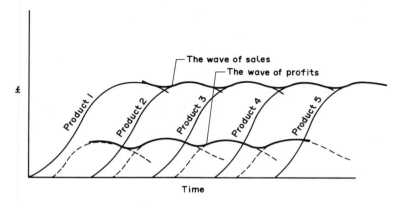

FIG. 9 *The wave of products concept*

performance and potential of businesses have, because they are monofunctional in their perspectives, provided somewhat blinkered insights. The various portfolio approaches help to overcome this narrowness of vision.

These approaches assert that the actual, or expected, financial performance of a SBU (say its cash flow or ROI) is not sufficient for strategic planning purposes — it is also important to know about the SBU's *position vis-à-vis* other SBUs in the corporate portfolio and also its position *vis-à-vis* competing SBUs in the industry. It is the graphic positioning of SBUs, both in relation to the company itself and in relation to the industries in which the company competes, plus their ability to display, simply, in two dimensions, complex multi-attribute strategic positions, that give the portfolio approaches their strategic edge. This positioning also enables strategic planners to decide which SBUs should receive additional funding, which should be starved of cash, which should be maintained in a "neutral" cash position and which should be sold.

For example, the Irish multinational packaging company Jefferson Smurfit has divided its worldwide operations into a number of SBUs delineated by geographical location and products. The company is organised as shown in Fig. 10. This structuring of the company enables corporate planners to assess and plan for the company as a whole and simultaneously to appraise the performance of and plan for the individual SBUs.

Defining the Business and Its Mission

In the section below it is assumed that the business being defined is a single SBU and that the business definition will fit happily with the organisational delineation of the SBU.

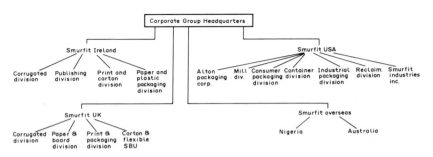

FIG. 10. *Schematic representation of the major divisions of the Jefferson Smurfit group*[12]

While there is widespread agreement among strategists on the fundamental importance of correctly defining the business as a prerequisite to successful strategic planning, there is unfortunately no generally accepted methodology for doing this. A conventional approach is to define the business along two dimensions — the product and the market.

In many respects the product definition is quite straightforward — it is frequently defined by its name. However, the total definition can become much more complicated when the product is aligned with the market. Thus the market definition, for a firm, is ultimately the subjective (but not necessarily uninformed) view of the strategist, and this can have fundamental effects upon a firm's planning and subsequent success. For example, if a firm has a national rather than a global perception of its market this can have a fundamental influence on its perception of its success. Thus, the U.K. automobile manufacturer British Leyland (BL) enjoyed the highest market share of the U.K. automobile market during the years 1969–1975. During this period BL had a national rather than an international view of its business to the extent that around 1980 about 80% of its passenger car sales in Western Europe were within the United Kingdom. However, over much of this period, BL's leading U.K. competitor, Ford, which had a much more international conception of its business, enjoyed a much higher Return on Investment. For BL its national perception of its market was extremely costly. BL was, in reality, a "little league" player playing in the "big league" which was dominated by competitors who had global supranational perspectives of their businesses.[13]

In a similar fashion it can be extremely costly to misdefine the business by taking too broad a view or too narrow a view. For example, in the post-World War II era many European shipbuilders failed to segment their markets and narrow the focus of their business sufficiently to compete with the rising Japanese dominance in this industry. These shipbuilders continued to think of themselves as being in the "shipbuilding business" rather than being in specific sectors of the business such as "tankers" or "specialised standard carriers". In contrast to this industry, there are many businesses which have missed opportunities through having too narrow a focus. For example, the U.K. national telephone company, until its loss of monopoly status in 1982, had tended to think of itself as being in the business of "providing telephone services and installing telephone equipment". Post-1982 the company began, increasingly, to consider itself in the highly competitive "national and international communications" business.

These examples should illustrate the difficulty of defining the business. However, a comprehensive and practical solution to this difficult problem is provided if a Porter view is adopted. Thus when an industry structure analysis, of the type outlined on pages 3 to 7 above, is undertaken, and the five forces which determine an industry's competitive position have been ascertained, then the industry definition will automatically evolve.

When the industry has been thus defined, the strategist can, through more detailed analysis of the five forces, define firstly the strategic group of firms of which his is a member and then finally define his own particular business.

Closely related to the definition of the business is its mission. Frequently, in the literature, the terms are used interchangeably. Here it is assumed that the mission of the business is that set of long-range goals and targets which the top decision-makers in the business have determined that the company shall have. For example, the Irish multinational group Jefferson Smurfit has defined its business as the "packaging business and associated activities" and its primary mission is to stay in that business and to grow.

Finally, the definition of the business and its mission are interrelated — the choice of business definition will affect the mission and the choice of mission will affect the business definition. It may be helpful to think of these two crucial strategic concepts as being linked in an iterative fashion as shown in Fig. 11. The figure shows that the concepts are mutually dependent.

A Model of Strategic Management

As mentioned previously, the nature of strategic management is different for single-SBU and multi-SBU firms. In the section immedi-

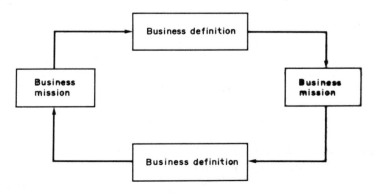

FIG. 11. *The mutual dependence of business definition and business mission*

ately below a single-SBU firm only is considered. This is expanded on page 28 to include the multi-SBU firm.

Strategic management, in this book, is considered to be that type of planning and those activities through which a firm adapts itself so that it obtains a good fit with its environment. This good fit is essential for the long-term survival of the firm and consequently The Strategic Problem is defined as *"obtaining a good fit with the environment"*. Therefore, strategic management is concerned, primarily, with those fundamental decisions which affect the nature, culture and structure of the business and, conventionally, are described as long-run decisions, i.e. decisions which have a time horizon of greater than three years.

A conceptual model of the strategic problem is provided by Fig. 12 and is discussed below.

The Environment

The environment is considered to be a simple envelope within which the organisation operates, i.e. it is not subdivided into relevant constituent segments but is considered to be an undifferentiated all-enveloping universe. Just two aspects of the environment are made explicit. These are, firstly, the competitive forces that determine where a business is located in its industry and, secondly, the contemporary phenomenon of discontinuity. The latter aspect is represented, in Fig. 12, by the environment being fragmented into three irregular sections — this is meant to convey the impression that the past is not a good guide to the future and that the environment is being frequently and irregularly rocked by unforeseen and traumatic shocks.

The Firm

The firm is portrayed as a black box divided schematically into the various functional areas into which a business is conventionally divided: Production, Finance, Personnel, Marketing, General Management, Management Information Systems and Research and Development. This division is not meant to be exhaustive and consequently, in the interests of generality, two rectangles have been left blank to allow the reader to insert those functions which he feels should be included. It is assumed that the firm takes various Inputs — land, labour, finance, equipment, raw materials, energy, information and entrepreneurship —

from the environment and converts them into Outputs, i.e. products or services which are sought by the environment.

In passing, it should be noted that in the 1960s and early 1970s strategic management was focused almost exclusively on the Output side of the strategic fit equation. For example, Ansoff[3] suggested that strategy should be guided by a two by two matrix which focused on the output of the organisation — its products and its mission. Similarly, the Boston Consulting Group[1] and many other strategists focused on this side of the strategic fit equation. This bias reflected an era when the key to strategic success was growth. Growth made possible, in part anyway, through such elements as cheap and plentiful supplies of raw materials and energy, relative environmental and political stability and an attitude of optimism about the future. This prevailing attitude of continuing plenty and the attendant aura of hope was, in most Western industrialised nations, severely buffeted in the 1970s and by the 1980s had been transformed into a realisation that the, previously believed, rosy prospects were at best uncertain and at worst unobtainable. It could be argued that the commencement of this process of disillusionment began with the oil crisis of 1973. Certainly, a strategic consequence of the evaporation of "growth" as the simplest, most effective and most natural strategy has been that many strategists have downgraded their expectations about the future and place an increasing emphasis on the Input side of the strategic fit equation, i.e. there has developed an increasing awareness of the strategic and practical implications imposed by the cost and the finite nature of the natural resources of the "spaceship earth".*

Finally, although the firm, as a whole, has the grand strategic objective of obtaining a good fit with its environment, it is assumed that this grand objective is refined into lower level objectives for each of the functional areas designated in Fig. 12. Then each of these functional areas has own strategies which are designed to enable it to simultaneously achieve its own (lower level) functional strategic objectives and also fulfil its contribution to the total firm's grand strategic objective. Thus the overall grand strategy is disaggregated into an integrated web of functional strategies.

For the multi-SBU firm an additional level of complexity must be included. In this case, strategic management, in addition to the concerns outlined above, is also concerned with managing the corporate portfolio of SBUs that the firm has, i.e. strategic planners are concerned with deciding which SBUs to fund for growth, which to dispose of, which to maintain, etc., in order to achieve corporate objectives. In passing it should be noted that this additional level of complexity is frequently a

*This is taken from Ref. (6).

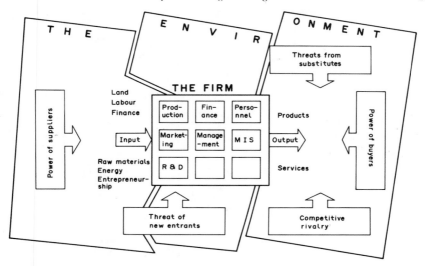

FIG. 12. *A model of strategic management*

source of conflict between corporate and divisional planners. This may arise because corporate and divisional objectives are incompatible. For example, corporate planners may take the view that in the interest of the total corporation that a particular division should receive reduced corporate funding — a strategy that rarely has divisional appeal.

A simplified portfolio for a firm with just four SBUs, and the suggested strategy for each SBU, is shown in Fig. 13.

Summary

This chapter sets the stage — in terms of the context in which strategic planning takes place and also in terms of introducing some of the fundamental concepts which are employed — for the tools and techniques of strategic management.

The chapter commenced with a consideration of the broader, and frequently less apparent, context in which strategic decisions must be made. This was done because an appreciation of the Competitive, Geographical, Informational, Quantitative, Spatial, Environmental and Behavioural aspects of strategic planning is frequently a necessary condition for successful strategic management.

Subsequently, various fundamental concepts in strategic management — the Influence of Structure, the Product Life Cycle, the Portfolio Concept and the Definition of a Business — were considered.

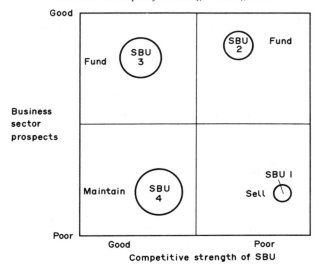

FIG. 13. *Hypothetical portfolio showing suggested strategies for four SBUs*

Some knowledge of these concepts is essential for understanding the more complex topics that follow.

Finally, a simple model of strategic management which can be used for all firms, large and small, was developed. Throughout the book all analyses and decisions will be taken in the context of this model.

Note on the References and the Bibliography

In this and all other chapters there is a set of references and a bibliography. The references refer to specific issues that have arisen in the chapter and are numerically keyed to the chapter. The bibliography is broader and more general than the references. The objective of the bibliography is to provide extensive references to readers who wish to pursue the topic of the chapter to a greater depth. For this chapter the bibliography is primarily concerned with texts and articles which give: an introduction to strategic management, a comprehensive overview of strategic management and empirical studies of the "state of the art" in practice.

References

1.   Abell, D. F. *Defining the Business: The Starting Point of Strategic Planning*, Prentice-Hall Inc., 1980.

2. Ackoff, R. L. *Concept of Corporate Planning*, Wiley, 1970.
3. Ansoff, H. I. *Corporate Strategy*, Penguin, 1968.
4. Ansoff, H. I. *Strategic Management*, Macmillan, 1979.
5. *Basic Principles of Business Strategy, the PIMS Program*, Strategic Planning Institute, Cambridge, Mass., 1981.
6. Brower, D. "The Third Planet: Operating Instructions", *The New York Times Magazine*, March 1973, p. 111.
7. Christiansen, D. R., Andrews, K. R. and Bower, J. L. *Business Policy: Text and Cases*, R. D. Irwin, 1980.
8. Dickens, C. *Hard Times*, Penguin, 1972.
9. Henderson, B. Address to the Strategic Management Society, Annual Conference, Paris, October 1983.
10. Hosmer, L. T. "The Importance of Strategic Leadership", *Journal of Business Strategy*, Vol. 2, No. 2, Fall 1982, pp. 47–57.
11. Hussey, D. *Strategic Analysis Techniques: A Handbook*, Harbridge House, Europe, London, 1982.
12. *Jefferson Smurfit Group Worldwide: Facts and Figures*, Jefferson Smurfit, Dublin, 1982.
13. Leontiades, J. "Market Share and Corporate Strategy in International Industries", paper presented to the EIBA Conference, Insead, December 1982.
14. Particelli, M. C. "The Japanese are Coming: Global Strategic Planning in Action", *Outlook*, 4, Booz, Allen & Hamilton, New York, Spring 1981, pp. 36–44.
15. Porter, M. E. *Competitive Strategy: Techniques for Analyzing Industries and Competitors*, The Free Press, 1980.
16. Schoeffler, S. "The Unprofitability of Modern Technology and What to do About it", *PIMS Letter*, No. 2, The Strategic Planning Institute, Cambridge, Mass., 1980.
17. Tsurumi, Y. *The Japanese are Coming*, Ballinger Publishing Company, Cambridge, Mass., 1976.
18. Wasson, C. R. *Dynamic Competitive Strategy and Product Life Cycles*, St. Charles, Ill., Challenge Books, 1974.
19. Wells, L. (Ed.) *The Product Life Cycle and International Trade*, Boston, Mass., The Harvard Business School, Division of Research, 1972.

Bibliography
I. General Works on Strategic Management

Abell, D. F. *Defining the Business: The Starting Point of Planning*, Prentice-Hall Inc., Englewood Cliffs, New Jersey, 1980.

Abell, D. F. and Hammond, J. S. *Strategic Market Planning*, Prentice-Hall, Englewood Cliffs, New Jersey, 1979.

Ackoff, R. "On the Use of Models in Corporate Planning", *Strategic Management Journal*, Vol. 2, 1981, pp. 353–359.

Ansoff, H. I., *et al. From Strategic Planning to Strategic Management*, New York, Wiley, 1976.

Argenti, J. *Corporate Collapse*, McGraw-Hill Book Company (UK) Ltd., 1976.

Argenti, J. *Practical Corporate Planning*, Allen and Unwin, Hemel Hempstead, Herts., 1980.

Beck, P. W. "Corporate Planning for an Uncertain Future", *Long Range Planning*, Vol. 15, No. 4, Aug. 1983, pp. 12–21.

Chastain, C. E. "Strategic Planning and the Recession", *Business Horizons*, Nov./Dec. 1982, pp. 39–45.

Christiansen, C. R., Andrews, K. R. and Bower, J. L. *Business Policy: Text and Cases*, R. D. Irwin, 3rd ed.

De Kluyver, C. A. and McNally, G. M. "Developing a Corporate Planning Model for a Small Company", *Long Range Planning*, Vol. 15, No. 1, Feb. 1982, pp. 97–106.

Diffenbach, J. "Finding the Right Strategic Combination", *Journal of Business Strategy*, Autumn 1981, pp. 47–58.

Drucker, P. *Managing in Turbulent Times*, Heinemann, London, 1980.

Easterby-Smith, M. and Davies, J. "Developing Strategic Thinking", *Long Range Planning*, Vol. 15, No. 4, Aug. 1983, pp. 39–48.

Ghosh, B. C. and Nee, A. Y. C. "Strategic Planning: A Contingency Approach, Part I. The Strategic Analysis", *Long Range Planning*, Vol. 16, No. 4, Aug. 1983, pp. 93–103.

Glueck, W. F. *Strategic Management and Business Policy*, McGraw-Hill, 1980.

Gluck, F. W., Kaufman, S. P. and Walleck, S. A. "Strategic Planning for Strategic Advantage", *Harvard Business Review*, July–August 1980, pp. 154–161.

Grant, J. H. and King, W. R. *The Logic of Strategic Planning*, Little Brown and Co., Boston, 1982.

Green, G. J. L. and Jones, E. G. "Strategic Management Step by Step", *Long Range Planning*, Vol. 15, No. 3, June 1982, pp. 61–70.

Hammond, J. S. *Market Strategies: Concepts and Cases*, Prentice-Hall, 1979.

Haner, F. T. "Risk Management in Corporate Planning", *Long Range Planning*, Vol. 14, No. 6, Dec. 1981, pp. 12–16.

Harvey, P. F. *Business Policy and Strategic Management*, Charles E. Merrill Publishing Co., 1982.

Hofer, C. W. and Schendel, D. *Strategy Formulation: Analytical Concepts*, West Publishing, St. Paul and Cash House, Tunbridge Wells, 1978.

Higgins, J. C. *Strategic and Operational Planning Systems: Principles and Practice*. Prentice-Hall International, Englewood Cliffs, 1980.

Hussey, D. E. *Introducing Corporate Planning*, 2nd Edition, Pergamon Press, Oxford, 1979.

Hussey, D. E. (Ed.) *The Truth About Corporate Planning*, Pergamon Press, Oxford, 1983.

Lorange, P. and Vancil, R. F. *Strategic Planning Systems*. Prentice-Hall, Englewood Cliffs, New Jersey, 1977.

Michael, S. R. "Tailor-made Planning: Making Planning Fit the Firm", *Long Range Planning*, Vol. 14, No. 6, Dec. 1980, pp. 74–79.

Nagel, A. "Strategy Formulation for the Smaller Firm — A Practical Approach", *Long Range Planning*, Vol. 14, No. 4, Aug. 1981, pp. 115–120.

Naylor, T. H. *Corporate Planning Models*, Addison Wesley, London, 1979.

Naylor, T. H. *Corporate Strategy: The Integration of Corporate Planning Models and Economics*, North Holland, Amsterdam, 1982.

Naylor, T. H. and Tapon, F. "The Capital Asset Pricing Model: An Evaluation of its Potential as a Strategic Planning Tool", *Management Science*, Vol. 28, No. 10, Oct. 1982, pp. 1166–1173.

Smith, G. D. and Steadman, L. E. "Present Value of Corporate History", *Harvard Business Review*, Nov.–Dec. 1981, pp. 164–173.

Taylor, B. and Ferro, L. "Key Social Issues for European Businesses", *Long Range Planning*, Vol. 16, No. 1, Feb. 1983, pp. 97–105.

Thomas, R. E. *Business Policy*, Phillip Allan, Deddington, Oxon., 1977.

II. Strategic Management in Practice

Al-Buzzaz, S. "How Planning Works in Practice", *Long Range Planning*, Vol. 13, No. 4, Aug. 1980, pp. 30–42.

Bar-Zakay, S. N. "A National Strategic Planning Model", *Long Range Planning*, Vol. 14, No. 4, Aug. 1981, pp. 76–88.

Bhatty, E. F. "Corporate Planning in Medium Sized Companies in the UK", *Long Range Planning*, Vol. 4, No. 1, Feb. 1981, pp. 60–72.

Berry, L. L. "Retail Positioning Strategies for the 1980s", *Business Horizons*, Nov.–Dec. 1982, pp. 15–50.

Bouamrene, M. A. and Flarell, R. "Airline Corporate Planning — A Contemporary Framework", *Long Range Planning*, Vol. 13, No. 1, Feb. 1980, pp. 62–69.

Boulton, W. R., Franklin, S. G., Lindsay, W. M. and Rice, L. W. "How are Companies Planning Now? — A Survey", *Long Range Planning*, Vol. 15, No. 1, Feb. 1982, pp. 82–86.

Branat, W. K., Hulbert, J. M. and Vargas, F. G. "Pitfalls in Planning for Multinational Operations", *Long Range Planning*, Vol. 13, No. 6, Dec. 1980, pp. 23–31.

Cazes, B. "French Planning in the 1980's: A Political Agenda", *Futures*, Dec. 1978, pp. 452 .

Finlay, A. W. "Swedish Industrial Policy Planning — A Workshop Report", Stockholm, 6–7 March 1980, *Long Range Planning*, Vol. 13, No. 6, Dec. 1980, pp. 55–59.

Finlay, P. N. "Introducing Corporate Planning in a Medium Sized Company — A Case History", *Long Range Planning*, Vol. 15, No. 2, April 1982, pp. 93–103.

Dyson, R. G. "Participation in Planning — A Study of Two Organisations in the Netherlands", *Long Range Planning*, Vol. 12, No. 4, Aug. 1978, pp. 61–69.

Frazer, P. and Morrison, I. "Shaping the Future for Retail Banking", *Long Range Planning*, Vol. 15, No. 4, Aug. 1982, pp. 110–115.

Gouy, M. "Strategic Decision Making in Large European Firms", *Long Range Planning*, Vol. 11, No. 3, June 1978, pp. 41–48.

Grinyer, P. and Wooler, J. *Corporate Models Today*, 2nd Edition, Institute of Chartered Accountants in England and Wales, 1978.

Grieve Smith, J. "Strategy — The Key to Planning in the Public Corporation", *Long Range Planning*, Vol. 14, No. 6, Dec. 1981, pp. 24–31.

Hall, P. "Great Planning Disasters", *Futures*, Feb. 1980, pp. 45–50.

Holloway, C. and Pearce, J. A. II, "Computer Based Strategic Planning", *Long Range Planning*, Vol. 15, No. 4, Aug. 1982, pp. 56–63.

Kono, T. "Japanese Management Philosophy: Can it be Exported?", *Long Range Planning*, Vol. 15, No. 3, June 1982, pp. 90–102.

Kreikebaum, H. and Grimm, U. "Planning in a Free Market Economy", *Long Range Planning*, Vol. 15, No. 3, June 1982, pp. 103–115.

Kudla, R. J. "The Current Practice of Bank Long Range Planning", *Long Range Planning*, Vol. 15, No. 3, June 1982, pp. 132–138.

Lawler, E. E. and Drexler, J. A. "Entrepreneurship in the Large Corporation: Is it Possible?" *Management Review*, Vol. 70, Part 2, Feb. 1981, pp. 8–11.

Long Range Planning: Special Issue: Planning in North America, Vol. 16, No. 3, June 1983.

Marakami, T. "Recent Changes in Long Range Planning in Japan", *Long Range Planning*, Vol. 11, No. 2, April 1982, p. 2.

Mazzolini, R. "How Strategic Decisions are Made", *Long Range Planning*, Vol. 14, No. 3, June 1981, pp. 85–96.

McConkey, D. and Barrett, F. D. "Managing in the Age of the Robot", *Business Quarterly*, Vol. 4, No. 47, Dec. 1982, pp. 40–46.

Mendelow, A. L. "Setting Corporate Goals and Measuring Organisational Effectiveness — A Practical Approach", *Long Range Planning*, Vol. 16, No. 1, Feb. 1983, pp. 70–76.

Mitchell, Ford T. "Strategic Planning: Myth or Reality? — A Chief Executive's View", *Long Range Planning*, Vol. 16, No. 6, Dec. 1981, pp. 9–11.

Montebello, M. and Buigues, P. "How French Industry Plans", *Long Range Planning*, Vol. 15, No. 3, June 1982, pp. 116–120.

Morton, R. M. E. "Technology and Strategy", *Business Horizons*, Jan.–Feb. 1983, pp. 44–49.

Petroni, G. "Strategic Planning and Research and Development — Can We Integrate Them?", *Long Range Planning*, Vol. 16, No. 1, Feb. 1983, pp. 15–25.

Prahalad, C. K. and Doz, Y. L. "An Approach to Strategic Control in MNCs", *Sloan Management Review*, Summer 1981, pp. 5–13.

Robinson, R. B. Jr. "The Importance of Outsiders in Small Firm Strategic Planning", *Academy of Management Journal*, Vol. 25, No. 1, March 1982, pp. 80–93.

Sethi, N. K. "Strategic Planning System for Multinational Companies", *Long Range Planning*, Vol. 15, No. 3, June 1982, pp. 80–89.

Snyder, U. and Glueck "How Managers Plan — The Analysis of Managers' Activities", *Long Range Planning*, Vol. 13, No. 1, Feb. 1980, pp. 70–76.

Taylor, B. and Hussey, D. E. *The Realities of Planning*, Pergamon Press, Oxford, 1982.

Warrington, M. B. "Will Hong Kong's Entrepreneurs Move to Planning?", *Long Range Planning*, Vol. 15, No. 3, June 1982, pp. 168–175.

Wheelwright, S. C. "Japan — Where Operations Really are Strategic", *Harvard Business Review*, July–Aug. 1981, pp. 67–74.

Wright, D. "New Zealand — a Newcomer to Planning", *Long Range Planning*, Vol. 15, No. 3, June 1982, pp. 122–131.

CHAPTER 2

Finance for Strategic Management

Introduction

Although it could be argued that a knowledge of all the functional areas of business — finance, marketing, personnel and production — is necessary for a comprehensive understanding of strategic management, in this book it is the finance function alone which is singled out for particular attention. While it is accepted that a knowledge of the other functional areas is important, the finance function is unique both as an instrument of strategic analysis and as a creative strategic tool. The importance of finance in strategic management cannot really be overstated. This function has the responsibility of ensuring that the strategic plans and objectives of the firm are feasible for the (financial) resources which it has. Additionally, as all operations, including overall performance, are measured, ultimately, in financial terms, the finance function is uniquely placed to receive and act upon information from all parts of the firm and from outside stakeholders. Finally, through using published financial data, the strategist can analyse the behaviour and competence of rival firms within the industry and make judgements about his own firm's relative competitive position. Additionally, it is frequently the case that financial information is the only hard information available about competitors.

From the perspective of strategic management, finance has two linked major roles:

> The *controlling role*, i.e. how finance can be used to implement, monitor and evaluate a business strategy.
> The *creative role*, i.e. how finance can be used, in a creative fashion, to power an organisation towards its objectives and to give the firm advantages over its competitors.

Each of these roles is now explored through the medium of a hypothetical company, Company X, whose Balance Sheet and Income Statement for the years 1981 to 1983 are given on pages 35 to 36. The data from this company is used to calculate, manually, in this chapter the various financial techniques which are considered. Additionally, the data is used in Chapter 8 in the FINA suite of financial computer packages.

Table 2. Balance Sheet for Company X for the Years 1981–1983

Balance Sheet for Company X, 1981–1983
(Note: all figures are in thousands of pounds)

	1983		1982		1981	
Fixed Assets (at cost)						
Land		4		4		2
Buildings		50		48		40
Equipment	120		100		70	
Less Depreciation	70	50	60	40	55	15
Net fixed assets		104		92		57
Investments and other assets		8		8		8
Current assets						
Inventory	140		150		148	
Accounts receivable	110		100		90	
Short-term investments	11		—		—	
Prepaid expenses	2		2		1	
Cash	39		16		10	
Total current assets		302		268		249
Total assets		414		368		314
Financed by:						
Shareholders' equity						
Common stock*		170		161		125
Retained earnings		64		40		24
Total equity		234		201		149
Long-term debt		44		59		67
Other nonconcurrent liabilities		15		15		15
Current liabilities						
Accounts payable	12		6		4	
Notes payable	31		29		27	
Accrued expenses	60		44		40	
Taxes	18		14		12	
Total current liabilities		121		93		83
Total liabilities		414		368		314

The average number of shares outstanding in 1981, 1982 and 1983 were 54,000, 55,000 and 57,800 respectively.

Using Finance for Control and Creativity

In this section the objective is to give strategists the fundamental tools which should enable them to make financial analyses of their own and other firms. Although the techniques discussed are mainly cast as devices for analysis and control, in practice, as the text shows, they can be used in a creative manner to help a firm compete more effectively. Three sets of "tools" are considered — Ratio Analysis, Sources and

Table 3. Income statement for Company X for the Years 1981–1983

Income Statement for Company X for the Years 1981–1983.
(Note: all figures are in thousands of pounds)

		1983		1982		1981
Net sales		620		550		480
Less cost of sales		440		400		348
Gross profit		180		150		132
Less expenses						
Selling general and administrative expenses	105		95		85	
Interest	4		6		6	
Depreciation	10	119	5	106	5	96
Profit before tax		61		44		36
Provision for tax		30		22		18
Net profit		31		22		18
Cash dividends		7		6		4
Retained earnings		24		16		14

Applications of Funds Statements, and Break-even Analysis.

Ratio Analysis

Ratio analysis is a widely used method of analysing a firm and it is frequently employed by outside stakeholders — creditors, investors and financial institutions. The technique can be used firstly to give a "moving picture" of the performance of the firm; i.e. trends over a number of years can be analysed. Secondly, the ratios of a particular firm can be compared with the industry average (or competitors' ratios) at a single point in time and hence a judgement about the firm's position within the industry can be made. Figure 14 shows these two aspects of ratio analysis graphically. Here it can be seen that there has been a steady decline in Company X's Current Ratio from 3.0 in 1981 to 2.5 in 1983. However, when the industry average Current Ratios are examined, it can be seen that Company X's Current Ratio has been considerably above the industry average and is now moving towards the industry average.

Ratio analysis is a very quick and effective way of obtaining insights into a firm's operations and performance. However, the approach must be used with circumspection and in conjunction with complementary analytical tools as it has several limitations. The most serious limitation is that the approach is based exclusively on the past and this may not be a good guide to the future. Additionally, the quality of the analysis is determined by the quality of the accounting information upon which it is based and it is not unknown for "creative" accountants to mask the true

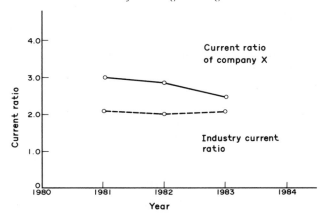

F<small>IG</small> 14. *Company X and industry current ratios, 1981–1983*

state of a firm's position. For example, an analysis of the accounts of the U.K. aero engine manufacturer Rolls Royce immediately prior to its collapse in 1979 would not have predicted its imminent bankruptcy.

Traditionally, financial ratios are divided into four broad categories. These are:

Liquidity Ratios: these measure the firm's ability to meet its short-term obligations.

Profitability Ratios: these measure management's overall performance and show the returns which management has been able to achieve.

Leverage Ratios, or Gearing Ratios: these measure the extent to which the firm has been financed by debt and by shareholders' funds.

Activity Ratios: these measure how well the firm is using its resources.

Each of these broad categories is now discussed in greater detail.

Liquidity Ratios

Liquidity shows how capable a firm is of meeting its short-term obligations, i.e. those which are due within one year. Firms generally meet these obligations by using their current assets, i.e. those assets which can quickly and easily be converted into cash. Adequate liquidity is particularly important in times of high inflation and also when businesses are just starting up. The liquidity of a firm is usually related to its cash flow position (see pages 57 to 59) and a cash flow analysis as well as a Liquidity Ratio analysis should be carried out.

Perhaps the best-known broad measure of a firm's ability to meet its short-term obligations is the Current Ratio.

Current Ratio

The Current Ratio is defined as: current assets divided by current liabilities. The Current Ratios for Company X for the years 1981 to 1983 are shown below.

Current Ratio	=	$\dfrac{\text{Current assets}}{\text{Current liabilities}}$

	1981	1982	1983
Current ratios of Company X	$\dfrac{249}{83} = 3.0$	$\dfrac{268}{93} = 2.9$	$\dfrac{302}{121} = 2.5$
Industry average = 2.2			

The ratio has declined, over the period, from 3.0 to 2.5, and has, in the process, moved closer to the industry average. However, it is important to bear in mind that a high Current Ratio is not necessarily either good or bad. Thus a high Current Ratio could be an indication that a company is not using its current assets efficiently. However, such a ratio could also indicate that the firm is maintaining a high ratio as an insurance against suspected forthcoming economic uncertainty. In conclusion, an excessively high, or an excessively low, Current Ratio should be a trigger for the strategist to investigate the reason more deeply.

Quick Ratio

Another measure of liquidity which is used frequently is the Quick Ratio, or Acid Test Ratio, which is defined as current assets minus average inventories divided by current liabilities. This ratio, rather than the Current Ratio, is used because it could be claimed that the inclusion of inventories (some of which may be obsolete and difficult to sell) in the Current Ratio overstates a firm's ability to meet its short-term obligations. The Quick Ratios for Company X for the years 1981 to 1983 are shown on page 39.

In general a Quick Ratio of 1 is considered satisfactory, as such a ratio indicates that a firm can meet its current liabilities quickly. Thus these two measures of liquidity indicate that Company X appears to have more liquidity than it needs, and this may be having an adverse effect upon its profitability.

From a strategic analysis point of view, it is probably sensible to commence with an analysis of the Liquidity Ratios, as these should reveal

Quick ratio $=$ $$\frac{\text{Current assets} - \text{Average inventories*}}{\text{Current liabilities}}$$

	1981	1982	1983
Current ratios of Company X =	$\frac{249-144}{83} = 1.3$	$\frac{268-149}{93} = 1.3$	$\frac{302-145}{121} = 1.3$
Industry average = 2.2		1.3	

how pressing the firm's commitments are and help determine the time available for strategic action.

Profitability Ratios

In spite of the increasing weight being afforded to the stakeholder, rather than the profit maximising view, of the role of business, it is the case that managerial and business success are still largely viewed in terms of profits. Managers ignore profits at their peril. Accordingly it seems appropriate to commence this section with some comments on profitability and how selected profit measures can be used as an aid to creative strategy.

Profitability is the ultimate measure of management's performance. Management can use the profitability measures to monitor its performance and to help plan strategies. A summary of how selected measures of profitability can be useful is given in Table 4 below.

The various measures of profitability are considered in more detail below.

Gross Profit Margin

Gross Profit Margin is defined as net sales minus cost of sales divided by net sales. The gross profit margins for Company X for the years 1981 to 1983 are shown below.

---

*Average inventory is calculated as follows.

$$Average\ inventory = \left(\frac{Inventory\ for\ year\ end\ +\ Inventory\ at\ previous\ year\ end}{2}\right).$$

(Note: *in the above example, in order to calculate the average inventory for 1981, it has been assumed that the value of the inventory at the end of 1980 was £140.*)

Table 4. Selected Measures of Profitability and Their Strategic Uses

Measure	Definition	Use
Gross profit margin	$\dfrac{\text{Net sales} - \text{Cost of sales}}{\text{Net sales}}$	How well are costs being controlled? How effective is marketing?
Net profit margin	$\dfrac{\text{Net profit}}{\text{Net Sales}}$	Shows return on sales. How effective is marketing?
Return on investment	$\dfrac{\text{Net Profit}}{\text{Total assets}}$	Can show how effective marketing and production are (see page 49)
Return on equity	$\dfrac{\text{Net profit}}{\text{Equity}}$	A crucial measure for shareholders, management and financial institutions. Shows performance and indicates potential for growth (see page 56)
Earnings per share	$\dfrac{\text{Earnings available}}{\text{Average no. of shares}}$	Of interest to shareholders and financial institutions
Payout ratio	$\dfrac{\text{Total dividends paid}}{\text{Total earnings available}}$	Of interest to shareholders

$$\text{Gross profit margin} \quad = \quad \frac{\text{Net sales} - \text{Cost of sales}}{\text{Net sales}}$$

Gross profit margins for Company X are:

1981	1982	1983
$\dfrac{480 - 348}{480} = 27.5\%$	$\dfrac{550 - 400}{550} = 27.3\%$	$\dfrac{620 - 440}{620} = 29.0\%$

Industry average = 25%

Company X has, over the period, had a higher and improving gross profit margin than the industry in general. This could indicate either a reduction in costs or an increase in the market price, and perhaps, overall, a strengthening of Company X.

Net Profit Margin

Net Profit Margin, or Return on Sales as it is frequently called, is defined as net profits after taxes divided by net sales. The net profit margin for Company X for the years 1981 to 1983 are shown below.

Net profit margin = $\dfrac{\text{Net profit}}{\text{Net sales}}$

Net profit margins for Company X are:

1981	1982	1983
$\dfrac{18}{480} = 3.8\%$	$\dfrac{22}{550} = 4.0\%$	$\dfrac{31}{620} = 5.0\%$

Industry average = 5.2%

The improvement of the net profit ratio could indicate a strengthening of the marketing effectiveness of the company as each £1 of net sales is now generating a higher net profit. This measure should be of considerable help to companies in assessing their marketing effectiveness.

Return on Investment

Return on Investment (ROI) is calculated by dividing net profits after taxes by total assets and measures how effectively the company's assets have been managed. The Return on Investment for Company X is shown below.

Return on investment = $\dfrac{\text{Net profit}}{\text{Total assets}}$

Return on investment for Company X:

1981	1982	1983
$\dfrac{18}{314} = 5.7\%$	$\dfrac{22}{368} = 6.0\%$	$\dfrac{31}{414} = 7.5\%$

Industry average = 8%

Although Return on Investment is an excellent measure of the overall performance of a company,* it is however such a broad measure (it is a single measure which captures the effects of many diverse and often opposing influences) that its diagnostic ability is somewhat limited. This limitation, to a certain extent, can be reduced by breaking down the Return on Investment Ratio into two other key ratios which can give strategists further insights into the management of the firm. Thus:

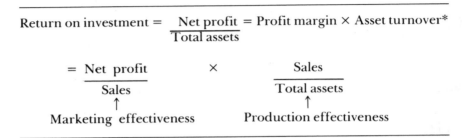

Return on investment = $\dfrac{\text{Net profit}}{\text{Total assets}}$ = Profit margin × Asset turnover*

$$= \underset{\underset{\text{Marketing effectiveness}}{\uparrow}}{\frac{\text{Net profit}}{\text{Sales}}} \quad \times \quad \underset{\underset{\text{Production effectiveness}}{\uparrow}}{\frac{\text{Sales}}{\text{Total assets}}}$$

When Return on Investment is broken down in the above fashion, the resulting ratios may show that improvements or disimprovements in performance may be traced to marketing effectiveness or production effectiveness. The breakdown of the Return on Investment for Company X is given below.

Return on investment for Company X = Profit margins × Asset turnover

1981	1982	1983
= 3.8% × 1.5 = 5.7%	4.0% × 1.5 = 6.0%	5.0% × 1.5 = 7.5%
↑ ↑	↑ ↑	↑ ↑
Market-ing effective-ness / Produc-tion effective-ness	Market effective-ness / Produc-tion effective-ness	Market effective-ness / Produc-tion effective-ness

As can be seen, the improvement of Company X's Return on Investment has been due exclusively to improvement in profit margins on sales. For this company an investigation into why its sales generation on assets has remained static could be worthwhile; any improvement in this ratio — say reducing the total assets — will automatically increase ROI.

*It is the method advocated by Ansoff.[1]
*See page 49 below for an exposition of the Asset Turnover Ratio.

Using Return on Investment Creatively

So far the analyses have looked backwards towards the past achievements of the firm. Now ROI is considered from a forward looking/planning perspective. This is achieved by answering the question:

"If a company, say Company M, has achieved a ROI of 4% in the last planning period, what ROI is possible, and realistic, in the next planning period, and how should the company strive to achieve this return?"

Firstly, consider ROI from a graphical point of view. Thus recalling from page 42 that ROI can be broken into two constituent ratios:

$$\text{ROI} = \frac{\text{Net profit}}{\text{Total assets}} = \frac{\text{Net profit}}{\text{Sales}} \times \frac{\text{Sales}}{\text{Total assets}}$$

ROI can be represented by a graph such as Fig. 15. In this graph the parabola *XYZ* represents all possible combinations of $\frac{\text{Net profits}}{\text{Sales}}$ and $\frac{\text{Sales}}{\text{Total assets}}$ that can yield a ROI of 4%.

Thus the point *X* is obtained by having:

$$\frac{\text{Net profit}}{\text{Sales}} = 4\% \text{ and } \frac{\text{Sales}}{\text{Total assets}} = 1\%, \text{ yielding a ROI of 4\%.}$$

Similarly, point *Y* is obtained by having:

$$\frac{\text{Net profit}}{\text{Sales}} = 2\% \text{ and } \frac{\text{Sales}}{\text{Total assets}} = 2\%, \text{ yielding a ROI of 4\%.}$$

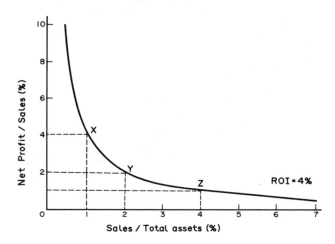

FIG. 15. *An ISORI line of 4%*

And point Z is obtained by having:

$$\frac{\text{Net profit}}{\text{Sales}} = 1\% \text{ and } \frac{\text{Sales}}{\text{Total assets}} = 4\%, \text{ yielding a ROI of } 4\%.$$

The line *XYZ* can be thought of as an ISOROI line — i.e. a line along which all points have an identical ROI. The ISOROI line shows that it is possible to achieve a given ROI by varying either $\frac{\text{Net profit}}{\text{Sales}}$ or $\frac{\text{Sales}}{\text{Total assets}}$ or both. Company M is at point *Y* and has achieved a ROI of 4% by having a $\frac{\text{Net profit}}{\text{Sales}}$ of 2% and a $\frac{\text{Sales}}{\text{Total assets}}$ of 2%.

ISOROI lines can be drawn for any desired ROI value. Thus Fig. 16 shows ISOROI lines of 4%, 8% and 16%.

Returning to the question of what ROI is feasible in the next planning period for Company M, this can be determined by answering the following two questions:

(a) What is the best Net profit/Sales ratio in the entire industry?* Let us assume in this case that it is 4%. This is displayed by the horizontal line *EC* in Fig. 16.

(b) What is the best Sales/Total assets ratio in the entire industry?* Again let us assume that it is 4%. This is displayed by the vertical line *HC* in Fig. 16.

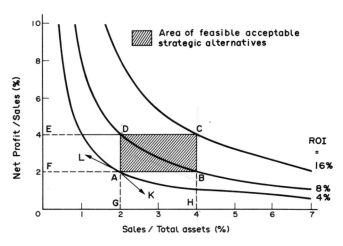

FIG. 16. *Setting a ROI target for the next planning period*

*This can be found through an examination of published trade and industry statistics

If it is assumed that the best Net profit/Sales ratio and the best Sales/Total assets ratio are possessed by different firms, then the theoretical maximum ROI for any company in this industry is 16%, and is shown by point *C*. Therefore, the strategy that Company M should follow is to move from point *A* towards point *C*. The rectangle *ABCD* delineates the area of feasible acceptable strategic alternatives. Any movement outside this rectangle, such as shown by *AK* or *AL*, is unacceptable because either of such movements will worsen Company M's ROI.

In conclusion, Company M has the following strategic options:

(1) It can improve its ROI by improving its Net profit/Sales ratio (through improvements in marketing effectiveness) and/or it can improve its Sales/Total assets ratio (through improving its production effectiveness).

(2) It knows that the theoretical maximum limit to its efforts is a ROI of 16%.

Finally, this approach to breaking single ratios into component ratios and then displaying them graphically can be employed with equal facility for many of the other ratios considered in this chapter.

Return on Equity

Return on Equity measures the rate of return on the owners' investment and is calculated by dividing net profits after taxes by stockholders' equity. The Returns on Equity for Company X for the years 1981 to 1983 are shown below.

Return on equity = $\dfrac{\text{Net profit}}{\text{Stockholders' equity}}$

Return on equity for Company X =

1981	1982	1983
$\dfrac{18}{149} = 12.1\%$	$\dfrac{22}{201} = 10.9\%$	$\dfrac{31}{234} = 13.2\%$

Industry average = 10.2%

As can be seen, the Return on Equity for Company X has been improving over the period somewhat more slowly than the other indicators of performance. This sluggishness in the Return on Equity must be a cause of concern for managers and shareholders. However, like the Return on Investment ratio, the Return on Equity ratio is too broad to provide diagnostic insights. This limitation can be overcome to some extent by breaking the Return on Equity ratio into other ratios as shown below.

Return on equity $= \dfrac{\text{Net profit}}{\text{Total equity}}$

$= \dfrac{\text{Net profit}}{\text{Total assets}} \times \dfrac{\text{Total assets}}{\text{Total equity}}$

$= \underset{\substack{\uparrow \\ \text{Marketing} \\ \text{effectiveness}}}{\dfrac{\text{Net profit}}{\text{Net sales}}} \times \underset{\substack{\uparrow \\ \text{Production} \\ \text{effective-} \\ \text{ness}}}{\dfrac{\text{Net sales}}{\text{Total assets}}} \times \underset{\substack{\uparrow \\ \text{Financial} \\ \text{effective-} \\ \text{ness}}}{\dfrac{\text{Total assets}}{\text{Total equity}}}$

Thus when Return on Equity is broken down, the resultant ratios may show that performance may be attributed to marketing effectiveness, production effectiveness or financial effectiveness. The breakdown of the Return on Equity for Company X is given below.

Return on equity for Company X

$= \dfrac{\text{Net profit }\%}{\text{Net sales}} \times \dfrac{\text{Net sales }^{Ratio}}{\text{Total assets}} \times \dfrac{\text{Total assets }^{Ratio}}{\text{Total equity}}$

1981	1982	1983
$= 3.8\% \times 1.5 \times 2.1$	$4.0\% \times 1.5 \times 1.8$	$5.0\% \times 1.5\% \times 1.8$
$= 12\%$	$= 10.8\%$	$= 13.5\%$

As can be seen, the improvement in the ROE is due mainly to an increase in the Net profit to Sales ratio. This helps confirm the previous analysis. Additionally, it may be noted that the Total assets/Total equity ratio appears to have inhibited the growth of ROE. This is confirmed on page 48.

Finally, ROE is considered to be a measure of such fundamental importance that it will be considered again, in greater detail, in the section "The Relationship Between Return on Equity, Leverage, Growth and Dividends" on page 52.

Earnings per Share

Earnings per share measures how much money each share earned during the period being considered and is calculated by dividing the earnings available for common stockholders by the average number of shares outstanding. The earnings per share for Company X for the years 1981 to 1983 are shown below.

$$\text{Earnings per share} = \frac{\text{Earnings available for common stockholders}}{\text{Average number of ordinary shares outstanding}}$$

1981	1982	1983
$\dfrac{18}{54000} = 33.3$ pence	$\dfrac{22}{55000} = 40$ pence	$\dfrac{31}{57800} = 53.6$ pence

As can be seen, the Earnings per share ratio has been improving strongly over the period.

Payout Ratio

The Payout ratio measures the extent to which the company pays cash dividends to the holders of common stock. This measure is obtained by dividing the total dividends paid by the total earnings available, i.e. the net profit. The Payout ratios for Company X for the years 1981 to 1983 are given below. As will be shown on page 57, the Payout ratio can have a fundamental effect upon a company's growth rate.

$$\text{Payout ratio} = \frac{\text{Total dividends paid}}{\text{Total earnings available}}$$

1981	1982	1983
$\dfrac{4}{18} = 22.2\%$	$\dfrac{6}{22} = 27.3\%$	$\dfrac{7}{31} = 22.6\%$

Industry average = 25%

Leverage Ratios

These ratios show who has supplied the firm's capital, i.e. owners or outside creditors (i.e. banks, bonds, etc.). Companies that have a high proportion of fixed obligations are said to be highly levered. The term "leverage" is used because the proportion of fixed obligations in a firm's capital structure will magnify (or lever) its profits or losses.

Debt to Equity

Probably the most commonly used leverage ratio is the Debt–Equity ratio* which is defined as the total long-term debt (liabilities) divided by the total of stockholders' equity. The Debt–Equity ratios for Company X for the years 1981 to 1983 are shown below.

Debt-Equity ratio $= \dfrac{\text{Total long-term debt}}{\text{Total equity}}$

Debt-Equity ratios of Company X are:

1981	1982	1983
$\dfrac{67}{149} = 44.9\%$	$\dfrac{59}{201} = 29.4\%$	$\dfrac{44}{234} = 18.8\%$

Industry average $= 48\%$

Another ratio which is used frequently in financial analysis is the ratio of total debt to total assets. However, this ratio is not included here as the Debt to Equity (D/E) and the Debt to Assets (D/A) ratios are simply transformations of each other. Thus:

$$\frac{D}{A} = \frac{\dfrac{D}{A}}{\left(\dfrac{1 - D}{A}\right)}$$

$$= \frac{\dfrac{D}{A}}{\dfrac{1}{A}(A - D)}$$

$$= \frac{D}{E}$$

$$\frac{D}{A} = \frac{D}{E + D}$$

$$\frac{A}{D} = \frac{E + D}{D} = \frac{E}{D} + 1$$

The Debt to Equity ratio has been falling quite dramatically and is now substantially below the industry average. This is confirmation of what had been suspected when the Return on Equity ratios were considered — the company's financial structure has too small a proportion of debt to equity and this is depressing the Return on Equity and giving stockholders suboptimal returns.

Debt Coverage

Another important measure of capital structure is Debt Coverage, which is defined as profit before interest and taxes divided by interest expense. This ratio shows the company's ability to *cover* its fixed charges. Company X's debt coverage ratio is shown below.

Debt coverage = $\dfrac{\text{Profit before interest and taxes}}{\text{Interest paid}}$

Debt coverage for Company X:

1981	1982	1983
$\dfrac{36+6}{6} = 7.0$	$\dfrac{44+6}{6} = 8.3$	$\dfrac{61+4}{4} = 16.2$

Industry average = 8.2

This ratio confirms the previous analyses: that the company has reduced significantly its dependence on debt and consequently its ability to meet its fixed charges has improved significantly.

Activity Ratios

These ratios measure how effectively, or efficiently, a firm is using its resources. The most commonly used activity ratios are given on page 50.

Fixed Asset Turnover

The Fixed Asset Turnover Ratio measures how effectively management is using the assets at its disposal and is computed by dividing the net sales by the total net fixed assets. The Fixed Asset Turnover Ratio for Company X for the years 1981 to 1983 is given below.

Fixed asset turnover ratio = $\dfrac{\text{Net sales}}{\text{Net fixed assets}}$

Fixed asset turnover ratio for Company X:

1981	1982	1983
$\dfrac{480}{57} = 8.4$	$\dfrac{550}{92} = 6.0$	$\dfrac{620}{104} = 6.0$

Industry average = 6.2

Fixed Asset Turnover has declined for Company X over the period and is now slightly below the industry average.

Inventory Turnover

Inventory Turnover Ratio measures how many times the company's inventory is turned over (or sold) each year and is computed by dividing the net sales by the average inventory* for the year. Obviously the faster inventories are turned over, the faster will be sales and the faster cash will flow into the company.

The Inventory Turnover Ratio for Company X for the years 1981 to 1983 is given below.

Inventory turnover ratio = $\dfrac{\text{Net sales}}{\text{Average inventory}}$

Inventory turnover ratio for Company X:

1981	1982	1983
$\dfrac{480}{144} = 3.3$	$\dfrac{550}{149} = 3.7$	$\dfrac{620}{145} = 4.3$

Industry average = 3.3

*The average inventory is obtained as shown in the footnote on page 39.

Inventory turnover for Company X has been steadily improving and is now considerably ahead of the industry average.

Accounts Receivable Turnover

The Accounts Receivable Turnover Ratio measures the average collection period for credit sales and is computed by dividing net sales by the accounts receivable. The Accounts Receivable Turnover for Company X for the years 1981 to 1983 is shown below.

Accounts receivable turnover ratio = $\dfrac{\text{Net sales}}{\text{Accounts receivable}}$

Accounts receivable turnover ratio for Company X:

1981	1982	1983
$= \dfrac{480}{90} = 5.3$	$\dfrac{550}{100} = 5.5$	$\dfrac{620}{110} = 5.6$

Industry average = 5.2

Company X is performing well. Over the entire period its Inventory Turnover Ratio has been better than the industry average and it is drawing further ahead.

Average Collection Period

Closely related to the Accounts Receivable Turnover ratio is the Average Collection Period of accounts receivable — this measures the number of days' sales that are held as receivables. This can be calculated by dividing 360* days by the Accounts Receivable turnover ratio. The Average Collection Periods for Company X for the years 1981 to 1983 are shown on page 52.

The figures indicate that Company X's average collection period is improving and it is better than the rest of the industry. If the average collection period for a firm is substantially different from the industry norm, this may indicate poor management or control. Thus if the collection period is excessively short, this may indicate an extremely strict credit policy which may inhibit sales, while if the collection period

By convention most analysts use a 360-day rather than a 365-day year.

Average collection period =		$\dfrac{360}{\text{Accounts receivable turnover ratio}}$	

1981	1982	1983
$= \dfrac{360}{5.3} = 68$ days	$\dfrac{360}{5.5} = 65$ days	$\dfrac{360}{5.6} = 64$ days

Industry average 69 days

---

is significantly longer than the industry average,* this may indicate poor control, and will cause excessive amounts of capital to be tied up in accounts receivable (this is particularly costly in an era of inflation) and may increase the probability of bad debts.

The Relationship Between Return on Equity, Leverage, Growth and Dividends[†]

In the section above the Return on Equity ratio and the Leverage ratio were considered separately and discretely. This is a somewhat artificial and limited perspective. The ratios are closely linked and are fundamental determinants in the growth of a firm.

ROE is a vitally important financial measure not just for the diagnostic insights, outlined above, that it can provide, but perhaps more importantly because this measure alone is the fundamental *variable* in a firm's financial strategy. Its historic value is a measure of management's past success in achieving growth and its current value is a key determinant of future growth. Its importance, and the importance of the closely related D:E ratio, are illustrated below by means of a simple example. In this example a firm is assumed to operate under the following conditions:

(a) the firm has total assets of £100;
(b) the rate of return on assets is 10% per year, each year;
(c) profits are defined as: profits = return on assets × assets;

---

*In a consultancy, the author noted that the accounts of the firm under investigation had allowed its average collection period to drift, in three years, from approximately 80 days to 273 days, in an industry with an average of 61 days. This appeared to indicate a lack of managerial control. After further investigation it was discovered that the company had, in this period, been attempting, unsuccessfully, to change from a manual information system to a computerised system. In the process of the attempted changeover, customers were not invoiced and this led to the catastrophic lengthening of the average collection period.

[†]The major substance for this section is taken from Ref. (2).

(d) all profits are retained in the firm (i.e. no dividends are paid);

(e) the rate of interest on debt is 5%;

(f) there are no taxes.

Consider now the balance sheet of this firm in three consecutive years under three different debt to equity conditions.

Condition I. No Debt at all

The firm's performance over the three years under this condition is shown in Table 5.

Table 5. Return on Equity under Conditions of No Debt

	Year 1 £	Year 2 £	Year 3 £
Total assets	100	110	121
Equity	100	110	121
Rate of return	10%	10%	10%
Profit	10	11	12.1
Reinvested	10	11	12.1
Return on assets	10%	10%	10%
Return on equity	10%	10%	10%

In this case it can be seen that each year there was:

(i) a return on equity of 10%;

(ii) a growth in assets of 10%;

(iii) a growth in equity of 10%; and

(iv) a growth in profits of 10%.

Condition II. A Debt to Equity ratio of 50:50

Under this condition the firm has the same amount of total assets as before but the capital structure is 50% debt and 50% equity. The firm's performance over the three years is shown in Table 6.

In this case it can be seen that each year there was:

(i) a return on equity of 15%;

(ii) a growth in assets of 15%;

(iii) a growth in equity of 15%; and

(iv) a growth in net profits of 15%.

Condition III. A Debt to Equity ratio of 75:25

Under this condition the firm has the same amount of total assets but

Table 6. Return on Equity under Conditions of a Debt to Equity Ratio of 50:50

	Year 1 £	Year 2 £	Year 3 £
Total assets	100	115	132.24
Equity	50	57.50	66.12
Debt	50	57.50	66.12
Rate of return	10%	10%	10%
Profit before interest	10	11.5	13.22
Interest (5%)	2.50	2.88	3.31
Profit after interest	7.50	8.62	9.91
• Net return on assets	7.5%	7.5%	7.5%
Return on equity	15%	15%	15%
Equity reinvested	7.50	8.62	9.91
Additional debt*	7.50	8.62	9.91
Total new investment	15.00	17.24	19.82

the capital structure is 75% debt and 25% equity. The firm's performance over the three years is shown in Table 7.

In this case it can be seen that each year there was:

(i) a return on equity of 25%;
(ii) a growth in assets of 25%;
(iii) a growth in equity of 25%; and
(iv) a growth in net profits of 25%.

These examples have two major strategic messages.

The first is that by using debt a firm can significantly magnify its
return on equity and its real growth rate. Thus the creative use of debt
by strategic planners can enable a firm to achieve and maintain a higher

Table 7. Return on Equity under Conditions of a Debt to Equity Ratio of 75:25

	Year 1 £	Year 2 £	Year 3 £
Total assets	100	125	156.25
Equity	25	31.25	39.06
Debt	75	93.75	117.19
Rate of return	10%	10%	10%
Profit before interest	10	12.5	15.62
Interest (5%)	3.75	4.69	5.86
Profit after interest	6.25	7.81	9.76
Net return on assets	6.25%	6.25%	6.25%
Return on equity	25%	25%	25%
Equity reinvested	6.25	7.81	9.76
Additional debt	18.75	23.44	29.3
Total new investment	25	31.25	39.06

*Needed to maintain the debt to equity ratio at 50:50.

rate of growth than its competitors. This can be of particular importance in industries which are subject to global competition. Thus it can be the case that although two rival companies in different countries have identical ROI ratios, that the company located in the country whose culture accommodates a higher level of debt financing can enjoy significant growth advantages. This is a strategic advantage that Japanese companies in particular have, for many years, enjoyed over their European and American rivals.

The advantage that having a higher debt to equity ratio than is rivals bestows upon a firm is illustrated in Fig. 17. Here two hypothetical firms

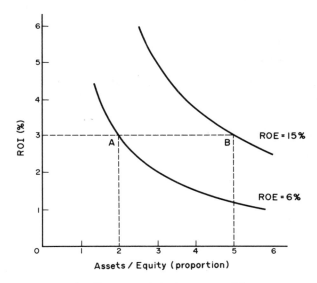

FIG. 17. *Illustration of the importance of leverage*

are portrayed. Firm A has a ROE of 6% while firm B has a ROE of 15%. Obviously firm B is performing in a much more satisfactory fashion than firm A. However, when the ROE ratios of each firm are broken into two constitutent ratios (Return on Investment and Assets/Equity), it can be seen that B's superior performance is due exclusively to having a much higher Assets/Equity (equivalent to Debt to Equity) ratio. The strategic implication for A is clear — its capital structure places it at a permanent disadvantage *vis-à-vis* B and for it to compete effectively it must increase its proportion of debt.

The second major strategic message is that ROE is equivalent to the maximum theoretical sustainable rate of growth that the company can achieve. As Tables 5, 6 and 7 show, the annual growth in assets of the firm is exactly equal to the return on equity. Based on this relationship, a formula for predicting growth is now derived.

The Maximum Sustainable Rate of Growth

The rate of growth is equal to the firm's return on equity, assuming no dividends are paid. Profit, or return, can be defined as the rate of return on assets minus the interest paid on debt. Thus:

$$\text{Profit} = r(TA) - ID \tag{1}$$

where r = rate of return,

TA = total assets,

i = interest rate,

D = debt,

E = equity.

Now as total assets must equal the sum of debt and equity, then (1) may be rewritten as:

$$\text{Profit} = r(D + E) - iD \tag{2}$$

$$\text{or, Profit} = rD - iD + rE \tag{3}$$

Dividing (3) by E (equity),

$$\frac{\text{Profit}}{\text{Equity}} = \frac{D}{E}(r - i) + \frac{rE}{E} \tag{4}$$

$$\frac{\text{Profit}}{\text{Equity}} = \frac{D}{E}(r - i) + r \tag{5}$$

i.e. Growth rate, $G = \dfrac{D}{E}(r - i) + r$ (6)

This is the maximum sustainable rate of growth assuming no dividends are paid. If dividends are paid, their effects may be introduced by multiplying (6) by p, the percent of earnings retained. Thus (6) becomes

$$\boxed{G = \frac{D}{E}(r - i)p + rp}$$

The growth rate G can be influenced by operating on one or more of the elements on the right-hand side of the above expression. To help perceive how alternative functional strategies can influence the rate of growth it is helpful to set out the growth formula as shown on page 57.

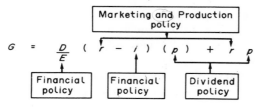

$$G = \frac{D}{E} \; (\; r - i \;) \; (\; p \;) \; + \; r \; p$$

In order to boost growth a firm can use one or more of the following broad strategies.

Financial Strategy I: increase the debt to equity ratio.

Financial Strategy II: reduce i, the interest paid on debt, by seeking cheaper sources of funds.

Marketing Strategy: increase r, the return on assets, by either selling more at the existing price and/or by increasing the price.

Production Strategy: increase r, the return on assets, by increasing the efficiency of production through unit cost reductions and/or producing the same quantity using fewer assets.

Dividend Strategy: reduce p, the proportion of profits paid out as dividends. Simply retain a greater proportion of the earnings.

In conclusion, the return on equity, is perhaps the most important ratio from a strategic management point of view and understanding how this ratio is linked to capital structure, return on assets and dividend payout is essential for formulating effective strategic plans.

Sources and Applications of Funds

Although the Income Statement and the Balance Sheet of a company show the amount of profit generated during the year and the state of the company's resources at the beginning and end of that year, these statements alone do not give an adequate or complete financial picture of the company's activities over that period. Thus movements in items such as assets, liabilities and capital, which may have material effects, are not shown explicitly in either statement. However, it is relatively easy to extract such movements and their effects. This can be done through a "Sources and Applications of Funds Statement".

The Sources and Applications of Funds Statement attempts to show how the company's financial resources have been obtained and how they have been used. Such a statement should enable planners to distinguish between using funds to purchase fixed assets and using funds to increase working capital. One aspect of the statement seems to be worthy of particular mention — its ability to show the net cash flow into, or out of, the company over the period of analysis. Cash flow, as the statement for Company X shows, is not the same as net profit (net profit and net cash flow for Company X in 1983 were £31,000 and £10,000 respectively) and it is important to distinguish between them. Net profit could be described as the amount of income accruing to a company after the various costs associated with sales, including depreciation and tax, have been met. Cash flow, however, measures the amount of *cash* that flows into (or out of) a company in a given period of time.

Finally, in passing, it is perhaps worth noting that cash flow is of vital importance in two particular situations.

(a) When a company is in a start-up and rapid growth situation a frequent cause of bankruptcy is overtrading — i.e. in its desire to grow quickly such a company may embark upon expansions which their asset base cannot sustain. In these circumstances cash flow problems are frequently a first manifestation of the problem.

(b) In periods of high inflation interest rates tend to be high and debtors tend, because of the high interest rates, to try to defer payments. This can lead to cash flow problems.

A statement showing the sources and applications of funds for Company X is shown in Table 8. As can be seen, the net cash flow was £10,000 and £11,000 in 1983 and 1982 respectively.

Break-even Analysis

A key decision in strategy formulation or appraisal is the pricing decision. The price which is charged for a good or service will have fundamental effects upon the company itself and may have, depending on the industry, material effects upon competitors. Break-even analysis can be used as an aid to strategic price determination.

Break-even analysis shows the relationships between volume, fixed costs, variable costs and revenue. The primary objective of the analysis is to see at what volume of production total costs equal total revenues, i.e. what is the break-even point. Additionally, the analysis can be used to test how sensitive profitability is to changes in price, changes in fixed costs and changes in variable costs. Break-even analysis is presented below in the context of a hypothetical company, Company Z.

Assumptions

In order to build a break-even model, several simplifying assumptions are made. These are:

Table 8. Sources and Application of Funds Statement for Company X for the Years 1982 and 1983

Company X
Statement of Sources and Application of Funds
(Note: all figures are in thousands of pounds)

	This year (1983)		Last year (1982)	
Sources of Funds				
Profit before tax		61		44
Adjustments for items not involving the movement of funds:				
Depreciation		10		5
Total Generated from Operations		71		49
Funds from Other Sources				
Issue of Shares for Cash		9		36
		80		85
Application of Funds				
Purchase of fixed assets	(22)		(40)	
Redemption of long-term debt	(15)		(8)	
Dividends paid	(7)		(6)	
Tax paid	(26)	(70)	(20)	(74)
		10		11
Increase (Decrease) in Working Capital				
Increase in stocks	(10)		2	
Increase in Prepayments	—		1	
Increase in Accounts Receivable	10		10	
Increase in Accounts Payable	(6)		(2)	
Increase in Notes Payable	(2)		(2)	
Increase in Accrued Expenses	(16)		(4)	
Movement in Net Liquid Funds				
Increase in Cash	23		6	
Increase in Short-term Investments	11		=	
		34		6
		10		11

(a) *Fixed costs*
   Fixed costs are independent of the number of units manufactured. These costs typically include such items as interest payments, salaries, rent, etc., and are shown in Fig. 18 by the line *FC*. As can be seen, fixed costs for Company Z are £10,000.
(b) *Variable costs*
   Variable costs are assumed to vary directly with the volume produced. In the case of Company Z, it is assumed that each unit costs £3 irrespective of the volume produced. Thus the line *OV* shows how total variable costs vary with output.

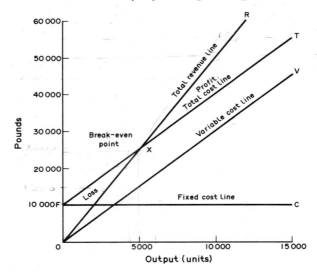

FIG. 18. *Break-even analysis, graphic method*

(c) *Total costs*
Total costs* are the sum of fixed costs and variable costs and are represented by the line *FT* in Fig. 18.

(d) *Price and revenue*
The selling price is fixed — it cannot be reduced or increased by the manufacturer — and consequently revenue is a fixed percentage of sales. In Company Z, price is £5 and total revenues are shown by the line *OR*.

(e) *Time*
It is assumed that the time period of the analysis is one year.

The Break-even Point

The intersection of the total cost line *FT* and the total revenue line *OR* gives the break-even point *X* for Company Z. It can be seen that for this company, output must exceed 5000 units in order to generate any profit. At this break-even point, variable costs plus fixed costs are equal to total revenue, or algebraically:

$$F \; + \; V(O) = P(O) \tag{1}$$

where F = fixed costs,

*It is pointed out that, for the sake of simplicity, semi-variable costs have been omitted.

V = variable costs per unit,
P = price per unit,
O = output (i.e. volume of production).

Alternatively (1) may be written as:

$$O = BE = \frac{F}{P-V}$$

where BE = break-even point,

and this equation gives the output required to break even.
Thus in the case of Company Z

$$BE = \frac{£10,000}{£5-£3} = 5000 \text{ units}$$

Sensitivity Analysis

As well as showing the relationship between profits* and volume, break-even analysis permits analyses of how sensitive these elements are to changes in fixed costs and changes in variable costs. The effects of changes in each of these factors are now considered.

Case 1. A 10% Change in Price

Table 9 shows how a 10% change in price would affect the operating profit before interest and taxes and break-even point for Company Z.

Table 9. How a Price Change would Affect the Profit B.I.T. and Break-even Point of Company Z

Price (£) Volume (units)	0	5,000	10,000	Break-even point (units)
		Profit B.I.T. (£)		
Original price i.e. £5	−10,000	0	10,000	5,000
10% Price increase i.e. £5.50	−10,000	+2,500	15,000	4,000
10% Price decrease i.e. £4.50	−10,000	−2,500	7,500	6,667

*By profit is meant operating profit before taxes, excluding interest and other income and expenses. It will subsequently be referred to as "Profit B.I.T."

Case 2. A 10% Change in Fixed Costs

Table 10 shows how a 10% change in fixed costs would affect the profit B.I.T. and break-even point of Company Z.

Case 3. A 10% Change in Variable Costs

Table 11 shows how a 10% change in variable costs would affect the profit B.I.T. and break-even point of Company Z.

As can be seen from Tables 9, 10 and 11, price is the most sensitive of the variables: i.e. for a given percentage change it has the greatest effect on profit B.I.T. and break-even point. Variable cost is the next most sensitive and fixed cost is the least sensitive.

Although this type of analysis can be of some help in making a pricing decision, it is extremely limited — it assumes linear relationships.

Table 10. How a Change in Fixed Costs would Affect the Profit B.I.T. and Break-even Point of Company Z

Volume (units)	0	5,000	10,000	Break-even point (units)
Fixed costs (£000)				
	Profit B.I.T. (£)			
Original case, i.e. F.C. = £10,000	−10,000	0	10,000	5,000
10% Decrease, i.e. F.C. = £9,000	−9,000	1,000	11,000	4,500
10% Increase, i.e. F.C. = £1,100	−1,100	−1,000	9,000	5,500

Table 11. How a Change in Variable Costs would Affect the Profit B.I.T. and Break-even Point of Company Z

Volume (units)	0	5,000	10,000	Break-even point (units)
Variable costs (£)				
	Operating profit (£000)			
Original case, i.e. V.C. = £300	−10,000	0	10,000	5,000
10% Decrease, i.e. V.C. = £270	−10,000	1,500	13,000	4,348
10% Increase, i.e. V.C. = £330	−10,000	−1,500	7,000	5,882

However, it is a useful method for obtaining a quick indication of price/volume/variable costs/fixed costs combinations that are required in order to break even, an essential calculation in appraising or formulating a strategy.

Nonlinear Break-even Analysis

In the above analyses linearity was assumed. This simplifying assumption is unlikely to be universally true. In practice it will frequently be the case that both revenues and costs will be nonlinear. For example, prices may be reduced in order to gain market share or in response to competitive moves by rivals. Similarly, although variable costs may progressively decline as volume increases, it can be the case that variable costs increase (as Porter[6] has shown) after a certain volume has been reached. Figure 19 shows a break-even graph where price decreases as volume increases and variable costs decrease initially and then increase. As the figure shows, this firm has two break-even points — A and B. The point of maximum profit is where the vertical distance between the Total Cost Line and the Revenue Line is greatest.

It is impossible to give a general mathematical formula for establishing

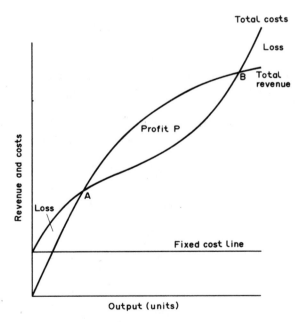

Fig. 19. *Nonlinear break-even analysis*

break-even points for nonlinear situations. It is suggested that the break-even points be obtained from a graphical plot based upon empirical data.

Using Break-even Analysis to Link Market Forecasts to Pricing Decisions

Although the above type of analyses are of some help in making a pricing decision, they suffer from the shortcoming that they do not link the pricing decision to market forecasts. This shortcoming is removed below.

It is now assumed that Company Z has received from its marketing department sales forecasts for its product. These forecasts are shown in Table 12 below.

Table 12. Sales Forecasts for Company X

Price (£)	Sales forecast (000s of units)
5.00	10,000
4.50	14,000
4.00	22,000
3.70	29,000
3.40	30,000
3.25	32,000

The sales forecast can be used with break-even analysis to determine the optimal price for the product using the maximum profit B.I.T. as the selection criterion.

As Table 12A shows, if the selection criterion is the maximisation of profit B.I.T. then the price should be set at £4.00.

Table 12A. How Operating Profit and Break-even Point are Affected by Price and Sales Forecast

Price (£)	Sales forecast (000s units)	Price — variable costs (£)	Break-even point (000s units)	Profit B.I.T. (£000)
5.00	10,000	2.00	5,000	10,000
4.50	14,000	1.50	6,667	11,000
4.00	22,000	1.00	10,000	12,000
3.70	29,000	0.70	14,286	10,300
3.40	30,000	0.40	25,000	2,000
3.25	32,000	0.25	40,000	−2,000

This exposition of break-even analysis has, in the interests of brevity and clarity, made a number of somewhat unrealistic simplifying assumptions. Thus the exposition has assumed that all relations are linear, that fixed costs are fixed for all volumes of output, that the variable costs per unit do not fall as the accumulated volume of production increases, that the original stock of assets will support any level of output and that maximising the profit B.I.T. is an appropriate selection criterion. In practice, frequently allowance must be made for these and other influences, and further information on how to accommodate these influences is given in Refs. (3), (4) and (5).

Conclusion

The rationale behind this chapter has been that some understanding of the power of the finance function is essential to sound strategic management. Accordingly, therefore, selected techniques which tend to be the most useful for strategic financial analysis have been presented. While it is accepted that there are many other financial techniques which might be considered as highly important in the area of strategic management — for example, investment appraisal, portfolio management, the tax environment, financial reporting, share valuation, etc. — the techniques which have been included are there firstly because they are probably the most useful and secondly because they are relatively simple and can be easily learnt by even the least financially sophisticated planner. Using the techniques given in this chapter, managers should be able to quickly obtain insights into their own and competitors' firms and students should, in their analysis of cases, be able to support their policy assertions with hard financial data. The FINA suite of computer programs should be of considerable help in the above tasks.

References

1. Ansoff, H. I. *Strategic Management*, Macmillan, 1979.
2. *Growth and Financial Strategies*, A Special Commentary published by the Boston Consulting Group, 1971.
3. Gup, B. E. *Guide to Strategic Planning*, McGraw-Hill Finance Guide Series, 1980.
4. Hawke, S. L. and Kroncke, C. O. "The Break-even Concept: A Guide to Profitable Decision Making", *Managerial Planning*, May/June 1977, pp. 11–28.
5. Ingham, H. and Harrington, L. T. *Interfirm Comparison*, Heinemann, London, 1980.
6. Porter, M. E. *Competitive Strategy*, The Free Press, 1980.

Bibliography

Note: This bibliography is shorter than the others in this book. This is because the field of finance is so wide that to attempt to provide a comprehensive bibliography in the context of this book would not reflect the scope and importance of the discipline. Instead a short selection of books and articles which the author has found useful for business strategy is given.

Bierman, H. *Financial Management and Inflation*, Collier Macmillan, 1981.
Branch, B. and Gale, B. "Linking Corporate Stock Performance to Strategy Formulation", *Journal of Business Strategy*, Vol. 4, No. 1, Summer 1983.
Brealy, R. and Myers, S. *Principles of Corporate Finance*, McGraw-Hill, London, 1981.
Dean, B. V. and Cowen, S. C. "Zero Based Budgeting in the Private Sector", *Business Horizons*, August 1979, pp. 73–83.
Dimson, E. and Marsh, P. "Calculating the Cost of Capital", *Long Range Planning*, Vol. 15, No. 2, April 1982, pp. 112–120.
Freear, J. *The Management of Business Finance*, Pitman, London, 1980.
Hardymon, G. F., De Nino, M. J. and Salter, M. S. "When Corporate Venture Capital Doesn't Work", *Harvard Business Review*, May–June 1983, pp. 114–120.
Hull, J. C. *The Evaluation of Risk in Business Investment*, Pergamon, Oxford, 1980.
Hobson, T. "Financial Modelling on Microcomputers", *OR*, Vol. 34, No. 4, April 1983, pp. 289–297.
McDonald, B. and Morris, M. H. "The Statistical Validity of the Ratio Method in Financial Analysis: An Empirical Investigation", *Journal of Business Finance and Accounting*, Vol. 11, No. 1, Spring 1984, pp. 89–97.
McInnes, J. M. and Carleton, W. J. "Theory, Models and Implementation in Financial Management", *Management Science*, Vol. 28, No. 9, Sept. 1982, pp. 957–978.
Miller, D. E. *The Meaningful Interpretation of Financial Statements: the Cause and Effect Ratio Approach*, American Management Association, 1972.
Naylor, T. H. and Tapon, F. "The Capital Asset Pricing Model: An Evaluation of its Potential as a Strategic Planning Tool", *Management Science*, Vol. 28, No. 10, Oct. 1983, pp. 1166–1173.
Pearson, J. V. "Zero-Base Budgeting — A Technique for Planned Organizational Decline", *Long Range Planning*, Vol. 14, No. 3, June 1981, pp. 68–76.
Rappaport, A. "Corporate Performance and Shareholder Value", *The Journal of Business Strategy*, Vol. 3, No. 4, Spring 1983, pp. 28–38.
Rudden, E. M. "Why DCF Doesn't Work", *BCG Perspective* No. 249, The Boston Consulting Group, 1982.
Samuels, J. M. and Wilkes, F. M. *Management of Company Finance*, Nelson, 1980.
Siegel, J. G. and Shim, J. K. "Quality of Earnings; a Key Factor in Financial Planning", *Long Range Planning*, Vol. 14, No. 6, Dec. 1981, pp. 68–75.
Simpson, L. *Management Accounting Techniques for Non-financial Managers*, Business Books, London, 1979.
Smith, J. E. *Cash Flow Management*, Woodhead-Falkner, 1980.
Stancill, J. M. "Growing Concerns", *Harvard Business Review*, March–April, 1981, pp. 180–225.
Tamari, M. *Financial Ratios: Analysis and Prediction*, Elek, London, 1978.
Tucker, S. A. *Profit Planning Decisions with the Break-even System*, Gower, Farnborough, Hants, 1980.
Wood, E. G. *Added Value: the Key to Prosperity*, Business Books, London 1978.
Wright, M. G. *Financial Management*, McGraw-Hill, 1980.

CHAPTER 3

Experience Curves

Introduction

In Chapter 1 the importance of having an informed strategic perspective was emphasised. One aspect of this perspective is having a knowledge of strategic approaches to cost reduction to enable a firm to gain cost advantage over competitors. A fundamental lever of cost reduction is the experience effect. A knowledge of how the experience effect can affect strategic management is essential for many industries. Without this knowledge planners will miss opportunities or, worse, will be crushed by those competitors who have such knowledge. Although the experience effect, i.e. the phenomenon whereby costs fall with accumulated volume of experience, has been known for many years, it is really only since the publication of the work of the Boston Consulting Group in this area in the 1960s and 1970s that it has come to be widely recognised as a major lever in business strategy and national economic strategy.

In the last twenty years, in particular, European and U.S. businesses have perceived, usually painfully, the very real effects of aggressive sales strategies based, at least in part, on the experience curve. The most obvious and best evidence of this is observed easily when the patterns of trade between Europe and Japan and the United States are examined.

Table 13 shows the overall pattern of trade between Japan and these

Table 13. Japanese Exports to and Imports from EEC and North America[6]

	Monthly averages ($ millions)									
	1969	1970	1971	1972	1973	1974	1975	1976	1977	1978
Japanese exports to:										
EEC	115	155	191	175	367	497	473	603	728	925
N. America	458	548	706	839	879	1209	1033	1454	1803	2251
Japanese imports from:										
EEC	99	129	134	163	264	33	281	302	350	501
N. America	397	541	499	584	941	1280	1177	1213	1275	1500

two blocs. The figures show that over the 10-year period Japanese exports to the EEC and North America have increased 7.04-fold and 3.91-fold respectively, while Japanese imports from the EEC and North America have increased only 4.06-fold and 2.78-fold respectively.

This phenomenal Japanese export achievement is of particular importance in experience influenced industries such as television and radio receivers, motor vehicles and vessels. Table 14 shows the extent of Japanese success in these areas. In fact, the Japanese strategy has been so effective that in certain industries, such as motor vehicles, European[4] and U.S.[8] manufacturers now concede that they cannot successfully compete in a free market.

Table 14. Japanese Exports of Machinery and Equipment to United States and Western Europe[6]

	1975 $m	1976 $m	1977 $m	1978 $m
Exports to United States				
Machinery and equipment	6,664	10,211	13,353	17,956
TV and radio receivers	615	1,317	1,326	1,469
Motor vehicles	2,281	3,529	4,926	7,030
Vessels	46	68	169	212
Exports to Europe				
Machinery and equipment	5,099	7,513	9,655	11,301
TV and radio receivers	496	751	839	961
Motor vehicles	917	1,358	1,692	2,247
Vessels	953	1,768	2,526	2,056

"The impact in Europe itself has been relatively dramatic. The Japanese share of sales in Western Europe has risen from 7.3 per cent at the end of 1979 to 9.6 per cent half-way through this year (1980) in spite of continued restrictions in major markets such as Italy, France and the UK.

But the major problems for the Europeans have been in 'neutral' territories where the Japanese products have been overtaking everybody else's mainly because the prices charged make the cars seem exceptionally good value for money.

Nowhere has this been more in evidence than in the US where the Japanese have pushed the market share to 22 per cent while the Europeans, mostly offering equally fuel efficient cars, have made only slight gains at the expense of the domestic manufacturers."[4]

Although it is not here claimed that the experience phenomenon is exclusively responsible for the singular success of Japanese exports, it is, as the following OECD quotation shows, a highly significant factor:

"The tendency towards a large current account surplus that has prevailed at the end of the 1960s up to the oil crisis has been attributed mainly to volume developments. The rapid growth of Japan's export volume which over the period exceeded that of world trade by some 90 per cent was largely due to the country's ability to adopt the commodity structure of exports in response to the changing world demand, as well as to increased price competitiveness and other non price factors such as high product quality, rapid and punctual delivery and adequate after sales services. *In particular the remarkable price stability of exports was due mainly to large productivity gains obtained through a rapid investment growth.** This orientation is clearly reflected in the pattern of relative prices which favour exports and fixed capital formation at the expense of personal consumption."[6]

This is shown in Table 15. There are signs, however, that certain sectors of European business now recognise the importance of the experience

Table 15. Relative Prices, International Comparisons. Percentage Change Divided by Percentage Change[6]

	Gross fixed capital formation deflator relative to private consumption deflator		Export deflator relative to private consumption deflator	
	1960–70	1974–77	1960–70	1970–77
Japan	0.399	0.771	0.190	0.356
United States	1.135	1.259	0.820	1.624
Germany	1.412	0.751	0.300	0.790
France	0.976	1.092	0.395	0.920
United Kingdom	0.872	1.650	0.777	1.363
Canada	1.200	1.285	0.869	1.425
Italy	1.199	1.276	0.232	1.059

phenomenon as a fundamental strategic lever. One of the clearest explicit examples of this recognition has been provided by France's Alcatel-Electronique.

In April 1981 Alcatel-Electronique was chosen by the French government[4A] postal and telecommunications authority (PTT) to provide the first 300,000 small electronic data terminals for the PTT's new electronic data directory project. This is an ambitious programme

**Author's italics.*

which aimed to equip each of France's 30 million telephone subscribers with a free terminal by 1992. The company was planning for an annual production rate of 1.5 million units by 1983 with a target price of $100 each.

By providing a huge home market for the data terminals, the French market will enable Alcatel-Electronique, à la Japanese, to lower its production costs and then invade export markets, in Europe and the United States in particular, with its cheap terminals. This is clearly an experience curve strategy.

This chapter analyses the experience phenomenon and shows how it can be used in strategic management.

The Experience Curve

The underlying concept of the experience curve is that the manufacturing cost of a standard item declines in a regular and predictable fashion as the total quantity produced increases. At first it was assumed that this phenomenon applied only to learning costs* and this led to the use of learning curves in certain industries — particularly the aircraft industry — to help predict the unit costs of items manufactured.

For example, Fig. 20 shows learning curves used by the Britten-

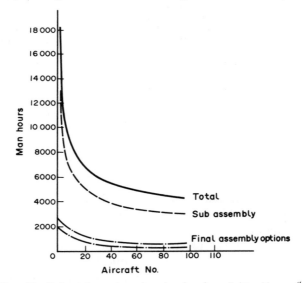

FIG. 20. *Estimated man-hour learning based on Britten-Norman*[1]

*Learning costs are the costs associated with the direct labour component of manufacturing costs, i.e. as the total number of a particular product increases, so the amount of direct labour time to make each item declines.

Norman aircraft company in the Isle of Wight, United Kingdom. These curves were used by the company to estimate the costs (and hence the final price) of the Islander aircraft.

However, largely through the work of the Boston Consulting Group, evidence was obtained that showed that for certain products each time the accumulated volume of production doubled, then the *total unit cost* of the product in real terms (i.e. constant money terms) can be made to fall by a constant and predictable percentage and that this decline is normally somewhere in the region of 20–30%. When this relationship between costs and experience is plotted as a graph, an experience curve is obtained.

Figure 21 shows an experience curve based on the data in Table 16. This is an 80% experience curve. This means that each time experience doubles, the unit costs of production decline by 20% or, in other words, each time experience doubles, costs per unit fall to 80% of the previous level. As Fig. 21 shows, the cost of producing the 80th item is 80% of the cost of producing the 40th item, which in turn is 80% of the cost of producing the 20th item, etc.

Table 16. Data for an 80% Experience Curve

Accumulated volume of production	2	4	8	16	32	64	128
Cost per unit (constant £s)	100	80	64	51	41	33	26

The Experience Function

The formula for the experience curve is*

$$C_n = C_1 n^{-\lambda} \tag{3.1}$$

where

C_n = the cost of the nth unit,
C_1 = the cost of the first unit,
n = the experience,
λ = the elasticity coefficient of the function.

This shows the cost of the nth unit expressed as a function of the first unit. This function is hyperbolic and can be represented as in Fig. 21. This hyperbolic function can be made linear by taking logs of both sides so that (3.1) becomes

$$\log C_n = \log C_1 - \lambda \log n. \tag{3.2}$$

This formula is taken from Ref. (16), Chapter 3.

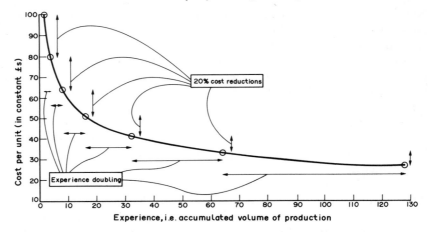

FIG. 21. *An 80% experience curve (based on data in Table 16)*

In practice the linearisation is achieved by plotting the data on double log graph paper. This is illustrated in Fig. 22 which shows the data in Table 16, this time plotted on double log paper.

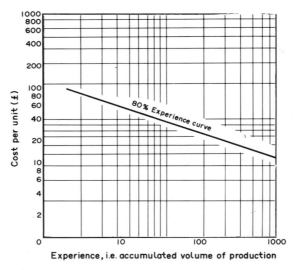

FIG. 22. *An 80% experience curve (based on the data in Table 16)*

The slope of the experience curve is represented by k and is defined as:

$$k = \frac{C_2 n}{C_n} \tag{3.3}$$

with $k \leqslant 1$

The slope indicates the strength of the experience effect. Thus $k = 100\%$ indicates no experience effect (i.e. the $2n$th item costs the same as the nth), while $k = 70\%$ indicates a strong experience effect (i.e. the $2n$th item will cost 70% of the nth item).

Experience curves with slopes of 70%, 80% and 90% are shown in Fig. 23. This illustrates one of the advantages of plotting experience curves

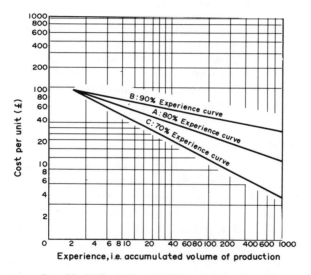

Fig. 23. *70%, 80% and 90% experience curves*

on double log paper: one can perceive very quickly the rate at which costs are being reduced and hence forecast future costs.

In equations (3.1) and (3.2) the slope of the experience curve is given by the elasticity coefficient λ. It is shown below that λ is equivalent to k. Thus from (3.3)

$$k = \frac{C_2 n}{C_n}.$$

Substituting for C_n and C_{2n} from (3.1)

$$k = \frac{C_1(2n)^{-\lambda}}{C_1 n^{-\lambda}} \tag{3.4}$$

Therefore $k = 2^{-\lambda}$.
Hence $\log k = -\lambda \log 2$.

$$\text{Therefore } \lambda = -\frac{\log k}{\log 2}. \tag{3.5}$$

Thus λ and k have a constant relationship, i.e. if k is known, λ can always be calculated and vice versa.

Causes of the Experience Curve

It is important to realise that the experience curve is not a natural law, i.e. it will not happen automatically. The cost reductions must be *made* to happen by managers. Therefore, in order to make the experience curve happen, it is important to understand the causes of this phenomenon. The causes are complex, overlapping and interrelated, but the main ones have been separated out below.

Labour Efficiency

As workers repeat a particular task, they learn to do it more efficiently, i.e. they learn short cuts and sequences which increase their total efficiency.* The learning effect is not confined just to the direct labour involved in manufacturing a certain product — as experience is gained, managers and supervisors are able to organise operations to reduce waste and increase efficiency. Again these gains in labour efficiency do not automatically occur. The personnel and training policies of the organisation must be designed to achieve them.

New Forms of Workforce Organisations

This can take the form of either increasing specialisation as production increases, i.e. a worker having fewer different tasks to perform, or of structuring the workforce organisation to suit the particular operation. For example, Volvo in their assembly plant at Kalinav, Sweden, have experimented with structures other than the traditional assembly line structure of the car industry.

*Any parent who has engaged in the labour-consuming activity of constructing children's model aeroplanes will appreciate that efficiency and speed are linked to experience.

New Production Processes

Innovations and improvements in the production process can be of great importance for cost reductions, especially in capital-intensive industries. For example, in the electronic semiconductor industry most of the experience effect is due to this source, and strong experience curves of 70% to 80% have been obtained, as can be seen in Fig. 29.

Varying the Resource Mix

As the products resources gain or lose comparative cost advantage, the mix can be varied to take advantage of this. For example, if the cost of skilled labour increases it may be possible to replace this labour by robots. In this respect it is instructive to observe the use of robots, as shown in Table 17. As Japan's labour costs have increased, so the resource mix is being varied. In passing, it is interesting to note that approximately 35% of Japan's robots were, in 1979, employed in the car industry — an industry usually in the forefront of hourly labour wage rates.

Table 17. Number of Industrial Robots in Use in Eight Countries[7]

Industrial robots* in use (March 1979)	
Japan	14,000
United States	3,255
West Germany	350
Italy	800
United Kingdom	185
Sweden	600
Norway	170
Finland	110

*Where robot is defined as excluding manual manipulators.

Standardising the Product

Without some degree of standardisation the replication of tasks necessary for learning cannot take place. For example, for the Ford Model T, the Ford Motor Company followed a strategy of deliberate standardisation with the result that its price over the years 1909 to 1923 followed an 85% experience curve.

Because of the dangers of standardisation (see Limitations of the Experience Curve on page 154 below) the motor industry has sought to achieve the best of both worlds, i.e. the cost benefits to be derived through standardisation plus the marketing benefits to be derived through offering a variety of models, through modular standardisation. See the example of the variety of cars marked by Ford in the United Kingdom on page 90 below.

Technical Conservatism

The process equipment itself is usually, initially, conservatively rated, so that as experience accumulates users can achieve a better performance than rated.

Product Redesign

As experience in producing a product accumulates, both the producer of the product and the product's customers increase their understanding of its performance requirements. Through value engineering the product can be redesigned to conserve material, labour effort, etc., while at the same time improving its performance.

Economies of Scale

Although these can be considered as separate effects,* and can occur independently of each other, the overlap between the two is so high that here they will not be separated. It has, however, been asserted that "the effect of static economies of scale on the slope of the experience curve is small in most cases".† However, the achievement of economies of scale is important for the time scale of improvement. Thus a firm which has a high volume of manufacturing will achieve not only static economies of scale, but it will also advance further and more quickly down the experience curve than its smaller rivals.

Costs, Prices and Experience

If costs and prices follow experience curves, then armed with this knowledge a planner can predict future costs, margins, cash flows, feasible strategic options, etc., not just for his own business, but also for his competitors.

---

*See Ref. (1), p. 114.
†Ref. (3), p. 7.

Forecasting Costs

If one knows the slope of the experience curve (k), the rate at which the firm accumulates experience* (ϱ), and the rate at which the market is growing (γ), then it is relatively easy to forecast future costs. Thus, using Fig. 24 it is easy to forecast the cost per unit will decline from £100 per unit at an accumulated experience of 20 units to approximately £20 per unit at an accumulated experience of 2000 units. This process is dealt with in greater detail on page 84.

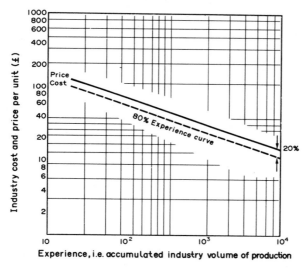

Fig. 24. *A stable cost-price pattern: price is set at 20% above costs*

Forecasting Prices

In *Perspectives on Experience*[13] the authors perceived just three basic price patterns. These are:

(a) *A stable pattern.* Here, as costs decrease due to experience, so also do prices. Profit margins remain at a constant percentage of price and average industry costs follow identically sloped experience curves. This pattern is illustrated in Fig. 24. An actual example of such a stable price pattern is the retail price of Japanese beer. This is shown in Fig. 25.

(b) *A stable–unstable pattern.* Here, as shown in Fig. 26, prices start briefly below cost; then, in spite of sharply decreasing costs, prices are kept constant by producers, i.e. the producers form a price

*This is defined as last year's observed production divided by previous experience.

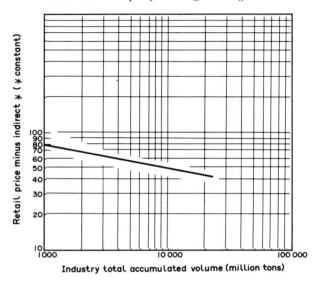

FIG. 25. *A stable price pattern: the retail price of Japanese beer*[16]

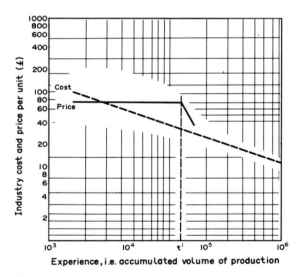

FIG. 26. *A stable–unstable pattern*

umbrella supported by the market leader. This umbrella lasts as long as demand exceeds supply; however, this is an unstable situation and at some point, such as t_i, a shake-out occurs, i.e. one producer reduces price in order to gain market share, and this leads to either a price war among existing competitors and the subsequent shake-out, as prices tumble, or else new producers are attracted by the high margins and the temporary overcapacity caused by these new entrants leads to a price war. An example of such a stable-unstable pattern is the price of paraxylene, as shown in Fig. 27.

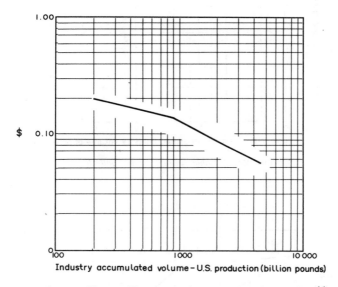

Industry accumulated volume – U.S. production (billion pounds)

FIG. 27. *A stable–unstable pattern: the U.S. price of paraxylene*[16]

(c) *A stable–unstable–stable pattern.* This commences when the price war is over and is illustrated in Fig. 28. At point t_2 marginal producers have been eliminated or else they have in some way made their product distinctive or different. The producers remaining will profit more from harmonious competitive relations than from a continued price war. So from point t_2 onwards profits return to normal and prices begin to follow industry costs down the experience curve, in a stable way. An example of a stable-unstable-stable pattern is the price of silicon transistors as shown in Fig. 29.

Using the Experience Curve: an Example

In industries where a significant element of cost can be assigned to

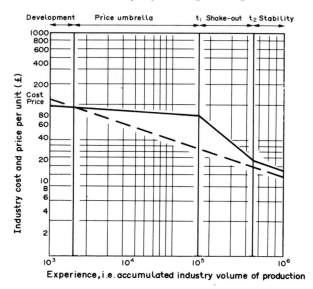

FIG. 28. *A stable–unstable–stable pattern*

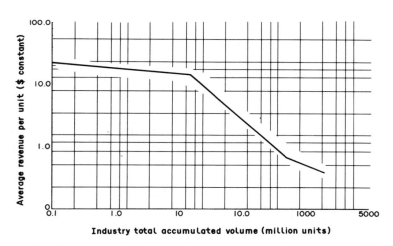

FIG. 29. *A stable–unstable–stable pattern: the price of silicon transistors*[10]

experience effects, it is important for individual firms in the industry (and national economic planners) to realise the cost advantages that can be gained by "riding the experience curve".

If, for example, in an experience influenced industry an individual firm knows its own profit margin, its own experience and the experience of its competitors, then the firm's planners can approximate competitors' costs (and hence profit margins), and subsequently develop a strategy with a knowledge of the likely impact of this strategy upon competitors and the types of reciprocal strategic reactions that are likely and feasible for competitors.

Consider an industry in which there are four manufacturers A, B, C and D of an undifferentiated product Z. These competitors compete in the same market and sell direct. Industry data available to all competitors is as shown in Table 18. On the basis of the above minimal information it is possible for any one firm to make informed strategic

Table 18. Industry Data for Product Z

Current price of product Z = £100
Annual growth rate of market for product Z = 20%
Slope of experience curve for product Z = 75%

Firm	Annual sales of product Z (units)	Market share (%)
Firm A	8,000	53
Firm B	4,000	27
Firm C	2,000	13
Firm D	1,000	7
Total	15,000	100

decisions. Consider the situation facing the strategic planners in Firm A. They know that Firm A's costs are £50 per unit and therefore its profit margin is £50 per unit. What now can be determined about A's competitive position and the strategic options that are available to it?

Firstly, it is possible for A to approximate B, C and D's profit margins on this product and hence the total profit contribution that this product is making to each firm. Thus:

A's market share is twice that of B, and if the relationship between A and B has been constant in the past, then A's experience should be twice that of B. If this is the case, then A's costs are, *ceteris paribus*, 75% of those of B.

Therefore B's costs are $\dfrac{£50 \times 100}{75} = £67$.

Similarly, C's experience is half that of B.

Therefore C's costs are $\dfrac{£67 \times 100}{75} = £89$.

And similarly, D's experience is half that of C.
Therefore D's costs are $\dfrac{£89 \times 100}{75} = £119$.

Thus the firm's profit margins for each unit of Z are as shown in Table 19.*

This situation is visually portrayed in Fig. 30 which shows the profitability advantages that accrue with experience.

Table 19. Costs, Selling Price and Profit Margins of Product Z for firms A, B, C and D

Firm	Annual sales	Cost £	Selling price £	Profit margin £
A	8,000	50	100	50
B	4,000	67	100	33
C	2,000	89	100	11
D	1,000	119	100	−19

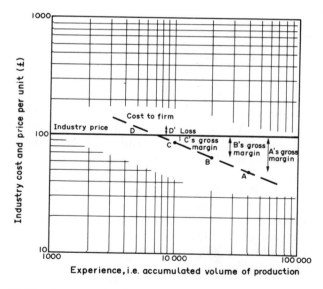

FIG. 30. *Visual representation of experience and cost/profit positions of firms A, B, C and D for product Z*

*All figures are rounded to the nearest £.

It is instructive to observe in Table 19 and in Fig. 30 that although A's sales are twice B's, B's are twice C's and C's are twice D's, that the same relationship doesn't hold for the profit margins of each firm. Thus D is selling the product at a loss, B's margin is three times that of C and A's margin is almost five times that of C. This numerical example illustrates the leverage effect that the experience phenomenon generates, i.e. firms which have the greatest experience have, all other things being equal, the disproportionately greatest profits.

Strategic Implications

Using the above information it is easy to see how experience information links to strategic planning.

Consider again the case of Firm A: armed with the above information, what strategies are available and which should be chosen?

First of all, it is important to bear in mind that A is dominant in the market and any pricing policy adopted by Firm A will have a major influence on competitors' actions and the industry price. Firm A has two basic strategic options:

Option I   It can let the current agreed industry price stay at £100.
Option II It can pursue an aggressive strategy of cutting prices in proportion to cost reductions, i.e. reduce costs by 25% each time experience doubles.

If Firm A chooses Option I, then it will continue to enjoy the cost reductions due to increasing experiences and thus its profit margins will improve.

Additionally, it is likely that Firm D will cease producing the product and this will increase the market size for A, B and C. However, pursuing this strategy will also allow competitors to improve their margins. This will lead to improvement in the financial health of B and C and may induce them to further improve their own performance by increasing their experience relative to A. Furthermore, the high level of industry profits may lead to the development of a price umbrella (see page 78) and may lead to a future traumatic shakeout.

If, on the other hand, Option II is chosen, then Firms D and C will be driven out of business and A and B will be left alone to share the market. However, the profit margins will be considerably reduced for both A and B.

To make a more informed and objective judgement on each option it is necessary to quantitatively analyse each. This can be done either mathematically or graphically. Both methods are illustrated below.

Mathematical Analysis of Option I

Assuming Firm D withdraws from the market and its market is shared, *pro rata*, among the remaining three competitors, then the production costs of each firm at the end of one year* are as follows:

A's production over the next year
= [current annual production] + [increased production due to market growth (20%)] + [its *pro rata* share of the market given up by D]
= [8000] + [20% × 8000] + [$^{8}/14$ {1000 + 20% (1000)}]
= 10,286 units.

$$\text{A's previous experience} = \frac{\text{production during last year of observation}}{\text{production growth rate}}$$

$$= \frac{8000}{0.2}$$

$$= 40,000 \text{ units}$$

A's marginal cost per unit at the end of the next year will be

$$C_{n+i} = C_n \left[1 + \frac{p_0}{n} (1 + \gamma)^i \right]^{-\lambda}$$

where[†] C_n = cost of the nth unit,
p_0 = the production during any given year,
n = previous experience, i.e. total experience up to and including the last period of observation,
γ = the annual rate of growth of the market for the product,
λ = the elasticity coefficient of the function,
i = the number of planning time periods under consideration.

In this case

$$C_{n+1} = £50 \left[1 + \frac{10,286}{40,000} (1.2)^1 \right]^{-0.415}$$

$$= £50 [0.8945]$$

$$= £44.72 \approx £45.$$

A's marginal profit margin at the end of the year will be

$$£100 - £45 = £55 \text{ per unit.}$$

One year has been arbitrarily chosen as the planning horizon. This is for the sake of simplicity. Obviously this could easily be amended to whatever horizon is appropriate.

[†]*This analysis is adapted from Ref. (16) which gives a much more comprehensive treatment and explanation.*

Similarly, B's production over the next year

$= [4000] + [20\% \times 4000] + [\frac{4}{14} \{1000 + 20\% (1000)\}\ ]$
$= 5143$ units.

B's previous experience $= \dfrac{4000}{0.2}$

$= 20,000$ units.

B's marginal cost per unit at the end of the year

$C_{n+1} = £67 \left[1 + \dfrac{5143}{20,000} (1.2)^1 \right]^{-0.415}$
$= £67 [0.8945]$
$= £59.93 \approx £60.$

B's marginal profit margin at the end of the year

$= £100 - £60 = £40$ per unit.

Similarly,

C's production over the next year
$= [2000] + [20\% \times 2000] + [\frac{2}{14} \{1000 + 20\% (1000)\}\ ]$.
$= 2571$ units.

C's previous experience $= \dfrac{2000}{0.2}$

$= 10,000$ units.

C's marginal cost per unit at the end of the year

$C_{n+1} = £89 \left[1 + \dfrac{2571}{10,000} (1.2) \right]^{-0.415}$
$= £89 (0.8945)$
$= £79.61 \approx £80.$

C's marginal profit margin at the end of the year
$= £100 - £80 = £20$ per unit.

Mathematical Analysis of Option II

Assuming that the 25% price reduction introduced by Firm A causes the immediate withdrawal of Firms D and C (because, as shown on pages 81 and 82, C and D will have production costs of £89 and £119 per unit at the start of this period), and that their market is shared, *pro rata*, between A and B, then the production costs at the end of one year are as follows:

A's production over the next year

= [current annual production] + [increased production due to market growth (20%)] + its *pro rata* share of the market given up by C and D]

= [8000 + [20% × 8000] + [$\frac{8}{12}$ {3000 + 20% (3000)}]]

= 12,000 units.

A's previous experience = 40,000 units

A's marginal cost per unit at the end of the year

$$C_{n+1} = £50 \left[1 + \frac{12,000}{40,000} (1.2)^1 \right]^{-0.415}$$

= £50 (0.8802)

= £44.01≈£44.

A's marginal profit margin at the end of the year

= £75 − £44 = £31 per unit.

Similarly,

B's production over the next year

= 4000 + 20% × 4000 + [$\frac{4}{12}$ {3000 + 20% (3000)}]]

= 6000 units.

B's previous experience = 20,000 units.

B's marginal cost per unit at the end of the year

$$C_{n+1} = £67 \left[1 + \frac{6000}{20,000} (1.2)^1 \right]^{-0.415}$$

= £67 (0.8802)

= £58.97≈£60.

B's marginal profit margin at the end of the year

= £75 − £60 = £15 per unit.

Tables 20 and 21 give summaries of the quantitative analysis for each option.

Option I

Table 20. Summary of Mathematical Analysis of Option 1

Firm	Unit selling price (£)	Marginal unit cost at year end (£)	Marginal unit profit at year end (£)	Expected next years sales (Units)	Expected market share (%)	Expected relative market share
A	100	45	55	10,286	57	2.0
B	100	60	40	5,143	29	0.5
C	100	80	20	2,571	14	0.25

Option II

Table 21. Summary of Mathematical Analysis of Option II

Firm	Unit selling price (£)	Marginal unit cost at year end (£)	Marginal unit profit at year end (£)	Expected next years sales (Units)	Expected market share (%)	Expected relative market share
A	75	44	31	12,000	67	2
B	75	60	15	6,000	33	0.5

Tables 20 and 21 clearly show the effects of each strategic option. If Option II is chosen, then A's profits per unit will fall by 44% while B's will plunge by 62%. Looking at this another way, the ratio of A's profit per unit to B's profit per unit would change from £55:£40, i.e. 1.4:1, under Option I to £31:£15, i.e. 2.1:1, under Option II.

In conclusion, it would appear that in this case Firm A would be in a relatively strong strategic position if it were to select Option II. The firm might, depending, among other factors, upon national monopoly legislation, be tempted to engage in a further bout of aggressive price cutting with a view to driving B out of business and becoming the monopoly producer.

Graphical Analysis

Alternatively, and indeed more easily, the above analysis can be carried out graphically. Option I is portrayed in Fig. 31 and Option II is portrayed in Fig. 32.

In Fig. 31 the shaded trapeziums on AA', BB' and CC' show the total profit contribution for Firms A, B and C respectively over the year if Option I is chosen. In Fig. 32 it can be seen that at the new price of £75 Firm C can only operate at a loss and that the trapeziums based on AA' and BB' show the total profit contributions for Firms A and B respectively over the year if Option II is chosen. Figure 32 also illustrates that Firm A has the option of reducing its price along the path $Z'Z'$ with a view to driving out Firm B.

Computer Based Analysis

The above analyses can be carried out using the program EXCU. Full details of this approach are given in Chapter 8.

Practical Considerations in Using the Experience Curve

The beguiling simplicity of the experience curve may, in practice, lead

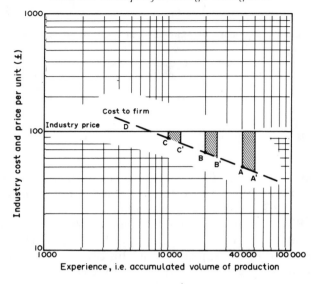

FIG. 31. *The total profit contributions to firms A, B and C over one year if Option I is chosen*

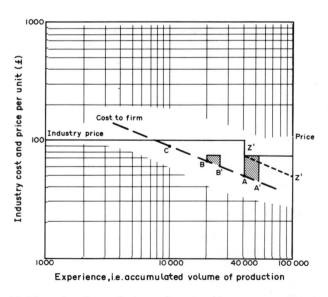

FIG. 32. *The total profit contributions to firms A and B over one year if Option II is chosen*

to a failure to recognise it when it occurs* or to the incorrect application of the tool. As pointed out in the section "Causes of the Experience Curve", "All experience curves, both normal and cross-sectional, are approximations of extremely complex interactions."[5]

Therefore, when the application of experience curves is being considered or their effects analysed, informed and careful judgement is essential. Among the more important practical considerations are the following.

The Unit of Analysis

Here careful judgement is required to ensure that the unit (or product or group of products or components) is defined neither too broadly nor too narrowly. For example, all the following units of analysis could be used in defining the unit of analysis for Porsche cars.

(a) The Porsche car is a car and competes with all other cars manufactured, hence Porsche experience and market share is relative to that of all other manufacturers.

(b) The Porsche car is a sports car and competes with all other sports cars and its experience and market share is relative to that of other sports car production lines only.

(c) The Porsche car is a high-quality "thoroughbred" European sports car and its experience and market share is relative to that of other similarly defined marques only.

(d) The Porsche single car concept is incorrect. There are really three main Porsche cars: the 924, the 911 and the 928, and each competes in a narrowly defined and specific market sector. Experience and market share for each model is relative to the defined sector.

This example illustrates, from marketing perspective, the difficulties in defining the unit of analysis and the strategic implications of different definitions: equally important is a correct definition of the unit of analysis from a production point of view. Thus if the unit of analysis is defined too broadly this may lead to experience advantages due to specialisation being missed. For example, a vehicle manufacturing company which makes a wide range of vehicles may miss significant experience advantages due to specialisation if it simply defines the unit of analysis as a vehicle. It may be more appropriate to define the unit(s) of analysis from a final use point of view, e.g. volume car, luxury car,

---

*When attempting to find European empirical evidence of the experience effect, the author has found that, even in industries where the effect has, in the United States, been found to apply, a standard initial management response has been "This effect doesn't apply to our industry."

trucks, etc. On the other hand, if the unit of analysis is defined too narrowly, then shared experience — such as common R and D marketing departments — may be missed. This indeed is one of the problems faced by Philips:[14]

> ". . . Philips should be paying more attention to technology flows in the other directions, too. Given the company's solid expertise in consumer recording technology, he wonders why Philips is not a leader in the hot market for computer memories. They have failed to transfer to the digital area the capabilities they developed in consumer products."

In practice, defining the unit of analyses is a challenging and important problem. It needs a balance of quantitative internal (production) and external (competitive) appraisal and flair in managerial judgement.

Shared Experience

Shared experience occurs when two or more products share a common resource or activity in a similar manner. This is because many products commence life with common resources and/or materials, and only acquire individuality late in the production process. For example, in March 1981 the Ford Motor Company offered (excluding the Mustang 2.3 Ghia 2-door Turbo) eighty-seven different cars for sale in the United Kingdom. In fact, the difference in many cases is superficial, as the models are built up from a total of only five different body types (Fiesta, Escort, Cortina, Capri and Granada) and nine different sizes of engine (the 1.0, 1.1, 1.3, 1.6, 2.0, 2.1 diesel, 2.3, 2.8 and 3.0).[11]

The possibility of shared experience should always be sought so that cost advantages over competitors can be gained. British Leyland's problems typify a company which has signally failed to exploit shared experience. Thus in March 1981 British Leyland offered seventy-three different cars for sale in the United Kingdom. The seventy-three models were based upon fourteen different body types (Mini, Metro, Allegro, Ital, Maxi, Princess, Jaguar XJ6, Jaguar XJS, Midget, MGB GT, Spitfire, Dolomite and TR7) and twenty-one different sizes of engine (in cubic centimetres: 998, 1098, 1275, 1296, 1485, 1493, 1700, 1748, 1789, 1798, 1993, 1998, 2227, 2350, 2498, 2597, 2997, 3442, 3528, 4253, 5343).[11]

A glance at the recent financial history of the above two motor companies shows the very real advantage of Ford's superior experience. Similarly, Japan's motor industry's successful striving for experience advantage over other producers has, as mentioned in the Introduction, in part been responsible for that country's current dominant position in that industry.

The cost importance of this shared experience can be seen quickly through the following simplified example.

A finished product p comprises two components, p_1 and p_2, which are used in equal proportion. These components, p_1 and p_2, have 70% and 80% experience curves respectively. Table 22 shows how the cost of manufacturing p is linked to the experience of the sub-component. In passing, it is interesting to note that although the proportion in which p_1 and p_2 are used has remained constant, the ratio of the costs of p_1 and p_2 has changed from 1.25:1 to 0.33:1.

Table 22. An Illustration of How Total Costs Decline with Shared Experience

Accumulated experience	Cost per unit of component p_1 (70% curve)	Cost per unit of component p_2 (80% curve)	Cost per unit for product P
100 units	£100	£80	£180
200 units	70	64	134
400 units	49	51.20	100.20
800 units	34.30	40.96	75.25
1,600 units	24.01	32.77	56.78
3,200 units	16.81	26.21	43.02
6,400 units	11.76	20.97	32.73
12,800 units	8.23	16.78	25.01
25,600 units	5.76	13.42	19.18
51,200 units	4.03	10.74	14.77
102,400 units	2.82	8.59	11.41

Time

Time can have three major influences on experience curve recognition and analysis. These influences are: the influence of short-term fluctuations, the effect of inflation, managerial confusion between experience and time. Each influence is considered below.

The Influence of Short-term Fluctuations

While the experience effect may hold for a product or an industry, it does not follow that costs will always decline in a smooth and continuous fashion. The experience function is essentially long run, and there may well be short-run fluctuations (caused, for example, by production or supply bottlenecks or fluctuations in costs of components) which may temporarily mask the long-run smooth trajectory.

The Effect of Inflation

All cost data used in experience analysis must be net of inflation, i.e.

the data must be in real money. Frequently uncorrected cost data may, over a period of time, show an increase; however, after deflation, by the appropriate inflation factor, a decrease in costs is observed.

Confusion Between Experience and Time

Managers may try to relate cost changes to the passing of time, i.e. they may expect costs to decline on an annual and regular basis. This is incorrect – cost reduction is related to the accumulation of experience and not the passage of time. Consider the case of a hypothetical volume car manufacturer whose production follows an 80% experience curve. If the initial production is 50,000 units per year and production increases at a rate of 10% per year, it will take 15 years approximately to achieve five doublings of experience. This is illustrated in Table 23 and Fig. 33.

Data Problems

When using experience analysis for one's own products, or those of a competitor or supplier, great difficulties may be encountered in obtaining the true cost and experience.

Thus, when attempting to ascertain one's own costs the data may not be available in an appropriate form. Costs may not be allocated on a product or component basis, or the constituent costs may be grouped in an unsuitable way, or costs may be allocated to departments rather than products. Furthermore, these may be gathered in an inconsistent method, i.e. some costs may be gathered on the basis of batches produced, etc. This problem is further aggravated by time — it is not unusual for methods of cost allocations or accounting procedures to be radically changed in the lifetime of a product or company. Whatever method of cost allocation is used, it is important that it is used consistently throughout the experience analysis. Probably the most appropriate approach to use is short-run average cost measured over say one quarter or one year's production.

Estimating costs for competitors or suppliers causes similar problems with the added complications that the data available usually cannot be verified, i.e. one does not know the details of the competitors' or suppliers' shared experience, nor does one know the competitors' or suppliers' total experience. Thus, if one is buying a component from a supplier one must, in order to forecast future prices, make good judgements about (among other things) the experience of the constituent sub-components and the effects of shared experience and also the total accumulated experience of the purchased component. This is particularly important because, as Table 16 shows, cost reduction during the first few years of a product's life is usually the greatest.

Table 23. Illustration of the Distinction between Annual Production and Experience

Year	1	2	3	4	5	6	7	8	9	10	11	12	13	14	15
Annual production*	50	55	60	67	73	80	89	97	107	118	130	143	157	172	190
Cumulative production* i.e. experience	50	105	165	232	305	385	474	571	678	796	926	1069	1226	1398	1588

*In thousands

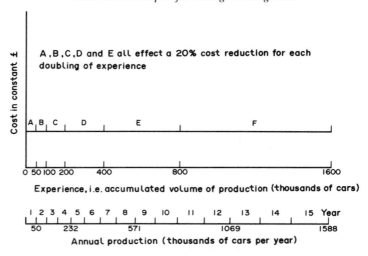

FIG. 33. *Graphical illustration of the distinction between annual production and experience*

A knowledge of the cost differences between competitors is vitally important for effective strategic planning, yet these differences are frequently difficult to ascertain and may frequently be more modest than a simple experience analysis would indicate. Any experience analysis should always include a consideration of the fact that competitors have different starting points. This can have many ramifications:

(a) Those competitors who enter late should be able to start at a lower initial cost than the early producers. This may be because they have learnt about the business from observation of the pioneers; there may have been technological advances in the equipment or components purchased from suppliers; there may have been cost advantages because the costs of goods and services purchased from common suppliers have fallen because of suppliers' experiences. Also late entrants may accelerate their learning by obtaining insights into the process currently employed by market leaders — say by "poaching" early entrants' staff.
The advantage of late entry is illustrated in Fig. 34. Here the lower initial costs enable the late entrant to make a profit. If this lower initial cost could not be achieved, it would not be profitable for the late entrant to enter the market.

(b) Late entrants may be able to exploit shared experience that early entrants cannot exploit.

(c) Late entrants may be able to structure their organisation to have

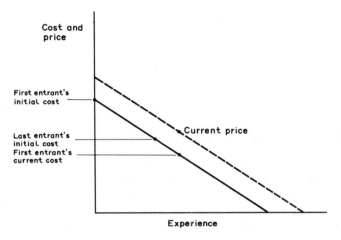

FIG. 34. *The lower initial cost advantages of late entry*

relative advantages in areas such as production and marketing. This could be done through, for example, vertical integration.

Limitations of the Experience Curve

Although the preceding would appear to indicate that following the experience curve is a simple but highly effective business strategy which, when followed, almost automatically leads to success, history indicates that exclusive adherence to a strategy based on the experience curve is fraught with danger – most strategic positions are multidimensional and a unidimensional experience curve strategy will generally be inadequate. Abernathy and Wayne[2] have shown convincingly that a strategy based upon increasing market penetration and reducing costs progressively may lead to reduced flexibility, a loss of innovative capability and an actual real increase in overhead due to efforts to cut costs.

They detail the case of the Ford Motor Company and the Model T. Because of the cost minimisation strategy of the company, the Model T had developed by the 1920s into a highly standardised product and had become the most successful motor car (in terms of sales) in the United States. The effects and success of this strategy can be seen in Table 24. However, this very success of Ford contained within it the seeds of failure. In order to achieve the cost reduction Ford had acquired companies which supplied raw materials and also a railway to transport these goods. In the process Ford had become an integrated giant diversified company oriented almost exclusively, and very inflexibly, towards Model T cost reductions and volume production. Unfortunately

Table 24. The Effects of Experience Curve Strategies on Ford Motor Company 1910 and 1921[2]

Year	List price of vehicle ($)	Motor vehicle sales (in thousands of units)	% of market share	Labour rate (in $ per hour)	Labour hours per vehicle	Profit $m
1910	3000	32	10.7	0.25	232	15
1921	1000	981	55.4	0.87	102	125

for Ford the market was changing: used cars were becoming plentiful and provided a cheap alternative to the Model T; also, rival car companies — particularly General Motors — were producing closed body and generally more sophisticated cars with which the Model T could not compete. Alfred Sloan of General Motors later wrote:

"Mr Ford . . . had frozen his policy in the Model T . . . pre-eminently an open car design. With its light chassis, it was unsuited to the heavier closed body and so in less than two years (by 1923) the closed body made the already obsolescing design of the Model T non-competitive as an engineering design.

. . . the old master has failed to master change . . . His precious volume, which was the foundation of his position, was fast disappearing. He could not continue losing sales and maintain his profits. And so for engineering and market reasons the Model T failed."[2]

Table 25. The Effect of Failing Sales on the Model T[2]

Year	Price $	Motor vehicle sales (in thousands of units)	% of market share	Labour rate per hour	Labour hours per vehicle	Loss $m
1927	N/A	424	10.6	0.87	475	−65

In fact, so inflexible had Ford become that in order to change its production to a more up-to-date and acceptable product (the Model A) Ford had to close its production line, replace 15,000 machine tools and lay off 60,000 workers in Detroit alone. The model change lost Ford $200 million.*

Ford of America announced record losses for 1980 and in many respects the causes of this failure are similar to the causes which led to the demise of the Model T.

The Model T Ford also provides a case study of how innovation is negatively correlated with experience. Abernathy and Wayne[2] analysed the innovative changes in the Ford Motor Company from 1900 to 1939 and found that as experience accumulates not only does the nature of innovation change, it becomes less significant and becomes increasingly concerned with process innovation rather than product innovation, but intensity also diminishes.

From this and other studies Abernathy and Wayne concluded that there was a negative relationship between product innovation and production efficiency. This phenomenon appears to be true for other industries as well and may be one of the factors behind the apparent inability of U.S. electronics companies to bridge the gap between radically different technologies, i.e. from vacuum tubes to germanium to silicon. As Mackintosh[10] has shown (see Table 26 below), only *one* of the leading U.S. tube manufacturers, RCA, in 1955 had survived as a significant integrated circuit manufacturer in 1975.

Table 26. The Leading U.S. Manufacturers of Vacuum Tubes, Semiconductors and Integrated circuits for the Years 1955, 1960, 1965 and 1975

	The Leading U.S. Manufacturers			
	1955		1960	1965	1975 Integrated circuits
	Tubes	Transistors	Semiconductors	Semiconductors	
1	RCA	Hughes	TI	TI	TI
2	Sylvania	Transitron	Transitron	Fairchild	Fairchild
3	GE	Philco	Philco	Motorola	MSC
4	Rathcon	Sylvania	GE	GI	Intel
5	Westinghouse	TI	RCA	GE	Motorola
6	Amperex	GE	Motorola	RCA	Rockwell
7	National Video	RCA	Clevite	Sprague	GI
8	Ranland	Westinghouse	Fairchild	Philco/Ford	RCA
9	EIMAC	Motorola	Hughes	Transitron	Signetics (Philips)
10	Landsdale	Clevite	Sylvania	Rathcon	AMI

Returning briefly to the instructive and cautionary tale of the Model T. In order to reduce costs, Ford invested heavily in plant, equipment, property, including coal mines, rubber plantations and forestry operations. The effect of this was that the rate of capital assets per dollar of sales rose from 11 cents per dollar in 1913 to nearly 33 cents per dollar in 1926. This greatly increased the fixed costs and therefore raised the break-even point.

Thus the experience curve was, for the Ford Motor Company, both a saviour and a destroyer.

Summary of the Practical Steps in Using the Experience Curve

In using the experience curve the following practical steps should be followed:

1. Remember that the experience effect is net of inflation, so all costs and prices must be deflated to a common base.
2. Obtain as much relevant historical cost data as possible. The greater the amount of experience, the more trustworthy are the results likely to be.
3. Determine which costs can be legitimately allocated to the product being analysed.
4. Group together cost components which appear to be similar in terms of their experience profile, i.e. group costs which have the same amounts of prior experience, the same rates of learning, etc.
5. For each grouping of costs plot, on double log paper, the average unit costs at different points in time and fit a straight line to the data points.
6. Use the fitted lines to project future costs of each grouping.
7. Combine the projected future cost in a fashion similar to that shown in Table 22.

Conclusions

This chapter's advocacy of the use of the experience curve as a fundamental tool for strategic planning is not unequivocal. This recommendation must be placed in a broader and a more questioning managerial context. Among the questions that can be raised are:

Does the success, in terms of sales, of a product always depend upon price alone?

While it is certainly true that certain products' sales are determined mainly by price (for example, basic calculators, basic radios), there are many other products whose sales are determined by price plus other factors such as quality image, durability, style, etc. Examples of such products are Hewlett-Packard calculators and computers, and Swiss watches.

Is a volume strategy always appropriate?

Experience strategy always implies pushing for large volumes, but this may not always be appropriate. It could be more appropriate, as the BMW Motor Company has done, to adopt a niche strategy and not to contest the market with large competitors.

Is a growth strategy appropriate in an era of stagnation?

In the early eighties the twin forces of zero or negative growth in industries which have previously been continuous growth (industries such as cars and ship building) plus concern about profligate depletion of finite natural resources (particularly oil) has led to a questioning of the ethics and appropriateness of growth strategies. It could be that if these conditions continue to obtain, then the relevance to the experience based strategies will decrease.

Is it rational to pursue an experience curve strategy without responding to the broader environment?

This is perhaps the most important factor to monitor in implementing an experience curve strategy. A recent example of an experience curve strategy which failed for this reason was the relative failure of the bubble memory market.[12] The first bubble memory* appeared in 1977 and it was expected to become a low price major competitor to the, sometimes unreliable, disc memory. U.S. industry sales, which were predicted to exceed $100m annually by 1979, in fact just hit $40m in 1981. Figure 35 shows actual and predicted sales of bubble memories and its competitors

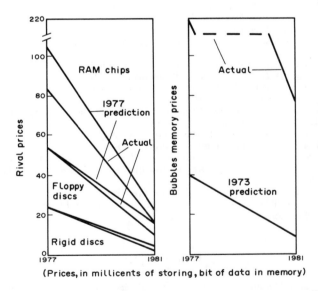

(Prices, in millicents of storing, bit of data in memory)

FIG. 35. *Actual and predicted sales of bubble memories, 1977–1981*[12]

A chip that stores data in the form of minuscule "bubbles" of magnetism.

over the years 1977–1981. The bubble memory's strategy was an experience curve strategy which failed because of production problems, marketing errors (Texas Instruments and Rockwell International Corporation were late in developing the adjunct electronics needed to make bubble memories as easy to use as discs) and the huge sales and consequent price reduction of discs.

Finally, any strategic decision should be based upon careful analyses along many axes (axes which are internal to the firm and axes in the total environment for the firm and its products), and the experience curve phenomenon should be viewed for what it is — a useful strategic tool which provides insights into productivity within the firm and a measure of how the firm is performing in comparison with its competitors.

References

1.   Abell, D. F. and Hammond, J. S. *Strategic Market Planning: Problems and Analytical Approaches.* Prentice Hall, Englewood Cliffs, 1979.
2.   Abernathy, W. J. and Wayne, K. "Limits of the Learning Curve", *Harvard Business Review*, September–October, 1974, pp. 109–119.
3.   Bodde, D. L. "Riding the Experience Curve", *Technology Review*, Vol. 78, No. 5, March 1976, pp. 53–59.
4.   European Motor Industry. *Financial Times Survey, Financial Times*, 13 October 1980.
4A. "France: An Export Flood of Low Cost Terminals", *Business Week*, 11 May 1981.
5.   Henderson, B. "Cross-sectional Experience Curves", The Boston Consulting Group, *Perspectives*, No. 208, 1978.
6.   Japan, *OECD Economic Surveys*, July 1979.
7.   "Japanese Industry", *Financial Times Survey, The Financial Times*, 29 October 1980, p. VII.
8.   "Japan's Edge in Auto Costs", *Business Week*, 14 September 1981, pp. 67–68.
9.   Lethbridge, D. G. "The Islander: Problems of the Innovational Entrepreneur", in Hayward, G. and Lethbridge, D. *European Case Studies in Business Policy: A Workbook*, Harper and Row, London, 1975.
10. Mackintosh, M. "Integrated Circuits: The Coming Battle", *Long Range Planning*, Vol. 12, No. 3, June 1979, pp. 28–37.
11. *Motor*, Wednesday 4 March 1981, Vol. 160, No. 4087, pp. 69–70.
12. "No Boom for Bubble Memory", *Business Week*, 4 May 1981, pp. 99–100.
13. *Perspectives on Experience, The Boston Consulting Group*, Boston, 1972.
14. "Philips: An Electronic Giant Rearms to Fight Japan", *Business Week*, 30 March 1981, pp. 62–67.
15. Porter, M. E. *Competitive Strategy*, The Free Press, 1982.
16. Sallenave, J. P. *Experience Curve Analysis for Industrial Planning*, Lexington and Teakfield, Fairnborough, 1976.

Bibliography

Abell, D. F. and Hammond, J. S. *Strategic Market Planning: Problems and Analytical Approaches*, Prentice Hall, Englewood Cliffs, 1979.
Allan, G. "Note on the Use of Experience Curves in Competitive Decision Making", ICCH 9-175-174, June 1976.

Baloff, U. "Start-up Management", *IEEE Transactions in Engineering Management*, EM-7, No. 4, Nov. 1970.

Barnes, J. H. Jr. "The Experience Curve — Artifact or Reality", *Omega*, Vol. 11, No. 2, 1983, pp. 209–211.

Bass, F. M. "The Relationship Between Diffusion Rates, Experience Curves and Demand Elasticities for Consumer Durable Technological Innovations", *Journal of Business* (University of Chicago), Vol. 53, No. 3, Part 2, July 1980, pp. S51–S67.

Beckenstein, A. R. and Gabel, H. L. "Experience Curve Pricing Strategy: The Next Target of Antitrust?", *Business Horizons*, Vol. 25, No. 5, pp. 71–77.

Byrd, J. Jr. and Moore, L. T. "IE's Skills Equip Them to Effectively Build and Implement Plans for Corporate Strategic Activity", *Industrial Engineering*, Vol. 14, No. 10, Oct. 1982, pp. 34–39.

The Boston Consulting Group Annual Perspective, 1981.

Bower, J. "The Business of Business is Serving Markets", *American Economic Review*, Vol. 68, No. 2, May 1978, pp. 322–327.

Bodde, D. L. "Riding the Experience Curve", *Technology Review*, Vol. 78, No. 5, March/April 1976, pp. 53–59.

Booz, Allen & Hamilton, *Outlook*, 4, Spring 1981.

Conley, P. "Experience Curves as a Planning Tool", in Rothenberg, R. *Corporate Strategy and Product Innovation*, New York, Free Press, 1977.

Day, G. "Gaining Insights Through Strategy Analysis", *Journal of Business Strategy*, Vol. 4, No. 1, Summer 1983, pp. 51–58.

Day, G. S. and Montgomery, D. B. "Diagnosing the Experience Curve", *Journal of Marketing*, Vol. 47, No. 2, Spring 1983, pp. 44–58.

Delombre, J. and Bruzelius, B. "Importance of Relative Market Share in Strategic Planning — A Case study", *Long Range Planning*, Vol. 16, No. 4, Aug. 1977, pp. 2–7.

Dolan, R. J. and Jeuland, A. P. "Experience Curves and Dynamic Models: Implications for Optimal Pricing Strategies", *Journal of Marketing*, Vol. 45, No. 1, Winter 1981, pp. 52–62.

Gup, B. E. *Guide to Strategic Planning*, McGraw-Hill, 1980.

Hartley, K. "The Learning Curve and its Applications to the Aircraft Industry", *Journal of Industrial Economics*, March 1965, pp. 112–118.

Hax, A. C. and Majluf, N. S. "Competitive Cost Dynamics: The Experience Curve", *Interfaces*, Vol. 12, No. 5, Oct. 1982, pp. 50–61.

Hedley, B. "A Fundamental Approach to Strategy Development", *Long Range Planning*, Dec. 1976, pp. 2–11.

Henderson, B. "Cross Sectional Experience Curves", Boston, The Boston Consulting Group, *Perspectives*, No. 208, 1978.

Henderson, B. "The Experience Curve Revisited: The Growth-Share Matrix of the Product Portfolio", *Perspectives*, Boston, Boston Consulting Group, 1973.

Hirschmann, W. B. "Profit from the Learning Curve", *Harvard Business Review*, Vol. 42, No. 1, Jan./Feb. 1964, pp. 125–139.

Hofer, C. W. and Schendel, D. *Strategy Formulation: Analytical Concepts*, West Publishing Co., St Paul, 1980.

Howell, S. "Learning and Experience Curves — A Review", *Managerial Finance*, Vol. 7, No. 1, 1981, pp. 26–28.

Jain, S. "Translating Experience into Growth", *Managerial Planning*, Vol. 23, No. 5, March/April 1975, pp. 1–5.

Kiechel, W. III, "Playing by the Rules of the Corporate Strategy Game", *Fortune*, Vol. 100, No. 6, 24 Sept. 1979, pp. 110–112.

Kiechel, W. III, "The Decline of the Experience Curve", *Fortune*, Vol. 104, No. 7, 5 Oct. 1981, pp. 139–146.

King, J. N. "Corporate Planning in the Chemical Industry", *Engineering and Process Economics*, Vol. 2, No. 3, Sept. 1977, pp. 171–1789.

Lofthouse, S. "Learning Costs and Market Share", *Rivista Internaziowale di Scienze Economiche e Commercial (RISEC)*, Nov. 1974, pp. 1015–1037.

Lorange, P. *Corporate Planning: an Executive Viewpoint*, Prentice-Hall Inc., Englewood Cliffs, 1980.

Mathey, C. J. "New Approaches to the Management of Product Planning", *Research Management*, Vol. 19, No. 6, Nov. 1976, pp. 13–18.

McMillan, C. J. "Production Planning in Japan", *Journal of General Management*, Vol. 8, No. 4, Summer 1983, pp. 44–72.

McNamee, P. B. "Comments on 'Aiding Life Cycles to Learning Curves by Louis Yelle'", *Long Range Planning*, Vol. 16, No. 6, Dec. 1983, pp. 102–104.

McNamee, P. B. *Strategic Management and the Experience Curve*, Strategic Management Monographs, No. 2, 1981.

Moore, L. T., Byrd, J. and Byers, A. "Experience Curves in Coal Mining", *AIIE Proceedings*, 1982 Conference, 23–27 May 1982, pp. 423–430.

Moose, S. O. "Barriers and Umbrellas", *Perspectives*, No. 232, Boston Consulting Group, 1980.

Newton, J. K. "Market Share — Key to Higher Profitability?", *Long Range Planning*, Vol. 16, No. 1, Feb. 1983, pp. 37–41.

Particelli, M. C. "The Japanese are Coming: Global Strategic Planning in Action", *Outlook* 4, Spring 1981, pp. 36–44.

"Perspectives on Experience", Boston, Boston Consulting Group, 1972.

Pessemier, E. A. *Product Management: Strategy and Organisation*, New York, John Wiley, 1977, pp. 51–59.

Ribon, B. "The Experience Effect and Pricing for Agricultural Products", *Long Range Planning*, Vol. 14, No. 4, Aug. 1981, pp. 65–75.

Robinson, B. and Lakhani, C. "Dynamic Price Models for New Product Planning", *Management Science*, Vol. 21, No. 10, June 1978, pp. 1113–1122.

Sallenave, J. P. *Experience Analysis for Industrial Planning*, Lexington Books, 1976.

"Texas Instruments Shows U.S. Business How to Survive in the 1980's", *Business Week*, 18 Sept. 1978, p. 68.

Yelle, L. "Industrial Life Cycles and Learning Curves: Interaction of Marketing and Production", *Industrial Marketing Management*, Vol. 9, No. 4, Oct. 1980.

Yelle, L. "Adding Life Cycles to Learning Curves", *Long Range Planning*, Vol. 16, No. 6, Dec. 1983, pp. 82–87.

CHAPTER 4

The Product Market Portfolio

Introduction

The tools and techniques which have been examined up to this point have implicitly assumed a single-product or a single-division firm. As was pointed out in Chapter 1, it is the case that most firms will be multiproduct firms and many firms will have many divisions. This additional complexity is considered here in the context of one of the seminal tools designed to handle this type of problem — the Product Market Portfolio.

For large diversified multiproduct companies strategic planning is an extremely complex and multidimensional process. Strategic planners are required to comprehend and allow for the many-faceted problems that accrue through diversity while simultaneously accommodating the overall strategic thrust of the company. For example, in a company organised on a two-division basis, one division may find that the products it manufactures are at the growth stage in the product life cycle and this division will therefore require inflows of cash in order to build market share, while the other division's products may be in the mature state of the product life cycle and consequently be generating cash. This obviously creates a dilemma for the planner — he must accommodate the very different strategic perspectives of the cash-absorbing division and the cash-generating division within common corporate parameters. If the above example is extended to a multidivision company (or at a different level of aggregation a multiproduct company) then the immensity of the problem of developing integrated corporate strategic plans becomes clear.

In the 1970s the Product Market Portfolio — an integrated corporate strategic planning technique capable of handling the above type of problem — came to prominence. This approach was developed mainly through the work of the Boston Consulting Group (BCG) and is now accepted by many* corporate planners as a substantial aid to planning.

Although there are many who are convinced of the approach's utility; see, for example, Refs. (26) and (28), there are, of course, those who remain sceptical; see, for example Ref. (19).

In many respects the Product Market Portfolio is the natural extension of the Experience Curve from a single-product dimension to multiproduct dimensions. Consider (as detailed in Chapter 3) one of the most basic strategic implications of the Experience Curve: in an appropriately defined market segment the competitor whose product has the greatest experience (which can be considered as equivalent to relative market share) should also be capable of having the lowest costs and therefore should also have the highest and most sustained profits.*

If, instead of a single-product firm, however, a multiproduct one is considered, then, because of the nature of the variety of products manufactured and because of the variety of market segments in which the various products are sold, each product will have its own unique relative market share. Hence each product will have a unique relative competitive position and therefore will require a strategy tailored to this position: some products may have commanding competitive positions and require little more than "maintenance", while others may have very small relative market shares and will raise fundamental strategic questions such as:

"Should the product be abandoned?"
"Should more cash be invested to give the product a stronger relative competitive position?"

Even in quite small businesses which manufacture a limited range of products, when strategies are considered from the perspective of the products' relative market shares only, the total number of possible combinations can be very large.† The complexity of the problem is observed very easily when one considers a multidivisioned and multiproduct company such as Akzo.[26]

Akzo was formed in 1969 by a merger of the two companies, Aku which was a multinational fibre company and KZO which was a diversified chemical company. In 1971 Akzo was, for strategic planning purposes, broken down into 100 planning units and portfolio planning was used as an integral part of the strategic planning process.

"At the same time the first articles on portfolio planning appeared. It was clear that portfolio planning theory was a useful contribution to our own approach.

It was decided by the Board of Management to integrate the

---

*This recognition of the very strong link between profits and relative market share is independently confirmed by the PIMS findings (see Chapter 6).
†For example, a company which manufactured just three products and had just three strategic options for each product could choose from a total of 27 different strategy combinations.

analytical frame-work of the product mix analysis and the portfolio planning theory into our strategic planning. . . .

After two years all businesses had been analysed in much more detail while divisional and corporate objectives and strategies had been formulated on the basis of portfolio analysis and portfolio planning theory. . . .

Furthermore we found that this portfolio planning approach is very useful in striking a better balance between centralisation and decentralisation in a large diversified company. It enables centralisation of the ultimate responsibility for strategy, and improves control over decentralised operations."[26]

Thus, for Akzo, the product market portfolio concept is seen as a most useful tool for strategic planning: it allows strategic planners to select the optimal strategy for individual planning units* whilst striving for overall corporate objectives.

Finally, it may be that the portfolio approach to strategic management will assume an even greater importance over the next twenty years because of organisational structure changes in companies. Thus, Sir Adrian Cadbury, Chairman of Cadbury Schweppes, takes the view that more and more companies in the future will be forced to centralise their operations and shed fringe activities while at the same time trying to maintain some central authority over subsidiaries.[7]

He has suggested that large companies — because of economic and social pressures — are likely to develop into federations of smaller enterprises and that to remain internationally competitive companies will have to cut costs and become more flexible in the face of less predictable market conditions.

"To achieve these aims means reversing the trend of the last 20 years towards large centralised organisations.

We will want to break these organisations into their separate business units and to give those units freedom to compete in their particular markets.

Large companies will become more like federations of small enterprises, not because 'small is beautiful' but because big is expensive and inflexible."[7]

---

*Although throughout this chapter portfolios based mainly on products will be used, the level of aggregation is decided by the firm's particular circumstances and the objective of the analysis. Thus on certain occasions it may be more appropriate to draw up displays on the basis of Strategic Business Units or Divisions rather than products. Similarly, a regional industrial development authority could draw up portfolio displays based upon the businesses within its region.

The Product Market Portfolio is a corporate strategic planning tool which has been developed to handle this type of complexity. It aims to enable strategic planners to select the optimal strategies for the individual products whilst achieving overall corporate objectives.

The Growth-Share Matrix and the Portfolio Concept

The Growth-Share Matrix is the primary tool in this approach to strategic management, and throughout this section reference will be made to a much simplified hypothetical example which will be used to illustrate its fundamentals. The hypothetical example comprises a single undifferentiated product (Product 1) which is manufactured and marketed by just three manufacturers (A, B and C). Data for the product is given in Table 27.

Table 27. Data for the Hypothetical Product, Product 1

Year	Company	Product name	Sales value £	Sales volume (units)	Market growth rate %
1979	A	1	500	100	12
1979	B	1	400	80	12
1979	C	1	100	10	12
1980	A	1	750	150	15
1980	B	1	500	100	15
1980	C	1	220	22	15

The matrix displays three fundamental determinants of a product's strategic position. These are:

The growth rate of the market.
The product's relative market share.
The monetary value of the product's sales.

Each of these factors is now considered in greater detail.

The Growth Rate of the Market

It is usually easier to penetrate a growing market than a static or low growth one. Thus if a new product is launched in a static market, the only way it can gain market share is at the expense of products which are currently in existence in the market. This usually will be more difficult and expensive than trying to gain market share in a fast growing market. Also, for existing products which have some market share, the cost of maintaining or improving market share may be greater in a low growth or static market than in a high growth market and indeed may well outweigh the benefits. An example of this is the history of U.K. shipbuilding yards which, in spite of efforts to halt the trend, have seen their relative and absolute market share of a declining market eroded. Thus, Table 28 shows how the world shipbuilding market has declined in the second half of the 1970s.

Table 28. Decline in the World Shipbuilding Market since 1975[8]

Market	Shipbuilding output (million compensated gross registered tonnes)		
	1975	1980 (forecast)	1980 (actual)
EEC	4.4	2.4	2.4
Rest of AWES*	3.2	1.5	1.6
AWES total	7.6	3.9	4.0
Japan	7.7	3.9	4.9
Rest of world	4.2	4.0	N/A
Total	19.5	11.8	N/A

*AWES = Association of West European Shipbuilding.

However, in 1980 there was the beginning of a market recovery which brought benefit principally to Japanese shipyards. Thus

". . . Europe's woes are not of Japan's doing. If anything, OECD officials noted, European shipbuilders are in trouble because they refused to take the tough measures that have enabled Japanese yards to emerge as lean, hyperefficient and strongly competitive.

Japan's ship industry has passed through a classic government inspired restructuring with flying colours. Roughly 120,000 workers have been shunted out of the industry since 1976 and over-all capacity has been shaved by more than a third. But dislocation has been minimal. Workers for industrial groups like Mitsubishi and Hitachi have simply moved from dry docks to assembly lines."[17]

The depressing and regressing plight of the U.K. shipbuilding industry in particular is underlined by the level of new orders for U.K. yards as shown in Table 29.

Table 29. Selected Shipyard Order Books in 1981[42]

	Shipyard order books (mil. dwt)*	
	1 October 1981	1 July 1981
Japan	25	21
S. Korea	5.2	4.3
Brazil	2.6	2.6
Spain	2.5	2.6
Taiwan	2.2	2.2
Romania	1.8	1.8
U.K.	1.8	1.4
Poland	1.6	1.4
Yugoslavia	1.5	1.4
Demark	1.4	1.5
World total	45.6	40.2

*Ships over 2,000 dwt.

In contrast to the recent history of the shipbuilding industry, Europe* has witnessed the birth and rapid growth of companies who have successfully found and exploited segments in fast growing markets. A good example of this is the Norwegian computer manufacturing company Norsk Data. This company was founded in 1967 and has had growth at 45% per annum from 1970 to 1980, a figure not unusual in the high growth computer industry.[16]

An area related to this which currently offers very attractive prospects, in terms of market growth rates, is that of information technology. Table 30 shows that in this area the lowest anticipated growth rate in the period 1980–1985 in any of the sectors is 7.9% (in Public Network Equipment) and the overall average growth rate is expected to be 14%. In passing, it should be noted that although the fruits of success in these sectors are indeed great, the rates of change, investments required, competitive pressures and levels of risk are all also extremely high.

The growth rate of the market is corrected for inflation and is plotted, as a percentage, on the vertical axis of the Growth-Share Matrix. The vertical axis of the matrix has a simple percentage scale. The market growth rates for Product 1 in 1979 and 1980 were 12% and 15% respectively and are plotted in Fig. 36.

The Product's Relative Market Share

By relative market share is meant a particular manufacturer's products market share relative to that manufacturer's largest competi-

*The implications of this for regional industrial development are plain to see.

Table 30. Market Summary of Worldwide Annual Shipments of Six Sectors of Information Technology (at constant 1980 prices)[25]

	£Bn per annum		Average annual growth rate %
The sectors	1980	1985	
Computer equipment	31.1	62.0	14.8
Computer services	8.5	17.3	15.3
Word processing	1.0	4.3	34.7
Business communication	3.3	5.4	10.0
Data transmission equipment	0.6	1.2	4.8
Public network equipment	9.9	14.5	7.9
Total	54.4	104.7	14.6

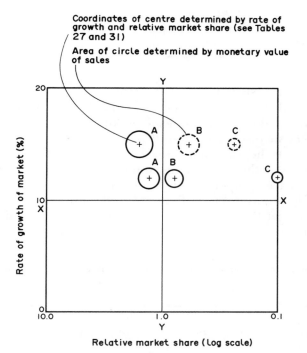

Fig. 36. *Growth share matrix for product 1.* ○ *1979 position;* ○ *1980 position*

tor. Returning to the hypothetical Product 1, the relative market shares for each manufacturer are given in Table 31.

It can be seen that Company A was the market leader in both 1979 and 1980; and that in 1980 this company actually increased its relative market share and hence improved its strategic position.

In passing it should be noted that if there is a clear market leader that this competitor will have a relative market share of more than 1.0 and market followers will have a relative market share of less than 1.0. A relative market share of 1.0 exactly indicates joint market leadership: i.e. two or more firms enjoy equal market leadership.

Table 31. Relative Market Shares for Product 1

Year	Company	Sales volume (units)	Relative market share = sales ÷ by sales of largest competitor
1979	A	100	100 ÷ 80 = 1.25
1979	B	80	80 ÷ 100 = 0.80
1979	C	10	10 ÷ 100 = 0.10
1980	A	150	150 ÷ 100 = 1.50
1980	B	100	100 ÷ 150 = 0.67
1980	C	22	22 ÷ 150 = 0.15

Relative market share rather than simple market share is used because it is believed that this measure more accurately reflects a product's true competitive position. For example, if it is known that two firms, D and Z, have market shares of 30% and 40% of their respective markets, this does not enable the true competitive positions of the firms to be gauged. In this case, on the basis of the information given so far, Z would apparently have a superior competitive position. However, when the industry figures, as given in Tables 32 and 33 below, are examined, it can be seen that D is in a much stronger competitive position (D has a sales volume three times greater than its nearest rival) than Z (Z has a

Table 32. Actual and Relative Market Shares for D and Competitors

Company	D	E	F	G	H	I	J	K
Actual market share (%)	30	10	10	10	10	10	10	10
Relative market share	3.0	0.3	0.3	0.3	0.3	0.3	0.3	0.3

**Table 33. Actual and Relative Market Shares
for Z and Competitors**

Company	Z	Y	X
Actual market share (%)	40	50	10
Relative market share	0.8	1.25	0.2

sales volume which is only 0.8 of Y's sales volume) even though Z has a higher *actual* market share.

Relative market share is an important determinant of a firm's strategic position. High relative market share usually indicates that the company has experience advantages over its competitors and that it will have lower costs with consequently higher profits. This implies that products which enjoy a high market share should generate cash for the firm.

The importance of having a dominant market position can be seen through an examination of Japan's marketing strategy. Particelli[24] has examined how Japan has "cascaded" through Western markets and has concluded that this success has been underpinned by a number of critical factors which include:

(i) Initial penetration of well-defined target segments:

> "The Japanese start with a large business in their highly protected home market, then enter periphery markets and then the U.S. and European markets. They aim at an extremely well defined target segment with a limited line — usually at the low end of the product range."

(ii) Volume stimulation and segment domination:

> "Their initial base secured, the Japanese then proceed to stimulate volume and *dominate that particular segment*.* This achieved, they move on to another segment and repeat the process, always concentrating on providing consumers with low price and extremely high quality, driving continually for price and cost (reduction) to increase consumer support and stimulate growth."

Particelli[24] shows how this Japanese expansion strategy, based in part on the above two factors,† has been particularly effective in the field of consumer electronics where the Japanese invasion has been achieved, as

---

*Author's italics.
†The other factors Particelli gives are "Resource Allocation: product and cost vs motivation"; "Establishing consumer value and building market pressure"; "Cost cutting in fronts"; and "Implementation in a global market place".

shown in Fig. 37, through a series of complementary series of steps from the transistor radio of 30 years ago to the videotape player of today.

The product's relative market share, or, depending upon the level of aggregation, the firm's relative market share, is plotted on a log scale* on the horizontal axis of the matrix. This is shown in Fig. 36 where it can be seen that the relative shares for Product 1 for Firms A, B and C were 1.25, 0.80 and 0.10 in 1979 and 1.5, 0.67 and 0.15 in 1980.

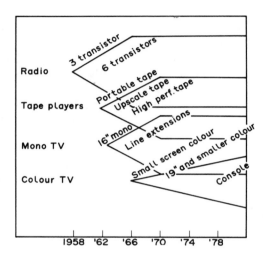

FIG. 37. *Japanese expansion: cascading segment penetration*[24]

Thus relative market share and the rate of market growth are the co-ordinates which fix the position of a product or strategic business unit or division or firm on the matrix. These co-ordinates are shown by crosses in Fig. 36.

The Monetary Value of the Product's Sales

The monetary value of the product's sales is shown by a circle whose area† is proportional to the value of the sales and is located at the co-ordinates of relative market share and rate of market growth. Figure

---

*A log scale is used so that a wide range of relative market shares can be accommodated easily. Thus, it is not a problem to accommodate on the matrix companies whose relative market shares range from, say, 0.05 to 5.

†There are those who advocate that sales should be represented by the diameter of a circle rather than its area (see Ref. (6)). However, in this book the area of the circle is advocated because it is felt that the comparative areas more accurately reflect comparative sales than do comparative diameters.

36 shows a completed Growth-Share Matrix for Product 1 for Companies A, B and C for the years 1979 and 1980.

This is a single-product multicompany matrix, i.e. the only product under analysis is Product 1, and the objective of the analysis is to ascertain one company's strategic position *vis-à-vis* its competition in this one product area alone.

Generalisation of the Growth-Share Matrix

A more frequently employed matrix is the multiproduct Growth-Share Matrix. Here, instead of just one product being displayed, the range[†] of products manufactured by the company is displayed. The co-ordinates fixing the positions of the products and the areas of the circles are calculated in exactly the same fashion as previously described. The multiproduct Growth-Share Matrix is now illustrated by means of a hypothetical example.

Table 34. Market and Sales Data for a Hypothetical Company, Company Q, which Manufactures Eleven Separate Products*

Product	A	B	C	D	E	F	G	H	I	J	K
Value of last years's sales (£000,000)	1	1	1.8	1.8	4	4	5.4	7.1	116	115	94
Relative market share	0.2	0.3	0.5	0.15	0.6	0.67	1.0	2.0	5.0	5.0	2.0
Market growth rate %	1	2	8	15	15	19	17	14	12	6	3
Last year's sales growth rate %*	0.5	2	2	2	19	18	13	15	12	7	5

This data is displayed in a Growth-Share Matrix in Fig. 38.

Interpreting the Growth-Share Matrix

In the matrix it is normal to divide market growth into areas of high growth and low growth. In Fig. 38 this dividing line is designated by XX and has been arbitrarily set at 10%. This value is not, however,

---

[†] *Or for a company with a large range of products, a portion of the range.*
**This data is also employed in the section "The Growth Gain Matrix" on page 120 below and is used in the computer program PROM in Chapter 8.*

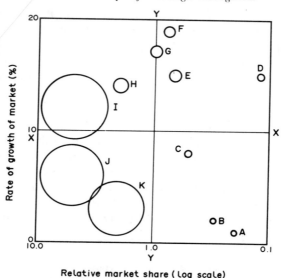

FIG. 38. *Growth-share matrix for Company Q*

sacrosanct — it can be set at whatever level the strategic planner deems to be appropriate, i.e. the planner will obviously bear in mind such factors as the historical average growth rate for the industry, the rate of growth of "high flyers" in the industry and the general economic conditions. Similarly a vertical dividing line YY has been drawn in at a relative market share of 1.0. Products that have a relative market share of 1.0 are joint market leaders, those to the left of YY have high relative market shares and are market leaders, while those to the right of YY are market followers and have lower relative market shares. As with the distinction between high and low growth, the decision about the delineation of the balancing point between high market share and low market share can be set by the strategic planner, after taking appropriate cognisance of factors such as the number of competitors, the strength of the competitors, the stage in the product life cycle of competitors' products, ease of entry to the market, etc., and whatever else he deems relevant.

In short, there is discretion about where the dividing lines XX and YY are drawn: generally they should be drawn so that the cash characteristics of the various products are as shown in Fig. 39.

The cash characteristics of each quadrant in the matrix have led to each quadrant or, more correctly, the products falling into each quadrant, receiving particular names as shown in Fig. 40.

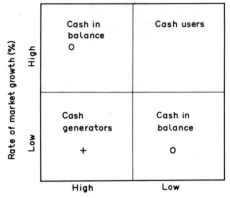

FIG. 39. *The cash characteristics of each quadrant*

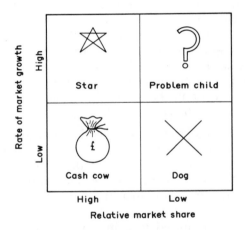

FIG. 40. *Different product categories in the product market portfolio*

As can be seen, products will fall into one of four categories — "Cash Cows", "Problem Children", "Stars" and "Dogs".

Cash Cows

These products are found in the lower left-hand quadrant. They have high relative market shares in low growth markets. These products should generate large amounts of cash — much more than is necessary for investment in these products. The extra cash is used to pay

dividends, overheads, provide debt capacity and, perhaps most impor
tantly, provide funds for investment in other parts of the company's
product portfolio. (See the section on Problem Children and Stars
below.)

The Ford Cortina was, certainly in the late 1970s, a Cash Cow for Ford
U.K.: it was a mature product with the leading market share in a static
market.

Problem Children

Problem Children or Question Marks have low market shares in high
growth markets. As their name suggests, these products can pose serious
dilemmas for strategic planners. Firstly, because the market is growing
relatively rapidly and if market share is to be maintained, or, as is more
likely desirable from a strategic point of view, increased, there must be a
substantial net cash input. This extra cash is needed to build market
share. This cash can be used in a variety of ways including price
reduction, product quality improvement, service improvement,
improvement of channels of distribution, etc. In short, there is a most
difficult problem for the planner: because Problem Children have low
market shares they will be low or negative net cash generators and yet, in
order to achieve a larger market share in this high growth market
(something which is often prerequisite to future profitability), even
larger amounts of cash must be invested. In summary, the planner has
the following difficult choices:

Do nothing. If nothing is done, however, these products will continue
to absorb cash in order to maintain their low market shares with
their consequent low profits. Indeed, if this policy is followed
problem children may consume ever-increasing amounts of cash*
and will eventually, as the growth of the market for the product
slows, become Dogs.

Invest as much as required to gain market share with the hope of
turning the product into the market leader and hence a Star. These
products are, after all, in markets where attempts to gain market
share should be easiest — overall market growth rate is relatively
high and therefore increases in market share do not have to be
wrested from competitors. However, simple as this sounds, in
practice, the building of market share, even under these circumstances, is usually extremely expensive (costs include building up
production facilities, developing marketing channels and facilities,
advertising, additional personnel costs, etc.) and has no guarantee

---

*i.e. will become "cash traps" (see Ref. (13)).

of success. However, this strategy may be the only way of ensuring the future viability of a Problem Child over the longer term.

Disinvest. This is really the only alternative to investment. If a Problem Child is absorbing cash, one way to stop the haemorrhage is surgery, i.e. through selling, to remove from the portfolio those products which are absorbing cash, and which will not receive the inputs necessary to convert them into stars. The sale of such problem children will raise cash for the company in the short term: this is preferable to having a cash trap.

An example of a European problem child which (in early 1982) had (although probably still a Problem Child according to the strict definition) met with some success was Siemens advanced electronics technology. Since 1965, Siemens had invested in R & D in this field (DM 500 mn between 1970 and 1980) but incurred losses almost every year up to about 1975. However, profits in the subsequent period just about wiped out past losses and in 1979 Siemens sold DM 500 mn of integrated circuits.

Stars

Star products are characterised by having high market shares in high growth markets and tend to generate large amounts of cash. However, in order to maintain this predominant market position, they must also spend large amounts of cash. Thus their overall cash position tends to be roughly in balance. These products really represent the best prospects for the company — when market growth slows, as it does for most products, the Stars will become Cash Cows and should generate large amounts of cash for the company. However, if the Stars fail to hold their relative market share they will slip to the right, become Problem Children and, as the growth of the market slows, eventually become Dogs, i.e. cash traps. Note also, that if planners attempt to capitalise on a Star's dominant position too early, through a high pricing policy, this may lead to the creation of a price umbrella (Chapter 3) with ultimately traumatic and disastrous consequences.

Dogs

These products have the twin characteristics of low market shares in low growth industries. Their current position tends to be poor with low profits, or else losses, and their future prospects are bleak. In the early 1970s (prior to the oil crisis and subsequent global economic stagnation) it was advocated (by BCG's founder and Chairman Bruce Henderson) that

"Dogs are essentially worthless."[14]

However, since then, prompted probably by among other things

the continuing success of many dog businesses,
slumping growth rates,
very high inflation rates,
rapidly shifting patterns of consumption,

the concept of the Dog product has been expanded to a kennel which includes two breeds of Dog.

Michael Goold of BCG has asserted that:

> "In assessing strategy, it must first be recognised that the value of market leadership differs between businesses. In many branded consumer products it is extremely difficult for second and third brands to come close to matching the performance of the leader, due to the cumulative effect of market share upon the price a company can charge and on unit marketing and distribution costs.

> Conversely, in large markets for commodity paper products where there is sufficient volume to allow several competitors each to employ scale papermaking facilities, the differences between competitors may be much more limited. The competitive difficulties faced by a dog business therefore depend heavily on the degree of differences between competitors in the business. Where there are no conclusive advantages to leadership it may be advisable to live with and maintain a dog position, rather than attempt to change it."[11]

Goold then distinguishes between the Cash Dog and the Genuine Dog. The Cash Dog is a business which is close to parity with the market leader, i.e. it is almost in the Cash Cow quadrant and it can maintain a positive cash flow, particularly if there is a stable market equilibrium.

The Genuine Dog, however, has a seriously weak competitive position and suffers from mature and direct competitors with little opportunity for developing an alternative niche marketing strategy. For such businesses liquidation, either immediate or gradual, is likely to be an appropriate strategy.

The recent history of Harland and Wolff, the Belfast shipbuilders[23] indicates particularly clearly the costs of maintaining a Genuine Dog. Over the past decade this business has absorbed an ever-increasing amount of government cash to sustain its existence. Thus in April 1970 the Belfast shipyard was warned by its then Chairman that it had "less than a year" to improve. Nine months later the company received £7 million pounds to "get the company out of its present financial crisis".

In July 1971 the company received a further £35 million pounds to develop an "expansion programme" which according to the then Chairman would promise profitability in 1974.

In July 1979 the Government gave the company another £22 million coupled with the warning that unless there were "early and marked improvements in performance there would have to be a final agonising reappraisal".

Finally(?), in June 1980 the shipyard received £46 million with clearance for "commercial borrowings" by the shipyard of a further £11 million.

In fact, the total amount of government money received by the shipyard since the 1960s is in excess of £250 million. In spite of this massive cash injection the shipyard has seen the total number of employees continuously decreasing and its level of orders also continuously decreasing.

Strategic Movements

As well as taking cognisance of the location of products on the matrix, it is also important for strategic planners to consider movements of the products over time. This can be accomplished easily by plotting a series of matrices at different points in time on acetate sheets and then superimposing them to see the movements.

Although movements in a vertical direction, i.e. movements caused by changes in the rate of growth of the market, are generally outside the control of the company,* planners should be aware that such movements may affect the matrix status of a product and hence influence the appropriate strategic action.

Horizontal movements, i.e. movements caused by changes in the products' relative market shares, are more within the control of the company.

For example, a company which has Cash Cows should be aware that these products normally only have a certain life: the market growth rate has declined from the buoyancy of earlier Star times and will continue to

---

Although this is not always the case. A company, or an industry may proactively stimulate the market. For example:

"... *They pick off volume channels where economical distribution can be achieved, with little concern for whether they market private label or branded products. ... Their initial base secured, the Japanese then proceed to stimulate volume and dominate that particular segment." (Ref. (24), p. 39.)*

decline and the products will eventually die. The excess cash generated from Cash Cows should be used firstly to maintain their relative market share. Secondly, this cash can be used to sustain (and indeed build) the relative market shares of Stars — Stars of today will fall vertically, as market growth rate declines, and become the Cash Cows of tomorrow.

Finally, the excess cash can be used to help finance the building of market share for a *limited number* of Problem Children. If Problem Children receive sufficient cash and are skilfully managed, they may* move in a westward direction on the matrix and hence become Stars.

Thus in summary, as shown in Fig. 41, the ideal movements of products are in the directions A–B–C, and complementing this movement of products are the ideal movements of cash which are shown by ZX and ZY.

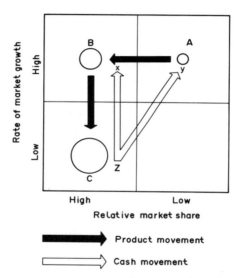

FIG. 41. *Ideal movements of products and cash in the portfolio*

The Growth-Gain Matrix

Another closely related matrix that can be used to help strategic planning is the Growth-Gain Matrix. This matrix shows how well a product† is keeping pace with the growth of the market. Like the

---

This movement, of course, depends on many other factors as well, such as strength of competition, being able to meet the volume required, having sufficient numbers of adequately trained manpower, etc.

†*Again, in the analysis given below, the level of aggregation is set at the product level. The same type of analysis could be used at the SBU or divisional level.*

Growth-Share Matrix, it displays the fundamental characteristics of a product's position. For this matrix these are:

The growth rate of the market — as before, this is plotted on a percentage scale on the vertical axis.
The growth rate of the product — this is plotted on the horizontal axis as a simple percentage.
The sales of the product — as before, this is represented by a circle whose area is proportional to the product's annual sales.

In constructing this matrix, an additional strategic factor which must be considered is the company's theoretical maximum sustainable rate of growth, which is defined as:[†]

$$G = \frac{D}{E}(r{-}i)p + rp$$

Where G =   the rate of growth,
      D =   the company's debt,
      E =   the company's equity,
      r =   the rate of return on assets,
      i =   the rate of interest charged on company
      p =   debt,
               the percentage of earnings retained by the company.

This formula gives the maximum sustainable rate of growth which the company as a whole can sustain. Thus, although a company may have, in its portfolio, products which are growing at a greater rate than G, the overall weighted average growth rate of all the products cannot be sustained at a level greater than G. G can be drawn on the matrix as a vertical line and is shown in Fig. 42 by ZZ. Although some products may be to the right of G (i.e. in the rectangle ZZRQ, in Fig. 42), the overall weighted average growth rate cannot be sustained at a level greater than G.* Figure 42 is a Growth Gain Matrix for Company Q. (See page 113 above.)

Interpreting the Growth-Gain Matrix

In Fig. 42 products whose growth is equal to that of the market are located along the diagonal PQ. Products which are growing at a faster rate than the market rate (gainers) are located in the triangle PQR, while products whose growth rate is less than that of the market growth rate

[†]*This formula was derived in Chapter 2.*
See Ref. (29) for a more detailed exposition.

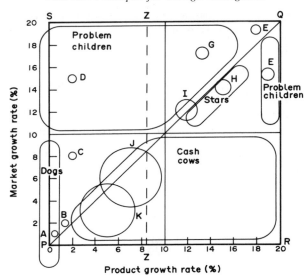

FIG. 42. *Growth-gain matrix for Company Q*

(losers) are located in the upper triangle PQS. Cash Cows, Problem Children, Stars and Dogs have the same characteristics as previously described, and are located in the areas designated in Fig. 42. Figure 42 shows that Company Q has a strong well-diversified portfolio.

As with the Growth-Share Matrix, it is possible to plot the position of a firm's products over time, make informed judgements about the firm's products' strategic position, the overall corporate strategic posture of the company and then promulgate appropriate strategies. Also it is possible, using industry data, to plot growth-gain matrices for competitors and to perceive their strategies and hence to evolve appropriate counter-strategies for individual products and the company as a whole.

Strategic Management of the Product Market Portfolio

Building market share, holding market share, harvesting and withdrawing are normally the four fundamental strategic options available. Which strategy is chosen should depend on other factors such as:

the overall composition of the firm's product market portfolio,
the position of the product in question in the matrix,
the firm's resources,
the nature of the industry,

the characteristics of the market for the product,
the strength and characteristics of competing firms,
the likely strategic actions of competitors.

Each of the four fundamental strategies is now considered in more
detail.

Building Market Share

Building market share is usually an appropriate and feasible strategy
when the market growth rate is high and when the product is in the
growth stage of its product life cycle — thus the strategy will be
appropriate mainly for products classified as Problem Children. Building market share will be found frequently to be least expensive during
the high growth period of the market — this is because under high
market growth, increasing a product's sales can be achieved without
having to "steal" sales from competitors. However, competitors will, if
alert, resist the erosion of their markets. This can be done by a variety of
devices, as outlined below. Note, however, that if the product is
experience related then the existing competitors with the largest market
shares should have cost advantages.

There are many ways in which a firm can attempt to increase its
market share. These include: simple price reduction; improving the
quality of the product or product innovation; improving the quality of
the associated service; improving the promptness of delivery; distribution innovation; advertising; narrowing the range of products offered or
concentrating on small segments of the market. This latter strategy has
been used with spectacular success by Japanese companies.

> "The fact is that strategies employed by the Japanese WORK. Simple
> and predictable though they are, they have been repeated with
> astounding success in many world markets and across many product
> lines. The power of their strategic approach arises not from their
> strategy *per se*, but from the discipline with which it is executed, from
> their *painstaking segmentation and analysis of all elements critical to their
> business, from the integration of those elements, and from their consistency and
> commitment to a highly targeted** strategic plan over the long term."[24]

Increasing market share, even in a growing market, is not always easy.
The difficulty and cost of increasing market share can be illustrated by
considering the case of Philips' (the Dutch electronics group) efforts to
grab market share for one of its Problem Children — the Video Cassette
Recorder (VCR). In 1981 Philips launched its V2000D series of VCR.

*Author's italics.

This was the third system that the company had launched since 1972, and not only was the system incompatible with the two Philips predecessors, but it was also incompatible with its Japanese rivals JVC and Sony.[27]

Philips hoped to gain market shares on the basis of technical superiority:

> the system could have up to eight hours of play on a single tape — roughly twice that of rival systems;
>
> it had a spare track which allows extra commentaries to be added to the recording without erasing the existing audio track;
>
> digital information could be recorded so that individual parts of the programme could be noted for further reference. This allowed skipping.

In 1981 JVC and Sony accounted for 90% of the world's production of VCRs and in the U.K. market (approximately one-third of the total European market) JVC alone had 70%. It was Philips' last chance to enter this growing world market. However, the costs for Philips were daunting and the prospects less than encouraging. Thus to produce the VCRs Philips spent in excess of £75m in video production in Europe.* By 1982 Philips hoped to produce in excess of one million units. However, even in 1981 Japanese capacity exceeded seven million units per year and Japanese companies were increasing production facilities as quickly as possible. From virtually zero in early 1981, Philips aimed to have 20% of the U.K. market by the end of 1982 and hoped eventually to have 50% of the total European market. However, by the end of 1982 the combined production of all companies endorsing the V2000 system was enough to supply one-third of the European market, which itself was only about 30% of the total world market.

Even though this is a very high growth market with great opportunities for winners, the prospects of Philips becoming a high relative market share company do not look promising.

Finally, building market share is fraught with risks — for example, large sums may have to be spent in irreversible capital budgeting decisions to achieve the required volume of production (in excess of £75m in the Philips VCR case). It is worth noting that this is not always appropriate for particular products or particular industries. Thus Fruhan[10] has shown empirically that for the U.S. computer industry, the U.S. retail grocery industry and the U.S. domestic trunk airline industry that the major efforts of competitors to gain large market

---

The VCRs were produced at Grundig's Nuremberg factory and at Philips' Krefeld and Vienna factories.

shares were unsuccessful, costly and inappropriate. He suggests that any company striving for large market shares should first of all ask the questions:

"Are you operating in an industry where extremely heavy financial resources are required?

Are you in an industry where an expansion strategy might be cut off abruptly by a regulatory agency?

Are you in an industry where some agency is even now planning some new regulatory hurdles?

If the answer to any of these questions is YES, and if yours is the kind of company that fights for market share, then reassess your battle plan."[10]

Also, although it is important to realise that although there is a strong direct correlation between profitability and market share it is incorrect to infer that a business which has a low market share has really only two strategic options — build market share or withdraw from the industry.

There are many examples of firms which have low market share who consistently achieve better results than their larger rivals and who are content with their market share position, i.e. they do not wish to build their market share, nor do they wish to withdraw. This can be observed in the very many successful small businesses in, say, engineering, which are a feature of European industry.

Holding Market Share

Holding market share is usually an appropriate strategy when the product and its market have become more mature and it is considered desirable to maintain the status quo. Thus this can frequently be an appropriate strategy for products that are in the Star or Cash Cow quadrants. These products should have accrued greater experience than their rivals and hence the firm should have cost, and hence profitability, advantages. The firm could be said to be operating at an optimal level: optimal in the sense that the cost or the risk attendant upon increasing market share would be greater than the likely benefits, while any decline in market share would reduce profitability.

Holding this (optimal) market share is not always easy: competitors with lower market shares will constantly be attempting to snatch — through innovation, promotion, market segmentation, etc. — some of the share of the more stable established rivals. However, there are various actions that a firm with a dominant market share may take to preserve its position. These include:

"Keeping ahead of the posse",* i.e. the market leader should not be complacent about its position but should ensure its leadership through aggressiveness in product and service innovation, cost cutting, improving distribution methods and market segmentation. The Xerox company has experienced, somewhat painfully, the cost of being "caught by the posse".

"The September 23rd disclosure by Xerox Corp. that it was planning major cutbacks and a reduction in staff had nothing to do with the state of the economy. Rather, it was the first stage in a major corporate reorganisation aimed at making the copier giant more competitive with the Japanese.

Xerox was burned once by Japanese copier makers, and its management is determined not to let the same thing happen again. When a host of Japanese producers introduced low price copiers in the U.S. in the mid 1970's, the invasion not only sparked an explosion in sales but also nearly shut the Xerox out of a market segment that it had previously ignored. Largely because of the new wave of Japanese competition Xerox's shares of U.S. copier revenues plummeted from the 96% in 1970 to just 46% last year — and is still falling.

Now the Japanese are levelling their sights on the medium and high performance end of the copier market — the lucrative heartland of Xerox's business — but this time Xerox is ready for the onslaught."[22]

Black and Decker, the U.S. power tools and saw chains manufacturer, has, in contrast to Xerox, successfully "kept ahead of the posse" for more than 35 years. This company dominates the industry and while increasing its net worldwide sales from over $222 million in 1969 to $1.4 billion in 1980 has a sales growth rate and profit rates which are double that of the industry as a whole and has a 50% greater return on its investment.[24]

"Fingers in the dyke", i.e. the market leader should try to fill all related product niches to prevent competitors from doing so. This is what IBM did in 1981 through the introduction of its microcomputer system.

"Fight them straight (nearly)," i.e. the market leader defends its leadership through aggressive advertising or price cutting. The effect of this is to make the market so unattractive that potential competitors

The author is indebted to Eamon Brennan for this apt and colourful maxim.

are dissuaded from entering this market and smaller rivals are encouraged to limit their ambitions.

Harvesting

This strategy deliberately permits market share to decline. It may be adopted because:

the product has a poor market share in a market which is declining (i.e. it is a Dog product) and the future prospects are consequently dismal;

the product has a poor market share in a growing market (i.e. it is a Problem Child product); however, the company feels it cannot provide the resources necessary to enable the product to improve its relative market share;

the company feels that it has over-extended itself in the market (i.e. the company feels that its portfolio is not sufficiently diversified or fears that its domination of a market provoke anti-trust action by the government).

Harvesting allows the company to maximise its short-term earnings and cash flow both from the operation and the working capital released. The cash obtained through harvesting may be used to help other products which appear to offer better prospects.

Withdrawal

This strategy differs from harvesting in that there is no positive cash flow into the company. The strategy is employed when a product has less than the minimum market share necessary for viability. This, indeed, must be an option which is looming for many U.K. vehicle manufacturers. Table 35 shows that U.K. production of commercial vehicles has slumped dramatically over the period 1980–1 and in 1981 commercial vehicle production was approximately equal to the output in 1949. There must be a possibility of withdrawal, i.e. closure, for those manufacturers who have insignificant market shares.

Comments on the Fundamental Strategies

The above is a description of the fundamental product market portfolio strategies in simplified and straightforward conditions. In practice, before any strategies are adopted, it is important to consider:

factors other than those captured by the display;
the risk attached to a proposed strategy;
the actual nature of the product and its market;

Table   35.   U.K.   Commercial   Vehicle Production 1980 and 1981[5]

U.K. commercial vehicle production		
Manufacturer	1981	1980
BL		
Austin Morris	25,396	55,301
Land Rover	41,060	51,378
Leyland Vehicles	16,852	22,953
Total BL	83,308	129,632
Ford	85,324	138,373
Talbot/Dodge	8,457	16,334
Vauxhall/Bedford	48,311	96,424
Hestair Dennis	835	721
ERF	n/a	1,811*
Foden	613	1,340
MCW	641	618
Seddon Atkinson	1,353	2,943
Others	713	974
Total	229,555	389,170

*First nine months only.

the arbitrariness of the product's matrix position (i.e. a change in the definition of high and low growth, high and low market share, or the definition of the market could alter the matrix status of the product). However, the matrix repositioning of a product or business should be treated with extreme caution. This has been a standard response by businesses which are not performing satisfactorily. However, frequently this repositioning has merely consisted of minor changes to, for example, the customer focus of a business without analysing and treating underlying fundamental weaknesses.[12]

Practical Guidelines for Using Product Market Portfolio Matrices

For this type of analysis, it is important to realise that the two matrices, i.e. the Growth-Share Matrix and the Growth-Gain Matrix, are complementary and both should be plotted.

A portfolio analysis can be carried out in three main stages. These are:

Developing displays for one's own firm.
Developing displays for competitors.
Making strategic comparisons on the basis of the first two stages and hence generating strategies.

Each of these stages is now considered in greater detail.

Developing Displays for One's Own Firm

This stage can be further subdivided into a number of discrete steps as follows.

Correctly Identifying the Products and the Markets

The first stage of any analysis should be to identify exactly what the products are and what the markets are. In practice this can be a most difficult problem and is not always amenable to scientific appraisal, i.e. on many occasions a statistical analysis must be complemented by judgement. It is important to correctly identify the product-market group as it will affect the perceived relative market share and the perceived market growth rate, and hence it is the basis of the display. For example, the BMW Motor Company of Germany would be a Dog company if its relative market shares were reflective to all motor cars produced and its market segment was the "motoring public". However, if the BMW Motor Company's market segment is regarded as "fast, high quality, prestigious saloon cars", then its relative market share appears to be much higher. Testimony to the fact that the BMW company is not a Dog is afforded by the company's record over the years 1976–80 which is given below.

When the product and market have been correctly identified, then the task of gathering the data necessary to construct the displays can be carried out. This data comprises sales volume, sales value, market size, rate of market growth and competitors' sales.

Table 36. BMW's Five-year Record 1976–1980[2]

Year	1980	1979	1978	1977	1976
Turnover group (DM bn)	8.12	7.41	6.56	5.53	4.76
Turnover parent company (DM bn)	6.89	6.56	5.95	4.99	4.28
After tax profit (DM m)	160.0	175.0	150.6	125.3	126.0
Workforce (group)	43,241	41,926	39,817	37,581	34,030
Car production	341,031	336,981	320,853	290,236	275,072
Total car sales	339,232	335,132	321,196	288,260	275,596
Domestic car registration	185,900	153,900	154,600	140,200	130,100
% share of West German new car registration	5.9	6.0	5.9	5.6	5.7

Draw-up Displays

Matrices for each year over, say, the previous three years can be drawn up. These displays should be superimposed upon each other so that trends can be seen. Also displays for up to five years ahead should be drawn up. These displays should show where each product would be if current policies were continued. From this analysis it should be possible to draw up tentative strategic recommendations.

Assessing the Strength and the Potential of the Portfolio

The current year's portfolio should be examined for its balance and strength, i.e. does the firm have a "good" distribution of products and is there overall financial balance? More specifically:

Are there Cash Cows to fund Problem Children which will become Stars?
Are there Stars which will become, as the rate of market growth declines, Cash Cows?
Are there Problem Children which will become, with appropriate and sufficient support, Stars?
Are there Dogs and are they being properly controlled?
What is the current overall composition of the portfolio in terms of Cash Cows, Stars, Problem Children and Dogs?, i.e. is the portfolio balanced? By this is meant is the firm's distribution of products as shown in Table 37 and is the overall cash flow of the total portfolio in balance.

Table 37. Characteristics of a Balanced Portfolio

Type	Stars	Cash Cows	Problem Children	Dogs
Characteristics	Largest circles	Largest circles	Few products	Few products

Developing Displays for Competitors

Displays for one's competitors are developed in much the same way as for one's own firm, i.e. there should be a Growth-Share Matrix and a Growth-Gain Matrix for each competitor for each year over, say, the past three years.

Making Strategic Comparisons on the Basis of the Displays Drawn and Generating Strategies

On the basis of the displays drawn up it should be possible to make

(a) An assessment of the current strategic posture of the firm
  internally — in terms of the balance of its portfolio and the trends which individual products have been following;
  externally — in terms of firstly the strength of the company's overall portfolio *vis-à-vis* its competitors and also in terms of how well individual products are competing with rival products.
(b) Generate appropriate strategies for the company.

The latter can be achieved by developing future ideal or target portfolios for, say, two years hence, and then taking strategic actions to try to achieve this ideal portfolio (always bearing in mind, of course, the likely actions or reactions of competitors).

For example for Firm Q, Fig. 43 shows its current position and the planned portfolio it aspires to move to in the current planning period.

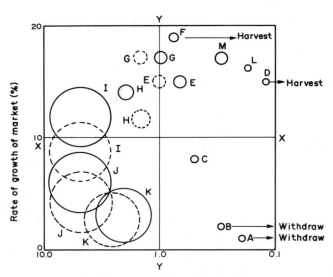

Relative market share (Log scale)

○ Current position

◌ Future planned position

Fig. 43. *Current and planned portfolio for Company Q*

Note that the firm intends to withdraw two Dogs — A and B — both have dismal prospects and the strategic planners believe that if they do not divest the portfolio of them these products will become cash traps. The Problem Children D and F will be harvested because the firm does not have sufficient resources to support all Problem Children. The Problem Children that will be supported are E and G. It is also anticipated that extra resources will be supplied to H and I and that both products will expand their sales and that I will become a Cash Cow. Products J and K will continue to be Cash Cows and their sales will continue to increase as competitors leave the declining market. Finally, it is surmised that C will continue to be a Dog (and if H may possibly become one) and that two new products L and M will be introduced during the planning period.

Limitations of the Approach

Although the product portfolio approach to strategic management has widespread support, there is now considerable questioning of the approach,[24A] and its use must be considered in the following critical context.

Firstly, the matrix relies for its analyses on just two factors — rate of market growth and relative market share. It could be argued that, although these are important factors, they do not exclusively determine a product's success or otherwise. It is this criticism (plus others) that has led to the development of strategic matrices such as the Directional Policy Matrix which incorporate other factors when displaying a product's strategic position.

Indeed, even the BCG itself has recognised this criticism, and its latest matrix (1982), as shown in Fig. 44, reflects this change. Thus BCG has replaced relative market share with "the size of advantage that can be created over other competitors" and it has replaced "rate of market growth" with "the number of unique ways in which that advantage can be created". These are the two factors which, BCG now argue, give both a "sense of the long-term value of a business and dictate the strategy requirements". This change by the BCG would seem simultaneously to expand the number of factors which a matrix is able to capture and also make the strategic positioning of a product a much more qualitative exercise and a more judgemental one. This matrix is shown in Fig. 44.[4]

The Product Market Portfolio has an implication that unless one's product is say in the top three or four in terms of relative market shares, then one should leave that market. There are many reasons why this implication should be treated with some scepticism. The principal one is that there is considerable evidence. (See Refs. (20), (21) and (15) to

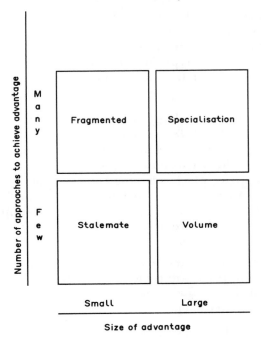

FIG. 44. *BCG's strategic planning tool (1981)*[4]

support the assertion that many businesses thrive in spite of a low relative market share.) Additionally, the link between profitability and market share may be weak because

Low share competitors (who entered later) may be on the steepest experience curves.

Low share competitors may have low cost suppliers or some other inbuilt cost advantage.

Not all products have experience related costs.

Large share competitors may be subject to more government regulation.

In the seventies such strategies, i.e. high market share and a low cost position, were, for many, fraught with problems as segment or niche speculation arose and multiple competitors reached economies of scale.

The Product Market Portfolio also implies that the most fruitful markets to enter, or stay in, are those which have the highest rate of growth. This may not always be so. Thus

entry barriers may be so high for a particular industry that even when growth is extremely rapid the returns are not sufficient to justify the cost of entry;

in the maturity stage of the product, especially, price competition may very adversely affect profitability, as has happened in the fast growing market for 64K RAM chips.

This can also happen in the growth stage.

"Because prices are falling so rapidly, industry analysts question whether any of today's players, including the Japanese, can be turning a profit today. Momichiro, Matsumura, associate senior vice president for semiconductors at Nippon Electric Co., concedes that his company, which is trailing Hitachi, Fujitsu and Motorola in its 64K RAM production, is making only 'marginal' profits on this type of chip. Of the six significant Japanese suppliers, he says, 'maybe two or three are making high profits and two or three are making marginal profits'.

. . . NEC's US chief Kerske Yawata predicts that the real test for 64K RAM suppliers will come in early to mid 1983. 'Don't think anyone will be profitable at the projected price of \$5 for that period. The latecomers will be shaken out.'"[17]

Finally, by definition, a very large number of European businesses must be Dogs, and must therefore be, according to BCG definitions, to some extent condemned. This is a harsh and really unrealistic way to view businesses,* but perhaps a more appropriate way is to adopt the view of Dogs postulated by Goold:

"The portfolio concept is about selectivity in the management of different businesses. In a period of low growth or recession, such selectivity becomes even more essential, but it is also important to identify strategies for the so-called Dogs that are realistic and will allow them to make as much contribution as possible within the corporate portfolio.

The fundamental guidelines for managing a Dog are to recognise that growth oriented strategies are likely to fail, and that a careful watch needs to be maintained on the cash flow performance of this quadrant."[11]

References

1.   Anderson, M. J. Jr. and Harris, J. E. "Strategies for Low Market Share Businesses", *Harvard Business Review*, Vol. 56, No. 3, May/June 1978, pp. 95–102.

*If this definition were to be applied to Ireland, practically all businesses would (because of their low relative market share due to Ireland having such a small population) be condemned as Dogs.

2. "BMW: Sharp Fall in Sales at Home, German Motor Industry", Financial Times Survey, *Financial Times*, 18 Sept. 1981.
3. Bloom, P. and Kotler, P. "Strategies for High Market Share Companies", *Harvard Business Review*, Vol. 53, No. 6, Nov./Dec. 1975, pp. 63–72.
4. Boston Consulting Group, *Annual Perspective*, 1981.
5. "Commercial Vehicle Output at 1949 Level", *Financial Times*, 19 Feb. 1982, p. 5.
6. Day, G. S. "Diagnosing the Product Portfolio", *Journal of Marketing*, Vol. 41, No. 2, April 1977, pp. 29–38.
7. Elliott, J. "Breaking the Mould of a Corporate Confection", *Financial Times*, 10 Feb. 1982, p. 16.
8. *Financial Times*, 28 Nov. 1981, p. 1.
9. *Long Range Planning*, Vol. 14, No. 6, Dec. 1981, pp. 58–67.
10. Fruhan, W. E. "Pyrrhic Victories in Fights for Market Share", *Harvard Business Review*, Vol. 50, No. 5, Sept./Oct. 1972, pp. 100–107.
11. Goold, M. "How 'Dogs' Can be Given More to Bite", *Financial Times*, 13 Nov. 1981, p. 16.
12. Goold, M. "Why Dicey Definitions Are So Dangerous", *Financial Times*, 16 Nov. 1981, p. 16.
13. Henderson, B. "Cash Traps", *Perspectives*, No. 102, The Boston Consulting Group, 1972.
14. Henderson, B. "The Product Portfolio", *Perspectives*, No. 66, The Boston Consulting Group, 1970.
15. "Hewlett Packard: Where Slower Growth is Smarter Management", *Business Week*, 9 June 1975, pp. 50–58.
16. "A High Flyer Comes in from the Cold", *Financial Times*, 30 Sept. 1981, p. 16.
17. *International Newsweek*, 6 April 1981.
17. "Japan's Strategy for the 1980's", *Business Week Special Issue*, 14 Dec. 1981, pp. 29–79.
18. "Japanese Shipyard Expansion Criticised", *Financial Times*, 16 March 1981.
19. Lofthouse, S. "Strategy, Cross-Subsidization and the Business Portfolio", *Long Range Planning*, Vol. 11, No. 4, August 1978, pp. 58–60.
20. Lorenz, C. "Why Boston Recanted its Doctrine of Market Leadership", *Financial Times*, 20 Nov. 1981, p. 10.
21. Lorenz, C. "Why Boston Theory is on Trial", *Financial Times*, 11 Nov. 1981.
22. "The New Mean Lean Xerox", *Business Week*, 12 Oct. 1981, pp. 82–86.
23. McCarthy Clippings Service: various sources, Belfast Central Reference Library.
24. Particelli, M. C. "The Japanese are Coming: Global Strategic Planning in Action", *Outlook*, 4, Spring 1981, pp. 36–44.
24A. Porter, M. E. *Competitive Strategy*, The Free Press, 1980.
25. "Office Equipment: Financial Times Survey", *Financial Times*, 12 Oct. 1981.
26. Tieleman, T. M. "Portfolio Planning at Akzo", *Long Range Planning*, Vol. 14, No. 6, Dec. 1981, pp. 17–23.
27. "Video Cassette Market Nears 200 million Mark", *Financial Times*, 16 Oct. 1981, p. 5.
28. Wind, Y., and Mahajans, V. "Designing Product and Business Portfolios", *Harvard Business Review*, Jan./Feb. 1981, pp. 155–165.
29. Zakon, A. *Growth and Financial Strategies*, Boston, The Boston Consulting Group, 1971.

Bibliography

Abell, D. F. *Defining the Business: The Starting Point of Strategic Planning*, Prentice-Hall, Englewood Cliffs, N.J., 1980.
Abell, D. F. "Strategic Windows", *Journal of Marketing*, Vol. 42, No. 3, July 1978, pp. 21–26.
Abell, D. and Hammond, J. S. *Strategic Market Planning: Problems and Analytical Approaches*, Prentice-Hall, Englewood Cliffs, N.J., 1979.

Anonymous, "Managing High Technology Portfolio Milks Cows, Kills Dogs", *Marketing News*, Vol. 13, No. 1, 13 July 1979.

Bamberger, I. "Portfolio Analysis for the Small Firm", *Long Range Planning*, Vol. 15, No. 6, Dec. 1982, pp. 49–57.

Barksdale, H. C. and Harris, C. E. "Portfolio Analysis and the Product Life Cycle", *Long Range Planning*, Vol. 15, No. 6, Dec. 1982, pp. 74–83.

Battacharya, K. "How Companies Can Escape Degeneration and Death", *Financial Times*, 27 Nov. 1981, p. 16.

Bettis, R. A. and Hall, W. K. "The Business Portfolio: Where it Falls Down in Practice", *Long Range Planning*, Vol. 16, No. 2, April 1982, pp. 95–104.

Boyd, H. W. and Headen, R. S. "Definition and Management of the Product Market Portfolio", *Industrial Marketing Management*, Vol. 7, No. 5, Oct. 1978, pp. 337–346.

Buckley, A. "Competitive Strategies for Investment", *Journal of General Management*, Vol. 2, No. 3, Spring 1975, pp. 59–66.

Buckley, A. "How to Plan for Successful Company Growth", *Accountancy (U.K.)*, Vol. 90, No. 1026, Feb. 1979, pp. 98–100.

Burke, M. and Weitz, B. "The Use of BCG Portfolio Model in Strategic Marketing Decision Making", *Educators' Conference Proceedings*, 1979, Vol. 44, pp. 468–473.

Burnett, S. C. "The Ecology of Building, Harvesting and Holding Market Share", *Research in Marketing*, Vol. 6, 1983, pp. 1–63.

Cardozo, R. N. and Smyth, D. K. Jr. "Applying Financial Portfolio Theory to Product Portfolio Decisions", *Journal of Marketing*, Vol. 47, No. 2, Spring 1983, pp. 110–119.

Carlson, R. D. "Planning Product Portfolio Strategies", *Mid South Business Journal*, Vol. 3, No. 1, Jan. 1983, pp. 3–7.

Christensen, H. K., Cooper, A. C. and De Kluyver, C. A. "The Dog Business: A Re-examination", *Business Horizons*, Nov./Dec. 1982, pp. 12–18.

Coate, M. B. "Pitfalls in Portfolio Planning", *Long Range Planning*, Vol. 16, No. 3, June 1983, pp. 47–56.

Cox, W. E. Jr. "Product Portfolio Strategy: A Review of the Boston Consulting Group Approach to Marketing Strategy", *American Marketing Association Combined Proceedings*, Series 36, 1974, pp. 460–464.

Day, G. S. "A Strategic Perspective on Product Planning", *Journal of Contemporary Business*, Vol. 4, No. 2, Spring 1975, pp. 1–34.

De Kluyver, C. "Innovation and Industrial Product Life Cycles", *California Management Review*, Vol. 20, No. 1, Fall 1977, pp. 21–33.

Delombre, J. and Bruzelius, J. "Importance of Relative Market Share in Strategic Planning: A Case Study", *Long Range Planning*, Vol. 10, Aug. 1977, pp. 2–7.

Frohman, A. T. "Co-ordinating Business Strategy and Technical Planning", *Long Range Planning*, Vol. 14, No. 6, Dec. 1981, pp. 58–67.

Gelb, B. D. "Strategic Planning for the Under-Dog", *Business Horizons*, Nov./Dec. 1983, pp. 8–11.

Goldgehn, L. A. and LaGarce, R. "Giving a New Dimension to Product Portfolio Analysis", *Management Review*, Vol. 72, No. 4, April 1983, pp. 57–61.

Gup, B. E. *Guide to Strategic Planning*, McGraw-Hill, 1980.

Guiltinan, J. P. and Donnelly, J. H. "The Use of Product Portfolio Analysis in Bank Planning", *Journal of Retail Banking*, Vol. 5, No. 1, Spring 1983, pp. 15–24.

Hambrick, D. C. and MacMillan, I. C. "The Product Market Portfolio and Man's Best Friend", *California Management Review*, Vol. 25, No. 1, Fall 1982, pp. 84–95.

Hambrick, D. C., MacMillan, I. C. and Day, D. L. "Strategic Attributes and Performance in the BCG Matrix — A PIMS-Based Analysis of Industrial Product Businesses", *Academy of Management Journal*, Vol. 25, No. 3, Sept. 1982, pp. 510–531.

Hammeresh, R. C., Anderson, M. J. and Harris, J. F. "Strategies for Low Market Share Businesses", *Harvard Business Review*, May/June 1978, pp. 95–102.

Hamermesh, R. G. and Silk, S. B. "How to Compete in Stagnant Industries", *Harvard Business Review*, Sept. 1979, pp. 161–168.

Haspeslagh, P. "Portfolio Planning: Uses and Limits", *Harvard Business Review*, Jan.–Feb. 1982, pp. 58–73.

Heany, D. F. and Weiss, G. "Integrating Strategies for Clusters of Businesses", *Journal of Business Strategy*, Vol. 4, No. 1, Summer 1983, pp. 3–11.

Hedley, B. "Strategy and the Business Portfolio", *Long Range Planning*, Vol. 10, Feb. 1977, pp. 9–15.

Hofer, C. W. and Schendel, D. *Strategy Formulation: Analytical Concepts*, West Publishing Co., St Paul, 1980.

Kitching, J. "Acquisitions in Europe", *Business International*, pp. 74–76.

Kotler, P. "Harvesting Strategies for Weak Products", *Business Horizons*, August 1978, pp. 15–22.

Larreche, J. C. "The International Product Market Portfolio", *American Marketing Association, Educator's Proceeding*, Series 43, 1978, pp. 276–281.

Larreche, J. C. and Srinivasan, V. "STRATPORT: a Model for the Evaluation of Business Portfolio Strategies", *Management Science*, Vol. 28, No. 9, Sept. 1982, pp. 1035–1044.

Linneman, R. E. and Thomas, M. J. "A Commonsense Approach to Portfolio Planning", *Long Range Planning*, Vol. 15, No. 2, April 1982, pp. 77–92.

Lorange, P. *Corporate Planning: An Executive Viewpoint*, Prentice-Hall Inc., Englewood Cliffs, N.J., 1980.

Lorenz, C. "Cows, Dogs and Drucker: the dangers of spoonfeeding", *Financial Times*, 15 Oct. 1982, p. 18.

Lund, R. T. and Denney, W. M. "Extending Product Life: Time to Remanufacture", *Management Review*, March 1978, pp. 21– .

MacMillan, I. C., Hambrick, D. C. and Day, D. L. "The Product Market Portfolio and Profitability", *Academy of Management Journal*, Vol. 25, No. 4, Dec. 1982, pp. 733–755.

Majaro, S. "Market Share: Deception or Diagnosis", *Marketing*, March 1977, pp. 43–47.

Mitchell, P. C. N. "Financial Analysis and Marketing Strategy", *Management Accounting (U.K.)*, Vol. 57, No. 2, Feb. 1979, pp. 16–19.

Mohn, N. C. and Hubbard, C. L. "How to Reduce Uncertainty in Sales Forecasting", *Management Review*, Vol. 67, No. 6, June 1978, pp. 14–22.

Newbould, G. D. "Product Portfolio Diagnosis for U.S. Universities", *Akron Business and Economic Review*, Vol. 1, No. 1, Spring 1980, pp. 39–45.

Newton, J. K. "Market Share — Key to Higher Profitability", *Long Range Planning*, Vol. 16, No. 1, Feb. 1983, pp. 37–41.

Patel, P. and Younger, M. "A Frame of Reference for Strategy Development", *Long Range Planning*, Vol. 11, No. 2, April 1978, pp. 6–12.

Pethia, R. F. and Saias, M. "Metalevel Product Portfolio Analysis: An Enrichment of Strategic Planning Suggested by Organization Theory", *International Studies of Management & Organization*, Vol. 8, No. 4, Winter 1978–79, pp. 35–66.

Porter, M. E. "Exit Barriers to Planning", *California Management Review*, Winter 1976, pp. 21–35.

The Product Portfolio, *Perspectives*, No. 66, The Boston Consulting Group, 1970.

Reece, J. S. and Coo, W. R. "Measuring Investment Center Performance", *Harvard Business Review*, May/June 1978, p. 28 etc.

Robicheaux, R. A. "GMROI/Share Product Portfolio Analysis", *American Marketing Association Proceedings*, No. 47, 1981, pp. 31–34.

Shanklin, W. L. and Ryans, J. K. Jr., "Is the International Cash Cow Really a Prize Heifer?", *Business Horizons*, Vol. 24, No. 2, March/April 1982, pp. 1–16.

Sherden, W. A. "Strategic Planning: Do the Concepts Apply?", *Best's Review Property/Casualty Insurance Edition*, Vol. 84, No. 6, Oct. 1983, pp. 28–30.

Sizer, J. "New Lamps for Old in Bazaars Ancient and Modern — Product and Market Planning in a Changing World", *Management Accounting (London)*, Vol. 55, No. 4, April 1977, pp. 160–163.

Sizer, J. "Pricing Policy in Inflation: A Management Accountant's Perspective", *Accounting and Business Research*, Vol. 5, No. 22, Spring 1976, pp. 107–124.

"Unless You Can Be Winner. Don't Play", *Forbes*, Vol. 120, No. 8, 15 Oct. 1977, p. 132.

"Why The (Smart) Rich Get Richer", *Forbes*, Vol. 113, No. 10, 15 may 1974, pp. 90–91.

Wind, Y. and Douglas, S. "International Portfolio Analysis and Strategy: the Challenge of the 80s", *Journal of International Business Studies*, Fall 1981, pp. 69–82.

CHAPTER 5
Matrix Displays

Introduction

As was argued in Chapter 4, strategic planning for large, diversified, multiproduct companies is an extremely complex and multidimensional process. The unique problem which this type of company presents is how to allow for the many-faceted problems that accrue through diversity while simultaneously accommodating the overall strategic thrust of the company.

A good example of the recognition of the importance of this problem and hence the importance of having structures (and hence strategic planning procedures) capable of handling this type of diversity is afforded by Sir Michael Edwardes' efforts to make British Leyland (BL) viable. Thus in May 1978, after less than one year in office, Sir Michael Edwardes reported, in his review of the group's corporate plan, that "first and foremost, BL's problems were in part due to the structure of the organisation";[1] he then proceeded to decentralise the organisation into a number of limited companies. By 1981 the company comprised four main groups — Unipart (components), Cars, Land Rover and Leyland (commercial vehicles including Leyland vehicles only). Each of these major groups was in a unique business sector with unique prospects, opportunities and expectations. Consequently, although BL had an overall strategy, this corporate strategy was disaggregated into group strategies, each of which was tailored to meet the unique challenges facing each group. A consequence of this approach to organisational structure and planning is that there must be a certain incompatibility between objectives at the corporate and the group (or divisional) levels.

This inevitable incompatibility of objectives at the corporate and the divisional levels and between divisions has been one factor that has led to the development of the types of matrix display considered in this chapter.

Another factor is the necessity for strategic planners to assess the overall strategic balance of the company. This strategic balance can be considered on two major axes: internal strategic balance and external strategic balance.

Internal Strategic Balance

There are, of course, many ways in which a company should be balanced internally. A judgement about this balance can be made after answering questions such as the following. Are there sufficient resources in each functional area to ensure that the objectives of each area can be met? Is the management and the workforce balanced in terms of skills? However, among the major factors which have been instrumental in the development of the type of approach considered in this chapter are:

1. *The age balance of the products.** By this is meant are there, in the corporate product range, a range of products at different stages of their life cycles which will provide a product dynasty?, i.e. are there, in the corporate product portfolio, products which are at the mature stage of their life cycles and which are generating sufficient surplus cash to:

   (a) nurture newer products which are at the growth stages of their life cycles, and
   (b) help maintain established products which require cash sustenance to sustain or improve their positions in high growth markets?

Returning again to the cautionary tale of British Leyland, it could be argued that one of that company's most difficult and intractable problems was its failure to establish, in the 1970s, a range of products which would sustain the company in the 1980s. The highly successful and innovative products of the 1970s[†] which dominated the U.K. market were not complemented, as they aged, by new products capable of sustaining BL in the 1980s. In fact, so aged had BL's line of products become, relative to the products available from their competitors, that the company was obliged in 1980 to enter into an agreement with Honda of Japan to manufacture in Britain, jointly with Honda, using Honda technology, a Honda designed car — the Triumph Acclaim — to plug a serious gap which was appearing in its product line.

The shortcomings in BL's total product range in the late 1970s and early 1980s had extremely adverse effects not just upon the external image of the car maker — it was increasingly appearing as a car maker which offered a limited range of dated products — but also upon its financial position. It could be argued that the lack of "age balance of products" was reflected in a lack of balance in BL's cash flows. Thus Fig.

The level of aggregation in this chapter has been changed from the divisional level of page 138 above to the product level. It is assumed that readers will most easily be able to conceptualise the arguments if they are couched in terms of products. The level of aggregation is, of course, determined by the strategic requirements.

[†]*The Economist's Intelligence Unit's "Motor Business" calls the years 1971 to 1973 BL's "Golden Years".[(2)]*

45 shows, schematically, how, because of the unbalanced age structure of its products, BL's profits were concentrated in "the golden years" to the detriment of subsequent years, while Fig. 46 shows, schematically, how a better age balance of products would have provided a smoother and more continuous pattern of profitability.

2. *The financial balance of the products.* By this is meant are there, in the corporate product range, a range of products whose cash characteristics are such that the sum of their cash contributions plus corporate cash inflows and disbursements are in balance? Figures 45 and 46 illustrate that for British Leyland this was not the case.

External Strategic Balance

Similarly, there are many ways in which judgements could be made about a company's external strategic balance. Areas of importance include relationships with customers, suppliers, government, etc. The area which has been instrumental in the development of this type of approach is the business sectoral balance of the company — i.e. are the products of the company spread in a variety of business sectors* such

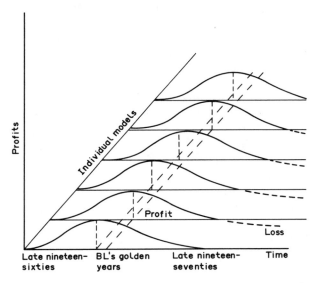

FIG. 45. *Schematic presentation of how BL's profits were concentrated in the "Golden Years" (not to scale)*

The term "business sector" rather than "market" is used as it is more general. For example, the most relevant business sector for certain businesses may be the "supplier", as is the case for the oil refining industry, rather than the "market".

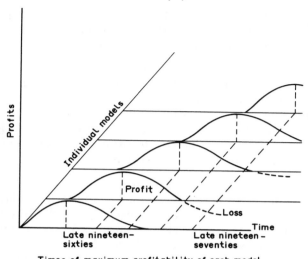

FIG. 46. *Schematic representation of how a better age balance of products would have provided BL with a smoother and more continuous flow of profits*

that the financial benefit to the company is maximised while overall corporate risk is reduced? This balance is of fundamental importance because of the necessity for strategic planners to ascertain the strategic positions each of their products in its unique environment, i.e. there is a necessity to be able to perceive not just how well each of the products is performing in relation to competing products, but how well each is performing in its business sector with particular reference to the major characteristics of its sector. For example, the Sinclair Timex computer company, although dwarfed in size by the major computer manufacturers, achieved, through its ZX81 computer, phenomenal success: over 500,000 ZX81s were sold worldwide by the end of 1982. The ZX81 achieved this spectacular success because it was a unique product — it was very much cheaper than its nearest rivals — and was the first such product in a new environment: the environment was the market for very low cost personal computers.

When the ZX81's business sector changed — the market became saturated, customers began demanding more technically powerful and sophisticated personal computers and other computer companies (Commodore, Texas Instruments, Acorn, etc.) brought out more powerful yet attractively priced personal computers — Sinclair-Timex introduced a new and more powerful personal computer: the Spectrum.

Although this new product was essential for Sinclair-Timex to remain a significant player in this changed business sector, the product faced much stiffer competition than the ZX81 had faced:

> "During its two years on the market, the Sinclair ZX81 has had to face little competition so far from similarly priced machines. With the Spectrum, the situation will be different; computers costing $200 or less are already on the market or promised from Commodore (Vic models); Acorn (Electron); Oric; Dragon; Computers (Lynx); Atari; Lowe Electronics (Colour Genie); Jupiter (Ace); Tandy; and Texas Instruments."[10]

The seminal, and perhaps best known, matrix which attempted to provide a technique to handle the types of complexities outlined above is the Product Market Portfolio Matrix developed by the Boston Consulting Group (BCG). However, almost since its introduction the BCG matrix has been the subject not only of considerable accolade but also of considerable criticism. The major criticisms are as follows.

It may be unrealistic to make a judgement about a product's strategic position solely on the basis of just two factors — relative market share and market growth rate. Even the most casual observation indicates that other factors — for example, quality of product, company reputation, nationalism of the market, etc. — may be of fundamental importance. For example, when IBM introduced its small business/personal computer in Europe in 1982 its strategic position could not properly be inferred from the growth rate of the market (very high) and IBM's relative market share in the area (by definition zero). Rather, IBM's initial strategic position in this particular business sector was considered strong by many industry watchers. This view was undoubtedly influenced by IBM's reputation as a manufacturer of quality products, its declared aspiration to become significant in this business sector and by the immense resources that IBM could provide to support such an aspiration.

The link between profitability and relative market share may not be so strong as the BCG writings[3] would appear to indicate. There are many examples of companies which have made handsome profits in business sectors where they were not among the market leaders and vice versa. For example, Leontiades[7] has examined the relationship between market share and Return on Investment of three pairs of firms (each pair comprising a major national competitor and a major international competitor) in three industries (automobiles, computers and semiconductors) operating in the United Kingdom. In each industry the national competitor enjoyed, for some years anyway, the leading market share, but no national competitor in any of the industries considered consistently achieved as good a return on investment as its international rival. This is illstrated for the automobile industry in Table 38.

Table 38. Ford (U.K.) and BL's Market Shares of U.K. Passenger Cars and Ford (U.K.) and BL's Returns on Investment[7]

Year	U.K. market share (%)		Return on Investment (%)	
	BL	Ford (U.K.)	BL	Ford (U.K.)
1969	39	27	16	18
1970	38	26	6	11
1971	40	19	13	Loss
1972	33	24	12	19
1973	31	23	16	28
1974	32.5	23	8	7
1975	30.5	22	Loss	9
1976	27	25	20	31
1977	24	26	9	55
1978	23	24	8	35
1979	21	28	Loss	49
1980	18	31	Loss	24

The BCG matrix implies that those markets with the highest growth rates are the most fruitful ones. This may not always be so. Thus, although the personal computer market already referred to will, it is predicted as shown in Table 39, grow at a phenomenal rate over the period 1981 to 1986, the dynamics of this industry — in terms of speed of change, price reductions, product obsolescence and the development of, and fury of competition — are such that participation in this industry is extremely risky and early death is a frequent occurrence.

Table 39. Projected Growth of Worldwide Portable Computer Market[7]

The worldwide portable computer market shipments and revenue forecasts 1981–1986*

	Shipments ('000 units)						
	1981	1982	1983	1984	1985	1986	CAGR[†]
U.S.	17.5	92	173	314	525	822	73
Total	26.5	115	230	449	808	1370	86

	Revenues ($m)						
	1981	1982	1983	1984	1985	1986	CAGR[†]
U.S.	45	192	345	566	975	1260	60
Total	73.8	239.7	460	808	1500	2100	72

*Excluding calculators and consoles.
†CAGR, compound annual growth rate, in percent.

By way of contrast, a more pedestrian, and perhaps seemingly unattractive, market is the market for milk products in Western Europe — the market is of fairly low growth and yet it has proved to be a most profitable one for certain companies. For example, the French company Sodima, which manufactures various milk products under the internationally famous Yoplait name, has had, over the past decade, continuous success in these products. Thus Yoplait's sales trends in France for the years 1980–81 (as shown in Table 40) show that the company has stolen market share from its competitors. For Yoplait anyway, the international milk products market is an extremely attractive one.

Table 40. Yoplait Sales Evolution 1980–1981 and Comparison with the Market (in France only)[12]

			Evolution 81/82	
	1980	1981	Yoplait	Market
Yoghurts (million cups 12cl)	992	1057	+6.6%	5.3%
Desserts (million cups 12cl)	258	271	+5.0%	−0.5%
Fresh cheese (tons)	33,074	39,672	+19.9%	+4.1%
Fresh cream (million litres)	16.6	18.2	+9.6%	+2.0%

The BCG matrix uses cash flow potential as the criterion for assessing a product's strategic position. There are other measures available — for example, ROI — which could be regarded, in certain circumstances, as being more appropriate. The criterion of assessment of the quality of a project assumes particular importance in industries which are subject to international competition and are global in perspective. This is particularly well illustrated when the measures of performance used by U.S. companies and Japanese companies are compared. Thus, in general, it is frequently the case that U.S. companies' performances are judged on the basis of quarterly earnings while rival Japanese companies may be judged on more multidimensional measures and over longer time horizons; for example, relative market share and return on investment over one decade. Such differences in time horizons have given Japanese companies substantial advantages in activities which have long lead times to profitability and which have high capital investment requirements.

In short, it could be argued that the original BCG matrix may view strategic problems too narrowly, and what is required is an approach which can incorporate a greater range of factors which help determine a product's strategic position, these factors being those characteristics which determine the particular competitive strength of the product and the attractiveness of the business sector in which the product is being sold. Returning again to the case of the Sinclair-Timex ZX81 computer, it could be argued that the particular competitive strength of the ZX81 was its price and the attractiveness of its business sector was its growth and the absence of real competitors.

An approach which incorporated this broader perspective was pioneered by Robinson, Hichens and Wade who developed the Directional Policy Matrix.[11] An amended version of this matrix is the major topic of this chapter and is presented below.

The Directional Policy Matrix

As was argued in Chapter 1, the fundamental way of assessing the strategic position of a business is to make a judgement about how well it fits in with its environment. The Directional Policy Matrix attempts to display this fit through examining the two major determinants of this fit. These are:

The attractiveness of the business sector in which the business is operating: the Business Sector Prospects.

The particular competences the business has that enable it to take advantage of the sector in which it is operating: the Business Position.

Each of these major sets of influence is now considered.

The Business Sector Prospects

The original BCG matrix appeared really to formally admit only one factor — market growth rate — as the determinant of Business Sector Prospects. As already referred to, European experience and casual observation would, however, seem to indicate that this is too narrow a way in which to judge the prospects presented by a business sector. However, when a more comprehensive appraisal is attempted, the problem of the very uniqueness of every business sector makes the formulation of a set of general rules for the appraisal of any particular sector extremely difficult. It will be the case that, in practice, a planner will appraise his business sector's prospects on the basis of those factors which he deems to be relevant.

In an attempt to overcome the difficulty of formulating a general set of guidelines, a non-exhaustive list of the criteria by which planners frequently judge the sector prospects for their business is now given.

Market factors

Size of the population or the relevant segment of the population.
Distribution of the population according to age, income, location, etc.
Population trends.
Size of the market in monetary terms and units.*[†]
Growth rate of the market.[†]
Seasonality of the market.
Maturity of the market.[†]

Competitive factors

The number of competitors.
The size of competitors in terms of sales, market share[†], relative market share[†].
The price level and the degree of competition.
Barriers to entry and exit.
Availability of substitutes.

Technological factors

Maturity of the market.
Speed of technological change.
Lead time for new products.
Patents.
Level of capacity utilization in the industry[†].

Economic factors

Degree of leverage within the sector.
The size of contribution margins.
Financial barriers to entry.
Capital intensity.

Government factors

Government subsidies.
Government purchases.
Government protection from "foreign competition".
Competition from "government companies".
Government monopoly/antitrust legislation.

Supplier factors

The availability and cost of raw materials or sub-assemblies.
The availability and cost of energy.

Geographical factors

The location of the business in relation to its suppliers and its markets.

*Factors marked thus [†] have been found by the PIMS Studies to be of most importance in determining ROI and cash flow (see Chapter 6).

The location of the business in relation to government tax and investment incentives.

Social factors
The power of pressure groups.
Trade union activity and power.
Social attitudes towards industry.

The Business Position

As was the case for the Business Sector Prospects, the BCG Matrix appeared to only formally admit one factor — relative market share — as the determinant of a firm's business position. This somewhat narrow perspective is expanded here.

Although the set of factors which determine the strategic position for any business will be unique to that particular business, factors which are frequently cited* as playing important roles are given below.

Market factors
Market share and relative market share[†].
Annual growth rate of sales[†].
Maturity of products relative to competitors[†].
Quality of products/services[†].
Product mix including width of product line[†].
Quality of marketing department.
Patent protection.
Pricing strategy.
Quality of distribution channels.
Quality of advertising.
Level of marketing expenses[†].
Level of customer loyalty.

Technological factors
Depth of technological skills.
Patent protection.
Quality of manufacturing technology.

Production factors
Costs relative to competitors.
Level of capacity utilisation[†].
Availability of raw materials and sub-assemblies.
Quality of inventory control.

---

*Once again factors marked thus [†] have been found by the PIMS Studies to be of crucial importance in determining ROI and cash flow.

Quality of maintenance.
Level of vertical integration.

Personnel factors
Quality of employees.
Balanced top management team.
Good industrial relations.
Quality of training and development.
Labour costs.

Financial factors
Total financial resources available.
Cost of capital.
Capital structure.
Margins.
Tax position.
Relations with suppliers of finance.
Quality of financial control system.
Inventory and asset evaluation policies.
Investment intensity[†].

What Factors are Relevant?

In practice, each business or industry is likely to be unique in the total list of factors (internal and external) that determine its strategic position. Thus, if an industry deals in highly differentiated products — motor cars, for example — then such factors as technical reliability, technical sophistication, image, price and market skills will be crucial factors, and when the matrix is being developed for such a firm, these factors will be instrumental in determining a motor company's business position. By contrast, a company engaged in, say, "the supply of energy business" will be less concerned with these factors and more concerned with external factors such as security of supplies, cost of supplies, prices of direct and indirect competitors. In short, there is a great deal of managerial judgement required in the process and it is really not possible to give a total list of factors for all industries.

Achieving Consistency

A major problem associated with this type of approach is that of achieving consistency during successive analyses — the judgemental

[†]*See footnote page 147.*

nature of the approach makes an element of subjectivity inevitable. For example, if a volume car manufacturer in 1980 shared its domestic market with four major domestic competitors and five major importers and in 1981 the following strategic changes occurred: the domestic competitors introduced two new models each and kept all prices constant in real terms; the Government imposed severe import quotas and reduced bank lending rate. A simple comparison, i.e. in some ways 1981 was better for the manufacturer in question and in some ways it was worse, is inadequate.

In this example it is insufficient to say that competitors' new models and the constant prices offered by competitors make the sector prospects more unfavourable: there must be a more precise judgement; there must be a ranking of the importance of the changes; but even this is not sufficient — there must also be a measurement of the strengths of the factors. For example, if in 1982 each competitor introduced three new models, rather than two, then this factor would have a much stronger impact than in 1981. A methodology for ranking the importance of measuring the strength and gauging the overall impact of each factor is now considered.

Tables 41 and 42 show the Business Sector Prospects and the Business Position quantified for a hypothetical company, while pages 150 to 151 give the method of quantification.

Table 41. Quantifying the Business Sector Prospects

Factor	Importance*	Strength†	Overall score (importance by strength)
Growth of market	5	+3	+15
Competition	3	+2	+6
Technology	5	+4	+20
Industry capacity	1	+1	+1
Stage of business cycle	4	−1	−4
Inflation	1	−1	−1
Government subsidies	1	+1	+1
Raw material costs	4	+2	+8
Location	2	+1	+2
Pressure groups	1	−1	−1

Total score	47
Maximum possible score	250
Percentage score	$\dfrac{47 \times 100}{250} = 18.8\%$

*Scale goes from 0 to 5.
†Scale goes from −5 to +5.

Table 42. Quantifying the Business Position

Factor	Importance*	Strength†	Overall score (importance by strength)
Market share	5	−4	−20
Product quality	5	−2	−10
Prices	4	−3	−12
Costs	3	−1	−3
Efficiency	3	−2	−6
Financial resources	3	−4	−12
Management skills	3	+1	+3

Total score	−60
Maximum possible score	175
Percentage score	$\dfrac{-60 \times 100}{175} = -34\%$

*Scale goes from 0 to +5.
†Scale goes from −5 to +5.

Quantifying the Business Sector Prospects and the Business Position

The same method of quantification is used for Business Sector Prospects and Business Position. It is explained below.

The *importance* of each factor is ranked on an ordinal scale of 0 to 5. Thus if a factor is of no importance at all, it scores zero (or, as in the above example, it is excluded from the table); if it is of only minor importance, it scores 1; if it is of average importance, it scores 3, and finally if the factor is of crucial importance, it scores 5. The *strength* of each factor is ranked on an ordinal scale from −5 to +5; −5 indicates that this factor has the strongest possible negative effect. For example, if a company required export licences and these were almost unobtainable, then the strength of this factor would be −5; +5 indicates that the factor has the strongest possible positive influence, and finally 0 indicates that the factor has no impact on the company in question.

Once the importance and the strength of each factor have been ascertained,* they are multiplied together to give an overall ranking for each factor. The rankings of all the factors are then summed and expressed as percentages. Two percentage figures are obtained — one for the Business Sector Prospects (18.8% in the above case) and the other for the Business Position (−34% in the above case), and these factors

*This can be done in a number of ways. Here it is suggested that a Delphi approach be used. See Refs. (4), (6) and (8) for methodologies.

form the coordinates which locate the business on the matrix. This is shown in Fig. 47, for the above example, by the point *A*. Additionally, the value of the company's sales can be shown by a circle whose area is proportional to its annual sales. In Fig. 47 each axis has been scaled from −100% through 0% to +100%; −100% indicates the weakest possible Business Position or the most unattractive Business Sector Prospects possible; +100% indicates the strongest Business Position possible or the most attractive Business Sector Prospects possible. 0% indicates either an average Business Position or else average Business Sector Prospects.

The Appendix to this chapter shows how the Business Sector Prospects were developed for the U.K. Credit Card industry.

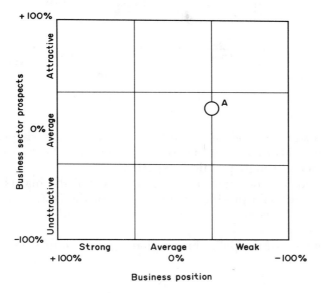

FIG. 47. *Quantifying the matrix*

Interpretation of the Matrix

As Fig. 48 shows, the matrix has been divided into a number of squares. Each square is associated with a different set of combinations of "Business Positions" and "Business Sector Prospects", and the labels in each square indicate policies that should be considered very seriously for businesses located there.* Although these areas are delineated in the

─────────

These policies are a reflection of the experience of planners who have had practical experience in using the matrix.

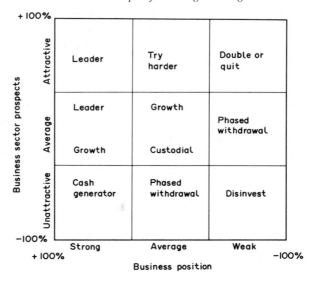

FIG. 48. *Companies' competitive positions*

figure as squares, it is suggested[11] that in reality the shapes are more irregular and fuzzy and in practice the boundaries can only be determined through practical experience.

It should be noted that in Fig. 48 the axes of the matrix are drawn such that the main product characteristics of the BCG matrix — Stars, Cash Cows, Dogs and Problem Children — would tend to occupy the same positions.

A summary of the policy implications of the products located in each position is now given.

Leader

This is the position occupied by the leader in the industry. This product will probably have advantages in most of the relevant criteria* which were used to assess the business's overall strategic position and the product may have especial advantages in areas such as relative market share, costs (due to experience effects and other factors), ability to influence the market and levels of profits. However, as the market is probably a fast growing one, this product will require considerable investment (in areas such as installing extra capacity, increasing the marketing expenditure, etc.) to maintain its superior position. Conse-

---

The "relevant criteria" will probably be selected from the list on pages 146 to 148.

quently, the net cash flow may be relatively small and indeed extra cash may even be required to maintain market share. However, as the market for the product matures and its growth rate declines, the product will fall vertically (provided its dominant position is adequately supported) in the matrix and become a greater net generator of cash. Thus this type of product is roughly equivalent to the BCG "Star" product.

Leader/Growth

For this type of product the days of heady growth and highly attractive Business Sector Prospects have ended and the prospects for the product are just average. Additionally, it may be the case that no single competitor in the market is extremely dominant, i.e. several products vie for leadership. In these circumstances the product tends to be a net generator of cash and should earn a rate of contribution to corporate funds. The fundamental strategy for this type of product should be to maintain its Business Position. This type of product falls somewhere between the BCG Star and Cash Cow.

Cash Generator

This type of product occupies a strong position in an unattractive (probably low or static market growth) Business Sector. Consequently the threat from existing (weaker) or new competitors will be small. This product will tend, therefore, to generate cash in excess of its requirements. This excess cash can be used to help fund promising products in more attractive sectors. This type of product is roughly equivalent to the BCG Cash Cow.

Try Harder

A product in this position is in a highly attractive Business Sector, but its Business Position is behind that of the Leader. Consequently this type of product will tend to have market share and cost disadvantages. Although this is a relatively attractive strategic position, the necessity to maintain (or build) Business Position, and the expenses associated with this, tend to make this type of product have a zero or even a negative cash flow. This type of product is somewhere between the BCG Problem Child and Star categories.

Growth/Custodial

A product falls into this category when it does not have any particular advantages in its Business Position and its Business Sector Prospects are average. This, typically, can happen when a product has no particular distinction, has no distinctive niche in the market and is competing against a large number of competitors. In such circumstances it may be appropriate to try to maximise cash flow without the commitment of further resources.

Phased Withdrawal

This type of product can be located in two squares on the matrix and will have one or other of the following set of characteristics:

it has an average Business Position in an unattractive Business Sector, or
it has a weak Business Position in an average Business Sector.

In both of these cases the prospects of the product are poor and there is a danger than such a product may turn into a cash trap.* Therefore, the appropriate policy here could be to withdraw or harvest the product and use the cash thrown off in the process for potentially more attractive projects. This type of product is somewhere between the BCG Problem Child and the Cash Cow.

Double or Quit

This type of product has the attribute of being in an attractive Business Sector but having a weak Business Position. To achieve the strength necessary to derive the benefits which can accrue from being in such an attractive Business Sector, the product will require considerable resources. Consequently, most companies normally will be able to fund only a limited number of such products. Therefore a company finding itself confronted with this type of problem must exercise great care in distinguishing between those products that are attractive and worthy of funding and those that, however regrettably, must be disposed of or harvested.

Disinvest

A product in this location has the twin traits of having a weak Business Position in an unattractive Business Sector. In general such a product will tend to lose money (at possibly an accelerating rate), and the appropriate strategy for such a product is disinvest. This type of product is roughly equivalent to the BCG Genuine Dog product.

See Ref. (3).

Strategic Movements

As well as taking cognisance of the location of products on the matrix it is also important, for strategic planners, to consider the movements of the products over time. This can be accomplished by plotting a series of matrices at different points in time on acetate sheets and then superimposing them to see the movements.

There are two main types of product movements — movements in a vertical direction and movements in a horizontal direction.

Movements in a vertical direction are caused by changes in the planners' perception of the Business Sector Prospects and consequently will usually be outside the control of the company.*

Movements in a horizontal direction are caused by changes in the product's Business Position. Such movements are, to some extent, within the control of the company and can be affected by company strategies. Thus a company can improve its business position by pursuing, say, a policy of product innovation or, say, by pursuing an aggressive marketing policy to improve its market share. A good example of a company which has made major efforts to improve its Business Position is afforded by the PSA Motor Company. In early 1982 this company introduced a new model in the United Kingdom — the Talbot Samba. By definition, the Business Position of this new product was weak. The company then engaged in an extensive marketing campaign in order to build up the Samba's Business Position.

Finally, although it is important to monitor (and where appropriate take action to change) to movements of products, it is also important to manage the movement of cash within the matrix.

As noted previously, products which are located in the Cash Generator quadrant have a strong Business Position in an unattractive Business Sector; consequently these types of products should be able to generate cash in excess of their requirements. This excess cash should be used to help finance the improvement of the Business Position of a limited number of products falling into the Try Harder or Double or Quit squares. If products falling into these positions receive sufficient resources and are skilfully managed, they may move in a westward direction on the matrix and arrive in the Leader square.

A simplified portrayal of these "ideal movements of products and cash" is shown in Fig. 49. This shows that the ideal movements of products are in the direction ABC, and complementing this movement of products are the ideal movements of cash which are shown by ZX, ZY and ZW.

*It is, of course, possible for a company to change its Business Sector Prospects. Thus a company, through marketing and promotion, could stimulate consumer need for a previously unneeded product.

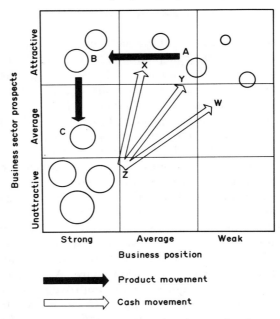

FIG. 49. *Ideal movements of products and cash*

An example, at the macro level, of the benefits to be derived from distinguishing, and taking advantage of, "ideal cash movements" and "ideal product movements" is given by the industrial policy of the Japanese Government and the subsequent development of Japanese business since World War II.

Japan's post-World War II industrial development can be divided into a number of eras, each era being defined by the particular industrial sector that was targeted and promoted by the Japanese Government and subsequently exploited by Japanese business. The major eras include: heavy industry — iron, steel and chemicals; shipbuilding; automobiles; electronics and more recently computers. When a targeted industrial sector had been developed and successfully exploited, the finances flowing from this sector would not be returned to it, but were instead directed to the next sector to be developed. Thus Tsurumi[13] has written:

> "After the mid-1950s, ships became the leading export product of Japan. The 'quality image' of tankers and freighters made in Japan helped to change the world market conception that Japanese products were shoddily made. Just as the foreign exchange costs of fostering the Japanese shipbuilding industry were financed by the

export earnings from such old export leaders as textiles, toys and ceramics, the tankers and freighters exported from Japan were in turn counted on to pay for the development of subsequent target industries such as automobiles and computers. The foreign exchange regulations of the Japanese Government were specifically designed to permit such allocation of export earnings. Newly selected industries (firms) were given a high priority in receiving foreign exchange needed for importation of raw materials, machinery and technology."[13]

These movements are schematically illustrated in Fig. 50.

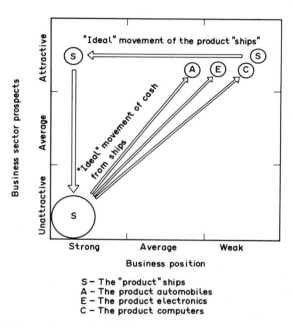

Fig. 50. *Schematic portrayal of ideal movement of the product "ships" and ideal movement of "cash" (not to scale)*

Using the Matrix to Guide Management

As the process of using the matrix to guide management is very similar to that employed when the Product Market Portfolio is used, the description given here is brief. The more detailed description given in Chapter 4 can also be used here. Briefly, the process can be divided into three main stages. These are as follows.

Developing matrices for one's own firm

This stage involves:
Correctly identifying the products and their business sectors.
Selecting and ranking the criteria for assessing the Business Position and the Business Sector Prospects.
Gathering the data.
Quantifying each product's position.
Drawing up matrices of one's own company which show its position over a number of years.
Assessing the strengths and potential of the final matrix.

Developing matrices for one's competitors

This stage involves developing matrices for one's major competitors over a number of years. This is done in much the same way as matrices are developed for one's own firm.

Making strategic comparisons on the basis of the first two stages and hence generating strategies

On the basis of the two sets of matrices drawn up, it should be possible to make:

(a) An assessment of one's firms' current strategic position internally (i.e. how balanced is the portfolio internally) and externally (i.e. how strong is the firm's portfolio *vis-à-vis* its major competitors), and
(b) then generate appropriate strategies for one's firm.

The latter can be achieved by developing further ideal or target portfolios for, say, two years hence and then taking strategic action to try to achieve this ideal portfolio. This is illustrated in Fig. 51. In Fig. 51 products A and B are considered to be future industry leaders and the strategy adopted for these products is substantial investment to improve their Business Position. In contrast, it is considered that product C is so weak in its Business Position (and the company can only support a limited number of Double or Quit or Try Harder products anyway) that it has been decided to harvest this product.

Products D and E are the leaders in their industries and they will receive sufficient resources to maintain these positions.

In contrast to these products, it is considered that products F, G and H present unattractive prospects — it is therefore planned to dispose of these products.

These are the core strategies for the company which are subsequently refined and reduced to specific functional targets for implementation purposes.

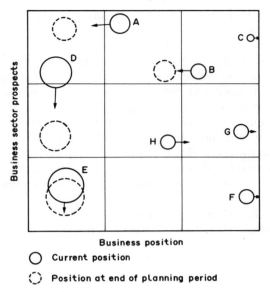

Business position

◯ Current position

◌ Position at end of planning period

Fig. 51. *Current and "ideal" portfolio*

Limitations of the Approach

Paradoxically, one of the major attributes of this type of approach — its ability to accommodate the many factors which determine a product's strategic position by a single set of coordinates — can also be considered a major shortcoming. Because of the very uniqueness of the factors affecting any product's Business Position and Business Sector Prospects, it is really impossible to give general guidelines for determining these parameters. Consequently all analyses will be tinged, to a greater or lesser extent, with subjectivity and this mitigates against making consistent comparisons over time either within the same company or between companies.

Additionally, it could be argued that although many factors are considered when locating a product's position on the matrix, the position is determined, ultimately, by just two somewhat nebulous and undefined coordinates and it may be unrealistic to assume that just two such measures can subsume all strategic factors and accurately portray a company's, or a product's, position.

The Hofer Matrix

Hofer[5] has taken cognisance of many of the criticisms that have been levelled against the Product Market Portfolio Matrix and the Directional Policy Matrix and devised a more comprehensive matrix — the Product Market Evolution Portfolio Matrix. In this matrix "Competitive Position" is plotted on the horizontal axis against "Stage of the Product Market Evolution" on the vertical axis, while circles represent the sizes of the industries involved and segments of the circles themselves represent an individual firm's or business's market share. This matrix is shown in Fig. 52. In this matrix it can be seen that Firm A has a market share of around 33%, it is almost in a strong competitive position and it is operating in an industry which is at the development stage. By contrast, Firm G has a market share of roughly 12%, has a weak competitive position and is operating in an industry which is at the decline stage of its life cycle.

Thus the Hofer Matrix gives a more comprehensive picture for the Product Market Portfolio but suffers from the disadvantage of being more complicated to construct.

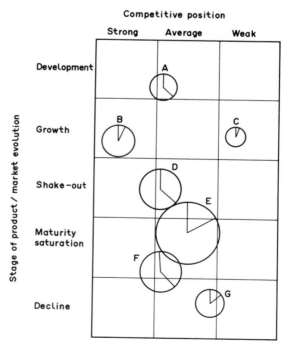

Fɪɢ. 52. *The Hofer matrix (Ref. (3), p. 168)*

Patel and Younger's Approach

Patel and Younger[9] considered that although many managers recognise and accept the value of strategic planning concepts such as the Experience Curve, the Product Market Portfolio, etc., they tend to be sceptical about their practical or operational value and consequently are inclined not to use them. In other words, there is a problem perceived in operationalising such approaches.

To help overcome this problem they advocated a "Frame of Reference for Strategy Development" which gives strategic planners explicit guidelines for assessing the strategic position of a company, formulating appropriate strategies and implementing these strategies at the operational level. Their analysis is carried out at two levels — the strategic planning required at the SBU* level and the strategic planning required at the corporate level.

Strategic Planning at the SBU level

They considered that strategic guidelines for a SBU could be derived from consideration of industry maturity and competitive position and suggested strategies appropriate to various "Industry Maturity" and "Competitive Position" coordinates. An amended version of their strategic guidelines table is given in Table 43.

As can be seen, in many ways this approach is a more general version of the Product Market Portfolio Matrix and also closely resembles the Directional Policy Matrix.

Patel and Younger suggest that the above table helps strategic planners select appropriate future basic strategies which can then be operationalised by reference to a "compendium of such detailed strategies . . .".[9] They also argue that since

> ". . . the only real value of a business unit to the corporation of which it is part is to provide cash now or more cash later on"[9]

that a key measure of a SBU's current performance and a good guide to its future potential is its "internal deployment" of funds. This is defined as the percentage of funds generated which are reinvested. Figure 53 shows how this method of measuring performance is portrayed. Thus Fig. 53 portrays a SBU which earned 22% on assets and has an internal deployment of 80%. This type of SBU would normally lie in the mature section of a company's portfolio and if it did not, then the company's strategic planners would need to question the corporate flow of funds among the various SBUs.

Table 43. Strategic Guidelines as a Function of Industry, Maturity and Competitive Position[9].

Industry maturity	Competitive Position					
	Dominant	Strong	Favourable	Tenable	Weak
Embryonic	All-out push for share Hold position	Attempt to improve position Push for share	Selective or all-out push for share Selectively attempt to improve position	Selectively push for position	Up or out
Growing	Hold position Hold share	Attempt to improve position Push for share	Attempt to improve position Selective push for share	Find niche and protect it	Turnaround or Abandon
Mature	Hold position Grow with industry	Hold position Grow with industry	Custodial or maintenance	Find niche and hang on or Phased withdrawal	Turnaround or Phased withdrawal
Ageing	Hold positions	Hold positions or Harvest	Phased withdrawal Harvest	Phased withdrawal or Abandon	Abandon

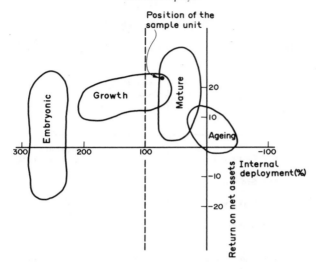

F<small>IG</small>. 53. *Patel and Younger's profitability and cash position matrix*

Strategic Planning at the Corporate Level

Patel and Younger maintain that while the objective of strategic planning at the SBU level is to gain competitive advantage over competitors, strategic planning at the corporate level is primarily concerned with developing

> ". . . business unit configuration, their organisational and management systems and their financial transactions in a manner conducive to the desired corporate growth, profitability and risk levels".[9]

Figure 54 and Table 44 together show how this corporate configuration is displayed. In Table 44 it can be seen that this company has only 10% of its assets in Growth businesses and 27% in Ageing businesses. Table 44 and Fig. 54 together show the fit between the industry maturity of the individual units: how profitable each is and the nature of their cash contributions (i.e. positive or negative). As can be seen, this company is taking cash from its largest growth business and giving to some of its mature businesses.

This approach can be considered as one which is complementary to the Product Market Portfolio approach. Although in many respects it is easy to see the close links between the Strategic Guidelines Table, the Profitability and Cash Position Matrices and the Product Market

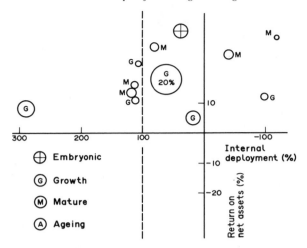

FIG. 54. *Patel and Younger's profitability and cash position matrix of a corporation — by business unit source*[16]

Portfolio Mix, it is important to recognise that Patel and Younger's approach relies primarily for its impact on financial data rather than marketing data. Consequently, this approach adds another dimension to the Product Market Portfolio approach.

The V Matrix

This matrix was developed by the author in 1981. It differs somewhat from most other matrix displays considered in this book, in that it relies for its strategic contribution principally on financial data.

This matrix arose out of an article by Ciaran Walsh and Edward Mock which was published in *Long Range Planning* in October 1979.[14] In summary, Walsh and Mock asserted that

> "A firm's earning power relative to the weighted cost of capital is the ultimate test of corporate performance. Earning power divided by the cost of capital is the first consideration in formulating a corporate plan."[14]

They also asserted that corporate strategy should be directed towards maximising this relationship. They showed that a firm can measure the quality of this relationship using a V (for valuation) factor which is defined as:

Table 44. Business Units and Their Assets Broken Down by Industry, Maturity and Competitive Position[9]

Industry maturity	Embryonic		Growth		Mature		Ageing		Total	
Competitive position	No. of units	Corporate assets %	No. of units	Corporate assets %	No. of units	Corporate assets %	No. of units	Corporate assets %	No. of units	Corporate assets %
Dominant			1	5	1	2	1	25	3	32
Strong			1	3	4	60	–	–	5	63
Favourable			1	2			1	2	2	4
Tenable					1	1			1	1
Weak										
Total			3	10	6	63	2	27	11	100

$$V = \frac{ROI}{K} \qquad \frac{\text{(Earning power)}}{\text{(Cost of capital)}}$$

where ROI is defined as

$$\frac{O(1 - T)}{A}$$

where O = operating income,
     T = the tax rate,
     A = the assets at risk,
and K = the weighted average cost of all funds in the business.

They also showed that if V is:

(1) less than unity, then investors' funds are being wasted and corporate performance can be said to be inadequate;
(2) equal to unity, then investors' funds are still intact and corporate performance can be said to be adequate;
(3) greater than unity, then investors' funds are growing and performance can be rated as good or excellent depending upon the size of the factor.

They concluded (on the basis of the above plus empirical studies) that the single objective of a (profit maximising) firm can be identified as the maximisation of V.

The Matrix

The V matrix visually portrays a firm's V factor. As shown in Fig. 55, the firm's weighted average cost of all funds employed in the business (K) is plotted along the horizontal axis and the firm's ROI is plotted along the vertical axis. Therefore, a firm whose ROI is equal to its K is located along the diagonal AD (i.e. along the line $V = 1$). By the same reasoning, a firm whose corporate performance was inadequate would fall somewhere in the "Inadequate" triangle ABC and a firm whose corporate performance was good or excellent would fall into the "Excellent Good" triangle AEF. Also included on the matrix are the "Just Adequate" and "Almost Adequate" triangles* (ADE and ACD respectively). A firm which finds itself in either of these triangles should monitor its performance extremely carefully as relatively small adjustments will turn its performance into either Inadequate or Good.

*In practice the Adequate Limit Lines (AE and AC) are set by decision-makers in the firm. For the purpose of this book they have been set arbitrarily at V = 0.9 and V = 1.1.

Finally, in order to give an impression of the significance of the business, size is indicated by the area of a circle which can be made proportional to either turnover or assets employed. Figure 55 shows a company (Company Z) which is performing inadequately with a K value of 16% and a ROI of 12%.

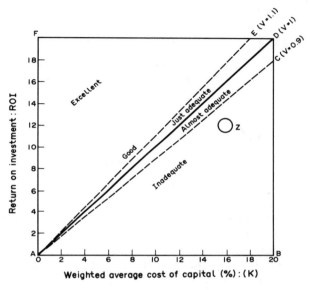

FIG. 55. *The V matrix*

Using the Matrix for Strategic Planning

The V Matrix can be used by an individual company in isolation to perceive its current position, the trends which led to this position and to plan feasible strategies to maintain or improve its position. Also, just as a company can draw up Product Portfolio Matrices or Directional Policy Matrices for its competitors' strategies, so also can this be done using the V Matrix.

Firstly, a company can perceive how it arrived at its current position if it constructs a series of matrices for various points in time. Such a series will give the trajectory of the company in terms of how its size is changing and how it is coping with the changing environment. For example, Fig. 56 shows how Company Y fared in the period 1976–80. As can be seen, this company, although it increased its sales and size, is always in the "Inadequate" triangle. It would appear from the trajectory that although the company has successfully employed strategies to boost

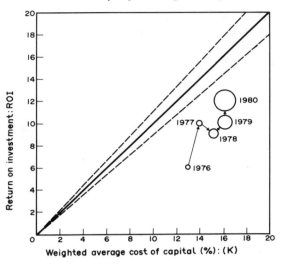

Fɪɢ. 56. *The trajectory of Company K for the years 1976–1980*

its ROI, the good effects of these strategies have been more than offset by continuously increasing cost of capital which, in the case of this company, was beyond its control.

Having observed the trends which led to the current position, the questions can then be raised:

"How does the V Matrix actually help plan strategies?"

Figure 57 shows Company Y's current position. It has a ROI of 12% and a K of 16%, giving

$$V = \frac{12}{16} = 0.75.$$

The company is in an undesirable situation. Obviously it will wish to move towards the V, diagonal (OI) as quickly as possible; but the questions must be asked:

"What *realistic* strategies should be employed to achieve this?"

The appropriate strategies may emerge after answering two questions:

1. What is the lowest weighted average cost of capital for any firm in this industry? When this is found* it is then drawn as a vertical

These figures can be found through companies' annual statements, industry publications, knowledge of industry, etc.

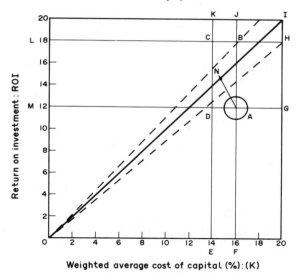

FIG. 57. *Company Y's current position*

line (on this occasion it is assumed to be 14% and is shown by the line *EK*), and

2. What is the best return on investment obtained by any firm in this industry? When this is found* it is then drawn as a horizontal line (on this occasion it is assumed to be 18% and is shown by the line *HL*).

The rectangle *ABCD* is now completed and this rectangle delineates the area of feasible† strategic alternatives, i.e. as a result of strategic decisions, the company should try, over time, to move in the direction *AN*. It may be possible to achieve this movement through operating on *K* and/or ROI. *K*, especially in times of high interest rates, would appear to be the less fruitful lever on which to operate. However, varying the proportion of total debt to equity could have some effect and could perhaps move the company from *A* towards *D*.

The return on investment would, however, appear to offer a more fruitful area in which to operate. Thus if ROI is broken into its constituent ratios:

These figures can be found through companies' annual statements, industry publications, knowledge of industry, etc.

†*The area is considered feasible because at least one firm in the industry is achieving a ROI of 18% and at least one firm (probably a different one) has a K of 14%. It is considered feasible to move towards one, or both, of these best rates.*

$$ROI = \frac{\text{Net profit}}{\text{Sales}} \times \frac{\text{Sales}}{\text{Assets}}$$

a ROI matrix, as described in Chapter 2, can be constructed. Company Y, as shown in Fig. 58, is at the point *D*. Appropriate strategies for the company may emerge after answering two questions:

1. What is the best $\dfrac{\text{Net profit}}{\text{Sales}}$ ratio obtained for any firm in this industry?* When this is found it is then drawn as a horizontal line (on this occasion it is assumed to be 6% and is shown by the line *HL*), and
2. What is the best $\dfrac{\text{Sales}}{\text{Assets}}$ ratio obtained by any firm in this industry?* When this is found it is then drawn as a vertical line (on this occasion it is assumed to be 6% and is shown by the line *FJ*).

The rectangle *ABCD* is now completed and this rectangle delineates the area of feasible strategic alternatives[†] i.e. over time Company Y should

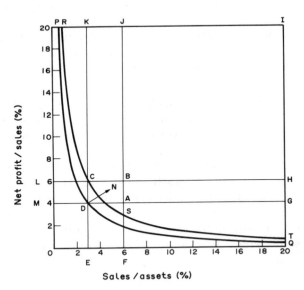

Fig. 58. *The ROI matrix for Company Y*

attempt to move in the direction *DN*. It may be possible to achieve the movement through operating on

the $\frac{\text{Sales}}{\text{Assets}}$ ratio or the $\frac{\text{Net profit}}{\text{Sales}}$ ratio or both.

Thus Company Y could improve its $\frac{\text{Sales}}{\text{Assets}}$ ratio by either increasing sales or decreasing assets or both, and the company could improve its $\frac{\text{Net profit}}{\text{Sales}}$ ratio by increasing its net profit, or decreasing its sales or both.

Thus the ROI Matrix can give a guide to the operational strategies necessary to achieve the desired movements, i.e. moving ROI from *A* towards *B* in Fig. 58 in the V Matrix.

The above strategies have been evolved by the company in isolation, i.e. without reference to its competitors. Another feature of the V Matrix is that it enables strategies to perceive the dynamic relationship between a company and its competitors and, on the basis of comparative displays, divine competitors' strategies. Thus Fig. 59 shows the V Matrix for Companies W and X. As can be seen, Company W has had a strategy of giving priority to increasing its ROI while maintaining its cost of capital at the 1978 level, while Company X has decided upon a strategy of

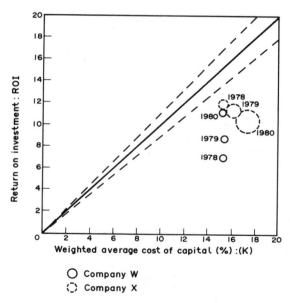

Fig. 59. *A V matrix for Companies W and Z for 1977–1979*

increasing its market and not being over-concerned with either the cost of capital or its return on investment. Presumably it is building market share (hence the cost of capital and ROI has declined because of the expenses involved in building market share) in the hope of a long-term pay-off. Thus the V Matrix allows Companies W and X to plan their strategies with some knowledge of what each other is doing.

Conclusions

The objective of this chapter was to explore how selected matrix displays can aid strategic management. Four types of matrix — the Directional Policy, the Hofer, the Patel and Younger and the V — were considered, and the particular contribution that each can make was examined. Each type makes a distinct and unique contribution and which type, or types, should be used by strategic planners should be a function of the objectives of the exercise and the data available. This chapter should be regarded as open-ended, i.e. a secondary purpose of the chapter is to encourage planners to think in two dimensions and to develop their own matrices to assist their planning. The great advantages of matrix displays over the more conventional tabular or text approaches to strategic management are:

they enable a planner to pinpoint a business's position in two dimensions (i.e. each axis of the display);

they enable a planner to perceive, easily, trends over time;

the display of quantitative information spatially facilitates comprehension, comparison and communication.

References

1. *Daily Telegraph*, October 1982.
2. "Financial Profile of BL", *Motor Business*, The Economist Intelligence Unit, No. 106, 2nd quarter 1981, pp. 66–84.
3. Hedley, B. "Strategy and the Business Portfolio", *Long Range Planning*, Vol. 10, Feb. 1977, pp. 9–15.
4. Hodgetts, R. M. "Applying the Delphi Technique to Management Gaming," *(SCS) Simulation*, Vol. 29, No. 1, July 1977, pp. 209–212.
5. Hofer, C. W. and Schendel, D. *Strategy Formulation: Analytical Concepts*, West Publishing, St. Paul and Cash House, Tunbridge Wells, 1978.
6. Korhonen, P. and Soismaa, M. "An Interactive Multiple Criteria Approach to Ranking Alternatives", *OR*, Vol. 32, No. 7, July 1981, pp. 577–585.
7. Leontiades, J. "Market Share and Corporate Strategies in International Industries", Unpublished paper, Manchester Business School, 1982.
8. McNamee, P. B. "The Application of Goal Programming to Capital Investment Under Conditions of Capital Budgeting, Unpublished M.Phil. Thesis, 1979.
9. Patel P. and Younger, M. "A Frame of Reference for Strategy Development", *Long Range Planning*, Vol. 11, No. 2, April 1978, pp. 6–12.

10.   "Personal Computers", *Financial Times Survey*, Tuesday, 18 January 1983, p. 15.
11.   Robinson, S. J. Q., Hichens, R. E. and Wade, D. P. "The Directional Policy Matrix — Tool for Strategic Planning", *Long Range Planning*, Vol. 11, June 1978, pp. 815–
12.   Sodima France, 1981 results.
13.   Tsurumi, Y. *The Japanese Are Coming*, Ballinger Publishing Company, 1976.
14.   Walsh, C. and Mock, E. "Setting Corporate Objectives Using Market Required Earnings", *Long Range Planning*, Vol. 12, Oct. 1979, pp. 54–64.

Bibliography

Abell, D. F. *Defining the Business*, Prentice-Hall Inc., Englewood Cliffs, N.J., 1980.
Buzzell, D., Gale, B. and Sultan R. G. M. "Market Share — A Key to Profitability," *Harvard Business Review*: Jan./Feb. 1975, pp.
Hussey, D. E. "Portfolio Analysis: Practical Experience with the Directional Policy Matrix", *Long Range Planning*, Vol. 11, No. 4, 1978, pp.   .
Glueck, W. F. *Strategic Management and Business Policy*, McGraw-Hill, 1980.
Newton, J. K. "Acquisitions: A Directional Policy Matrix Approach", *Long Range Planning*, Vol. 14, No. 6, Dec. 1981, pp. 51–57.
Schoeffler, S., Buzzell, R. and Heany, D. F. "Impact of Strategic Planning on Profit Performance", *Harvard Business Review*, March/April 1974, pp. 137–145.
Wind, Y. and Mahajan, V. "Designing Product and Business Portfolios", *Harvard Business Review*, Vol. 59, No. 1, Jan.–Feb. 1981, pp. 155–165.

The Business Sector Prospects for Credit Cards in the United Kingdom

Introduction

This appendix briefly considers the prospects for a particular business sector: Credit Cards in the United Kingdom. The various determinants of Business Sector Prospects are now examined.

Competitive factors

I. The Major Competitors

1. *Barclaycard (Visa)*: launched in 1965, owned jointly by Barclays Bank, the Bank of Scotland and Allied Irish Banks, is affiliated to the American Visa organisation. Holds U.K. franchise for Visa cards in conjunction with the Trustee Savings Bank (TSB). The first in the field, and currently has the largest number of cardholders.

2. *Access (Mastercard)*: launched in 1972 by the Joint Credit Card Company which is owned jointly by the National Westminster Bank, Lloyds Bank, the Midland Bank, Williams and Glyns Bank and the Royal Bank of Scotland. Member of the Inter Bank Card Association, the Master Charge Card Association and Euro Card. Was second in the field, but has the largest number of outlets.

3. *American Express* and *Diners Club*: introduced in the 1950s and aimed at the higher income bracket, particularly in the area of Travel and Entertainment (T & E).

4. *"In Store" Cards*: credit cards issued by individual stores — for example, Habitat, Telefusion, Tandy, John Collier. Very rapid growth during the 1970s, but not sustained in the 1980s. No single card has a substantial ownership.

This Appendix was prepared with the assistance of Marti Wilton, a student of the Ulster Polytechnic. It is stressed that this case is not meant to be an exhaustive analysis of this business sector but is meant to illustrate how Business Sector Prospects can be assessed.

5. *Trustee Savings Bank Cards*: introduced by Barclaycard in 1979 and not expected to break even until 1983.

II. Size of Competitors

The size of each competitor measured on a variety of axes is given below.

Table A1. Ownership of Credit Cards in the United Kingdom by Competitor

	1980		1981	
	Cards issued (millions)	No. of outlets	Cards issued (millions)	No. of outlets
Barclaycard	5.5	131,000	6.1	169,000
T.S.B.	1.5		1.54	
Access	6.3	107,000	5.3	174,000
Amex	0.6	36,000	0.53	53,000
Diners club	0.3	21,000	0.26	41,000
"In store" cards			4.5	

Total ownership after duplication is approximately 6.6 million people.

Table A2. Annual Turnover of Major Credit Card Companies (1982)

Company	Annual turnover ($ millions)
Access	2500
Barclaycard	?
Amex	500
Diners	150

Table A3. Growth in Recruitment of the Major Card Companies

Company	Recruitment	
	1979	1980
Barclaycard	30,000	40,000
Access	12,000	45,000
Amex	?	8,000
Diners	?	2,000

**Table A4. Advertising Expenditures of the Major
Card Companies in 1978**

Company	Advertising expenditure in $, 1978
Amex	1.0m — 1.3m
Barclaycard	550,000 — 650,000
Access	200,000 — 400,000

Other Competitive Factors

In 1981 Diners Club franchise was acquired by Citibank, who hope to revitalise the card in the United Kingdom. They have already mounted an extensive advertising campaign.

Amex has nearly tripled its number of U.K. card holders in the period January 1980 to April 1982.

Bank credit cards are increasingly encroaching on the traditional territory of the T & E cards.

The growth of Amex and Diners Club could be restricted in the future, as their main attraction of convenience is offered by bank credit cards without an annual subscription charge.

International acceptability is a major selling point and Access and Barclaycard have this feature through their international affiliations.

The bank card companies have now offered premium cards which offer more facilities and are aimed at higher earners, the primary markets of Amex and Diners Club.

The Market

1. Market Growth

It is difficult to get an exact size and growth rate of this market, but the following tables give some indication.

**Table A5. Percentage of Cash
Payments Made to Retailers**

Year	Percentage
1971	1
1976	5
1982	15

2. Characteristics of the Market

The characteristics of the market according to age, sex, income class and residential status are now given.

Table A6. Percentage of the Population Holding Credit Cards According to Age

	Percentage		
Age	1978	1980	1982
Under 25 years	9	10	25
25–34	27	31	?
35–44	21	24	37
45–54	18	20	31
55+	13.5	15	12

Table A7. Percentage of Cardholders According to Status in 1980

Status	Percentage
Single male	10
Married male	64
Single female	7
Married female	19

Table A8. Distribution of the Major Credit Cards According to Income Class

Income class	Percentage			
AB	36.8	37.7	69.9	61.3
C1	35.9	33.7	17.1	21.0
C2	18.7	20.0	5.5	4.0
C3	8.6	10.6	9.5	13.6
Card	Access	Barclaycard	Amex	Diners

Table A9. Distribution of Card Holders According to Residential Status

Residential status	1980 (%)
Home owner	22
Owner with mortgage	51
Tenant	18

Table A10. Usage by Outlets of Credit Cards in Terms of Total Turnover in 1978

Rank	Type of outlet
1	Garages
2	Travel
3	Entertainment
4	Department stores
5	Consumer durables

Additional Comments on the Market

"In Store" cards have grown very rapidly recently, and it is believed that the growth potential in this sector is very high: in the United States the average adult has four "In Store" cards.

Automatic cash dispensing facilities will grow, and this will lead to an increase in card use.

Petrol companies may, as in the United States, issue their own cards.

Building Societies are extending the range of services that they offer and may introduce their own cards.

Technology

It seems likely that there will be rapid technological advance in the following areas:

The major banks will be linked to point of sale terminals in larger retail outlets.

Automatic cash dispensing facilities will greatly increase.

Legal

Major enacted U.K. legislation includes:

1973   At least 15% of outstanding credit must be paid each month.

1977   Consumer Credit Act:

Companies not allowed to canvas for business off trade premises.

Credit cards cannot be renewed without credit card holders' permission.

Credit levels cannot be issued without agreement from card holder.

1978   Outstanding credit restriction relaxed to at least 5% of balance or £5, whichever is the greater, must be repaid each month.

1981   Retailers not allowed to impose a surcharge on customers making purchases by credit card.

The future: more legislation to protect the consumer in the near future seems likely at both national and international levels.

Social Factors

The conservatism of the British consumer in the field of credit cards. Comparable rates of uses are shown in Table A11.

Table A11. Percentage of the Working Population Paid Weekly in Cash

Percentage	Country
59	U.K.
5	France
1	U.S.A.

Credit card holders in the United Kingdom tend to borrow only up to 50% of their credit limits.

One-third of active credit card holders settle their accounts before any interest is payable.

Active cards comprise 80% of issued cards.

Economic Factors

Demand for credit cards should follow demand for consumer goods, which should be positively correlated with disposable income. However, as demand for credit cards has grown faster than disposable income, in the United Kingdom it may be that credit cards are being used to enhance buying power in this recessionary time. Thus credit card growth should not be less hard hit by recession than most consumer sectors.

Quantifying the Business Sector Prospects for Credit Cards

Table A12. Business Sector Prospects for Credit Cards in the United Kingdom for the Years 1983–1988

Factor	Importance	Strength	Overall score (importance by strength)
Competitive	4	−2	−8
Market	5	+4	+20
Technology	3	+2	+6
Legal	2	−1	−2
Social	3	+1	+3
Economic	3	+1	+3

Total score			$\dfrac{+22}{150}$
Maximum possible score			
Percentage score			$\dfrac{22 \times 100}{150} = 14.6\%$

Bibliography

Euromonitor, 1982, Credit Cards.
Keynote, 1981, Credit Cards.
Mintel, January 1979, Credit Cards.
Retail Business, No. 264, Feb. 1980, Special Report No. 3, Credit Cards.

CHAPTER 6

The PIMS Findings

Introduction

The various models of strategic management which have been considered so far — the Experience Curve, the Product Market Portfolio, the Directional Policy Matrix, the Hofer Matrix, and the Patel and Younger Matrix — have all, in their own particular fashion, made unique and substantial contributions to the understanding of this subject. However, each of these models was subject to certain limitations (see the relevant chapter) and, at a more general level, each could be criticised on the grounds that none of them is

(a) based upon a sufficiently large enough empirical base to be statistically robust, and
(b) sufficiently detailed in either their published analyses or proposals to make specific proposals to, and engage line managers in, the strategic process.

The PIMS approach (PIMS standing for Profit Impact of Market Strategy) is an alternative approach which attempts to overcome some of these, and other alleged, shortcomings of the above strategic management models.

History of PIMS

In the 1950s the General Electric Company (GE) in America changed to a divisionalised structure with many separate and diverse businesses. Consequently, corporate planners observed a variation in the Return on Investment (ROI) yielded by the various businesses. This variation prompted corporate planners in GE to begin enquiring into the factors that caused a particular business to have a particular ROI. In 1960, at the instigation of the then Vice-president–Marketing Services, F. J. Borch, a research project was set up under the direction of Sidney Schoeffler to investigate:

the relationship between market share and operating economies;

methods of strategically managing GE's large and growing diverse
businesses; and

the factors that determine ROI.

This research project, PROM (Profitability Optimisation Model), was
really concerned with using the plentiful historical data of GE's many
businesses to try to discover "the laws of the market place" which would
enable GE to predict, on the basis of experience, the future performance
of individual businesses. After several years of research a substantial
data base was established and a computer based model was developed
which, it was claimed, captured the major factors which explain a large
amount of the variability in ROI. This model was a cross-sectional model
which used data from GE's large number of diverse businesses. Today,
such cross-sectional models are a standard part of GE's corporate
planning system.

In 1972 the project was established at the Marketing Science Institute
(a research institute associated with the Harvard Business School) and,
with academic as well as GE personnel, it was extended to cover other
corporations in addition to GE. This enabled the earlier GE findings to
be verified on a wider cross-section of businesses* and also enabled
project staff to develop expertise in handling businesses from many
corporations. In this stage the software for subsequent operations was
developed. In 1975, in order to facilitate its evolution from an academic
to an operating entity, PIMS was set up as the Strategic Planning
Institute (SPI) in Cambridge, Mass. Today SPI manages the PIMS
program and is an autonomous, non-profit-making corporation gov-
erned by its member companies.

There are currently (1983) over 250 companies in the PIMS data base,
with over 3000 separate businesses. These companies are mainly
U.S.-based, tend to be large (by European standards), i.e. having annual
sales of $8 million to $25 billion, and tend to be biased towards
manufacturing. There are, however, a growing number of European
companies joining the data base, and now PIMS has a number of
European centres.

Objectives of the PIMS Program

Among the more important objectives of the program are the
following:

(a) To develop an up-to-date data base which truly reflects the
business experiences of the participating businesses.

*I.e. by increasing the size and heterogeneity of the sample, the accuracy of the statistical predictions
should be improved.*

(b) Through a research program, investigating the data base to discover "the laws of the market place" that govern business strategy.

(c) Through an applications program, to make the research findings available to participating businesses.

At a more specific level, the program hopes to provide managers with the information to enable them to answer questions such as:

What is the "normal" ROI, cash flow, profit level, etc., for a particular business?

What are the major factors that determine the particular levels of ROI, cash flow, etc., for various types of businesses?

What will be the effects of changes of strategy on a particular business?

What strategies should particular businesses pursue in order to meet their objectives?

How PIMS Operates

The PIMS organisation and activities are structured in a manner similar to that shown in Fig. 60 and are described below. Each business

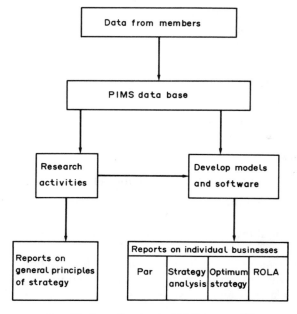

Fig. 60. *Data flow in the PIMS program*[10]

participating in the program supplies SPI, on standard data forms, with the data from its business which are necessary for the model. This data consists of more than 100 data items and includes information on the following:

Characteristics of the Business Environment

> Long-run and short-run market growth rates.
> Level of inflation.
> Number and size of customers.
> Purchasing patterns.

Competitive Position of the Business

> Share of the served market.
> Product quality, relative to competitors.
> Prices, relative to competitors.
> Marketing effort, relative to competitors.
> Labour costs, relative to competitors.
> Pattern of market segmentation.
> Rate of new product introductions.

Structure of the Production Process

> Capital intensity.
> Degree of vertical integration.
> Capacity utilisation.
> Levels of productivity.
> Inventory levels.

Discretionary Budget Allocations

> R & D budgets.
> Advertising and promotion budgets.
> Sales force expenditure.

Strategic Moves

> Patterns of change in the controllable elements above.

When this information has been obtained by SPI it is entered into the data base.

As Figure 60 shows, the data base is used to generate two types of reports:

(a) *Reports on the general principles of business strategy.* These reports give principles of business strategy and are not related to specific businesses, but rather related to business in general or classes of businesses.*

---

*In PIMS terminology, they are reports that enunciate "the laws of the market place".

Among the best-known PIMS reports in this category are:

"The Start-up Business Report" — a report dealing with the PIMS findings for new businesses;

"Businesses in Profit Trouble" — a report showing how businesses get into profit trouble and pathways out of trouble; and

"Basic Principles of Business Strategy" — a report which enunciates the "laws of the market place" that PIMS has divined.

Perhaps the best-known finding to emanate from this aspect of PIMS work is the PIMS regression model. PIMS claims that this model, which contains 37 independent variables, explains more than 80% of the variation in profitability among the businesses in the PIMS data base. It is the "general principles" aspect of PIMS work that is the major topic of this chapter.

(b) *Specific reports on each business that is a member*. These specific reports are PIMS strategic assessments for specific businesses which are made on an individual basis. These reports have two major characteristics — they make a statement about the particular business's strategic position at the time of analysis, and secondly they give strategic advice to the business.

Four major reports are (as shown in Fig. 60) provided. These are as follows.

The Par Report

This report gives the ROI that is normal or "par" for the particular business judging by the experiences of other businesses with similar characteristics. The report also identifies the major strengths or weaknesses that the business in question has that account for its particular par.

The Strategy Analysis Report

This is a simulation of the short-term and long-term consequences of several possible strategic actions.

The Optimum Strategy Report

This is really a refinement of the Strategy Analysis Report — it selects that combination of strategic changes which promises to yield the optimal results for the business.

Report on "Look-Alikes" (ROLA)

ROLA provides reports on businesses that are strategically similar to the business being analysed. The objective of this class of report is to help strategists operate with effective tactics by providing them with data on how similar businesses have achieved their objectives. Finally, in addition to reports, PIMS also provides members with access to computer models which are useful for strategic planning and simulation.

PIMS Definitions

When interpreting the PIMS findings it is important to be aware of the exact meaning of the terms used. Some of the more frequently used ones are defined below.

A Business

A "business" is the unit of observation in the PIMS researches and is defined as a single operating unit that has the following characteristics: it sells a distinct set of products or services to an identifiable group of customers and is in competition with a well-defined set of competitors. This unit of analysis is similar to the definition of the Strategic Business Unit given in Chapter 1.

A Market and a Served Market

PIMS distinguishes between a market and a served market. A market includes all of the products or services, customer types, and geographic areas that are directly related to the activities of the business. More precisely, it is considered to be a set of customers with similar types of requirements for certain products and/or services. A served market is not necessarily the total market, but is that segment of the total market where the business unit is focusing its effort. This concept is illustrated in Fig. 61.

A business focuses on a segment of total market by :

(1) Offering a product suitable   (2) Making a marketing
    for this segment   effort which reaches
                                            this segment

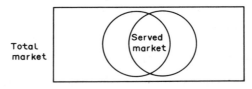

FIG. 61. *PIMS definition of a served market*[2]

Market Share

This is the ratio of monetary sales by a business, in a given time period, to the total sales by all competitors in the same market.

Relative Market Share

Relative market share is somewhat different from the Boston Consulting Group's concept. PIMS defines it as:

Relative market share = Your share divided by the combined share of your three largest competitors.

For example:

$$\text{Your share} = 20\%.$$
The combined share of your three largest competitors $= 50\%.$
$$\therefore \text{Relative market share} = \frac{20\%}{50\%} = 40\%.$$

Marketing Expenditures

This includes the total costs for sales force, advertising, sales promotion, marketing research and marketing administration, but does not include the costs of physical distribution.

Return on Investment

$$\text{ROI} = \frac{\text{Pre-tax income}}{\text{Average investment}}$$

where "Income" is after deduction of corporate expenses but prior to interest charges, and

"Investment" is equal to working capital plus fixed capital at book value.

Quality

Quality is assessed in terms of a "Quality Index" which is defined as:

Quality Index = Percentage of sales from superior products minus Percentage of sales from inferior products,

where the concept of "Quality" does not include price and is determined by:

The customer's judgement, not the producer's.

Both the product and the associated services.
The concept not being absolute but being relative to competitors.

R & D Expenditures

This comprises the total costs of product development and process improvement, including those costs incurred by corporate-level units which can be directly attributed to the individual business.

Level of Innovation

This is determined by the percentage of sales made by products introduced within the last three years.

The PIMS Nine Basic Findings on Business Strategy[12]

I. Business situations generally behave in a regular and predictable manner

This finding asserts that business situations can be understood by an empirical scientific approach. It could be argued that this is the cornerstone of the PIMS philosophy — after all, unless this is so, then an analytical approach to business strategy, based largely on "laws of the market place" as determined by investigation of a pool of experience, is doomed to failure.

In summary, PIMS claims to be able to make predictions, on the basis of pooled experience, which will be approximately correct for most businesses over a moderately long period (3–5 years).

II. All business situations are basically alike in obeying the same "laws of the market place"

This implies that there will be a tendency for all businesses to behave in the same way for given circumstances. This further implies that a trained strategist can function effectively in any business. It could be argued that this is "good news" for professional management, as an implication of this finding is that the trained professional manager can function equally well in any business.

III. The laws of the market place determine about 80% of the observed variance in operating results across different businesses

This implies that the profitability or unprofitability of any business is 80%, determined by the characteristics of the business and the environment in which it operates, and consequently only 20% of performance can be attributed to management. In other words, there are some businesses which are "inherently profitable" and some which are "inherently unprofitable". It could be argued that this is "bad news" for professional management, as an implication of this finding is that management is really only responsible for 20% of the performance of a business (on average) and that the "laws of the market place" are responsible for the other 80%. A further implication could therefore be that it is more important for the aspiring manager to be in the right business rather than to manage well.

IV. There are nine major strategic influences on profitability and net cash flow

Furthermore, these nine influences account for almost 80% of the determination of business success or failure. These influences are, in descending order of importance as follows.

1. *Investment intensity.* This is measured by two indexes:

(a) Investment/Sales expressed as a percentage, and
(b) Investment/Value Added expressed as a percentage.

In general, the higher the level of Investment Intensity, then the lower the ROI.

Some of the evidence that PIMS has advances in support of this assertion is presented below.

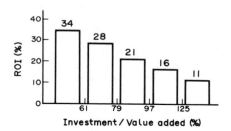

FIG. 62. *Investment intensity is the largest single drag on profitability*[2]

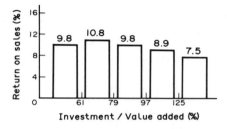

FIG. 63. *Investment intensity squeezes return on sales*[2]

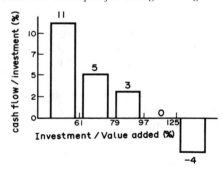

Fig. 64. *Investment intensity drains cash flow*[2]

Table 45. Fixed Capital Intensity Increases the Pressure to Load Plants[2]

	Capacity utilisation		
ROI	Low 70%	84% High	
Fixed capital / Sales — Low / 23%	22	27	33
23% / 50%	19	22	29
50% / High	11	14	21

Note on interpreting the table: This and subsequent tables attempt to isolate and cross-tabulate two variables and ROI. Thus in the above table a high level of Capacity Utilisation and a low Fixed Capital/Sales ratio yield a ROI of 33%.

Table 46. Any Kind of Investment Intensity Hurts Profitability[2]

	Working capital / sales		
ROI	Low 18%	30% High	
Fixed capital / sales — Low / 28%	38	26	16
28% / 50%	31	25	14
50% / High	22	18	7

Table 47. Heavy Marketing does not Relieve Profit Pressures Produced by Investment Intensity[2]

ROI	Marketing / Sales		
Investment value added	Low 5%	10% High	
Low	35	32	29
73%	25	25	17
106% High	16	12	5

Table 48. Weak Market Position Plus High Investment Intensity Leads to Disaster[2]

ROI	Relative market share		
Investment value added	Low 25%	60% High	
Low	25	29	39
73%	16	20	28
106% High	8	12	19

Table 49. Narrow Product Lines Hurt Earnings especially in Fixed-Capital-intensive Businesses[2]

ROI (%)	Product-line breadth (relative to competition)		
Fixed capital sales	Narrower	Same	Broader
Low	23	27	30
28%	19	20	29
50% High	12	17	18

Why should investment intensity have adverse effects?

The adverse effects that investment intensity can have are, as Schoeffler has written,[13] somewhat unexpected and controversial. This may be so because public (and business) perceptions tend to equate high investment intensity with good business strategy — i.e. it is a "good thing" for businesses to automate, increase capacity, increase efficiency, etc., and so lower costs. What is the cause of this seeming paradox? PIMS suggests that there are two major reasons.

(a) *The nature of the arithmetic.* By definition, those businesses that are most capital-intensive will have the largest denominators in their ROIs and therefore will tend to have the lowest ROIs.

(b) *The nature of investment-intensive industries.* Schoeffler[13] points out that although high investment intensity is often equated with good business strategy, this may well be untrue and, indeed, it is not necessarily in the best interests of business that this occurs. Thus although it is frequently the case that when this type of investment intensity occurs benefits to the public do accrue — increased investment intensity tends to lead to higher wages, lower prices and improved quality — the benefits to business may be illusory or non-existent. The cause of this may be due to the nature of the competition in investment-intensive industries being substantially different from the competition in other industries. The difference is caused by the intensity of the investment necessary to compete in this type of industry. The heavy investment requires that the primary objective of the business becomes that capacity must be as fully loaded as possible and therefore the kernel of all strategies must be volume and therefore the nature of the competition is "volume at all costs". This leads to strategies such as price wars and massive advertising to stimulate demand, with the consequent reductions in margins and ultimately catastrophe for a number of competitors. The recent history of the Japanese motorcycle industry — a highly investment-intensive industry — demonstrates the dangers.

> "Japan's world-dominating motorcycle industry has developed a slow puncture. And it is getting worse, despite the industry's frenzied attempts to pump fresh life into the world's markets.
>
> . . . Suzuki, Yamaha and Kawasaki have been bringing out new models at the rate of roughly one a month; Honda, the industry's giant, almost one a week.
>
> However, the world outside Japan itself — the only developed market where sales were increasing rapidly until very recently — is proving incapable of absorbing them.
>
> Industry estimates of world stocks of unsold motorcycles,

scooters and mopeds now range as high as 4m, with some 25 per cent of those languishing in warehouses in the U.S. alone. . . .

. . . Yet as late as the middle of last year, the Japanese producers, who account for about 65 per cent of world output, were publicly clinging to the belief that they would build 10m machines in 1982 — a 25 per cent increase from a year earlier.

The result is a fast-gathering crisis for the Japanese industry; one created not so much by shrinking markets as by its own over-production, based on exaggerated expectations of growth.

. . . It is this attitude which lies behind the proliferation of new models, yet which carries the risk of increasing investment for diminishing returns. This is already starting to show up in company results: the motorcycle operations of Kawasaki Heavy Industries group are mainly responsible for it omitting a dividend this year for the first time for 30 years. . . .

. . . Thus the pressures on the Japanese to find ways of disposing of existing stocks and sustaining existing markets are enormous — the entire industry has been built on the basis of high-volume plants operating close to capacity.

In every market which the Japanese have entered since the early 1960s, the strategy has been the same. Using the economies of scale already achieved in their domestic market, they identified the most valuable market segments and developed the marketing networks and products necessary to gain significant shares of them — irrespective of short term cost. Annual sales targets were set, based on assumptions about market penetration and market growth. And if it meant cutting prices, or bringing out new models, meeting the sales targets took top priority.

It has been a devastatingly successful strategy, wiping out the once world-leading UK motorcyle industry along the way as the Japanese makers moved from small machines into all sectors of the market.

The trouble is, it is no longer working.

Moreover, the Japanese manufacturers' tactics of very heavy discounting to shift the stock mountain has rapidly heightened trade tension with countries like the U.S., West Germany and Italy where sizeable indigenous manufacture still exists. . . .

. . . BMW's Dr. Safert warns that the world stockpile of machines is so large that even dramatically reduced prices may not be enough to dispose of it altogether — and prices are already down by up to 30 per cent. . . .

. . . While BMW acknowledged that, on the surface, consumers were benefiting from heavy discounting, it said the knock-on effects were an erosion of dealers' ability to invest in parts and service back-up and rising prices, which in turn would raise insurance premiums and accelerate the depreciation of used machines.

. . . . Only one thing is certain: the customers are having a field day".[7]

An implication of the above could be that a business is "dammed if it does become investment-intensive and dammed if it doesn't". The question then arises as to what should be done when a business is perceived to be becoming investment-intensive. Schoeffler suggests several courses of action. These include:

A very detailed scrutiny and appraisal of all investment that is greater than that required to enable capacity to match future demand, i.e. the often held belief that more automation of disproportionate size automatically is good for a business is untrue.

In evaluating an investment which is greater than that required to match future demand, the total strategic effects should be considered just as carefully as the cost effect. By this is meant: if the capacity increase leads to, say, volume grabbing strategies by competitors, or protectionism, then the hoped for benefits that should accrue through reduced unit costs will not materialise due to lower price levels.

Businesses should attempt to mimimise the profit-damaging effects of capital-intensive technology through:
    Concentration on a particular segment of the market.
    Having a broader product range.
    Increasing productivity.
    Engaging in capital-saving R & D, especially in areas where
        demand is elastic.
    Developing equipment which is flexible in terms of its capacity and
        purpose.
    Leasing rather than buying where possible.

2. *Productivity.* This is measured by the value added per employee, and in general the higher the productivity, the more profitable is the business.

Some of the evidence that PIMS has advanced in support of this assertion is presented below.

Table 50. Low-integrated Businesses are Damaged Most by Low Employee Productivity[2]

Value added / Employee

ROI	Low	19K	27K	High
Low	12	16	25	
Value added sales — 53%	16	15	17	
68%	23	19	22	
High				

Table 51. Productivity Reduces the Effect of Investment Intensity[2]

Value added / Employee

ROI	Low	19K	28K	High
Low	23	29	37	
Investment sales — 42%	20	19	25	
61%	7	10	15	
High				

3. *Market position*[1][5]. A high relative market share has a positive effect upon profit and cash flow. Some of the evidence that PIMS has advanced in support of this assertion is presented below.

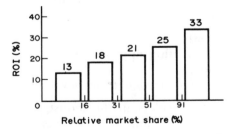

FIG. 65. *Market position boosts profitability*[2]

PIMS[2] advances three main reasons for market share having such a strong effect upon profitability. These are;

Economies of scale,
Experience effects, and
Bargaining power.

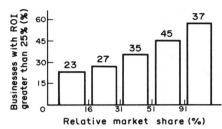

FIG. 66. *Strong relative market share makes an adequate return more likely*[2]

These findings are similar to those of the Boston Consulting Group.

PIMS suggests that, in certain circumstances, having a dominant market position can be especially valuable. Among the more important circumstances are the following:

When the market growth rate is high.
When the industry is at an early stage in the life cycle.
When the technology needs a high degree of vertical integration.
When the employees are not highly unionised.
When the business lacks major process or product patent protection.
When high marketing expenses are necessary.

Finally it is, as always, important to consider the normative advice that PIMS offers to businesses which wish to minimise the disadvantages of a weak market position or to maximise the advantages which can be obtained from their particular market position.

For businesses that have a weak market position, PIMS suggests that they should adopt a "safe" strategy which is appropriate to weak market share businesses; specifically they should

minimise R & D efforts,
avoid expensive marketing approaches,
keep capacity loaded,
be wary of investment needed to achieve vertical integration.

In other words, let the leaders in the industry take the risk and be satisfied to be an informed follower. For businesses in general, the advice is:

● Striving for increased market share is not always worthwhile. The cost of the marginal increase in market share may outweigh the benefits. The cost of increasing market share is especially high when

the market is growing rapidly,
the effort is made through price reductions,
the product is of only standard quality or lower.
● Build market share if the foreseen benefits outweigh the foreseen costs and no other better investments are available.
● Harvest, rather than build market share, if the cost of building appears high relative to the benefits.

4. *Growth of the served market.* In general, growth of the served market has a favourable effect upon monetary measures of profit, has a neutral effect upon percentage measures of profit and has a negative effect upon all measures of cash flow.
Some of the evidence that PIMS has advanced in support of this assertion is presented below.

Table 52. Rapid Rates of New Product Introduction in Well-growing Markets Damages ROI[2]

Long-term market growth rate	New products			
ROI	Low	1%	12%	High
Low				
	21	18	18	
6%				
	20	24	15	
9%				
	24	25	15	
High				

Table 53. Productivity is Most Important in High Growth Markets[2]

Long run market growth rate	Sales / Employee			
ROI	Low	32K	48K	High
Low				
	18	17	18	
6%				
	14	18	27	
9%				
	12	15	25	
High				

5. *Quality of the products and/or services offered*[1]. High quality has a generally favourable effect upon all measures of financial performance.
Some of the evidence that PIMS has advanced in support of this assertion is presented below.

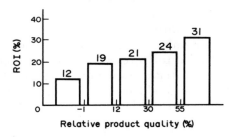

FIG. 67. *Relative product quality promotes profitability*[2]

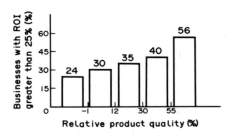

FIG. 68. *High product quality makes an "adequate" return more likely*[2]

Table 54. Market Position and Product Quality are Partial Substitutes for Each Other[2]

ROI	Relative market share			
	Low	25%	60%	High
Relative product quality −1%	10	10	21	
	14	19	27	
40%	22	27	35	

The PIMS findings show that quality has a fundamental influence on business performance. Some specific messages arise. These include:

(a) Quality and profitability are strongly linked. The findings show that businesses selling high-quality products and services tend to be more profitable than those with lower quality offerings and, furthermore, the impact of quality on profitability is greatest at the extremes of very high quality and very low quality.

Table 55. High Product Quality is Most Valuable in Concentrated Markets⁽²⁾

Share of big-4 competitors

ROI	Low	65%	85%	High
Low →	10	10	14
−1%	17	19	23
40%	24	29	35
High

Relative product quality

Table 56. R & D Activities are Very Unprofitable if They Don't Yield High Product Quality⁽²⁾

R & D / Sales

ROI	Low	0.7%	2.5%	High
Low →	14	15	8
−1%	20	21	18
40%	34	30	25
High

Relative product quality

Table 57. Heavy Marketing is No Substitute for Low Product Quality⁽²⁾

Marketing / Sales

ROI	Low	5%	10%	High
Low →	13	13	9
−1%	22	21	16
40%	33	30	26
High

Relative product quality

Table 58. New Products are Unprofitable when Introduced by Businesses with Low-quality Products[2]

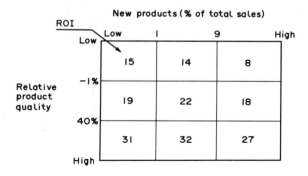

New products (% of total sales)

ROI	Low	I	9	High
Low / Low	15	14	8
−1%	19	22	18
40%	31	32	27
High			

Relative product quality

Table 59. Low-integrated Businesses Need High Product Quality[2]

Value added / Sales

ROI	Low	49%	63%	High
Low / Low	9	10	18
−1%	19	19	22
40%	31	23	23
High			

Relative product quality

(b) Quality and market share are strongly linked. Both tend to go together. However, PIMS has found that product quality is positively correlated to ROI independently of market share. This suggests that when a business has both a high market share and high quality, then it is indeed in an extremely profitable and powerful position. This is illustrated particularly well in Table 54 above.

(c) The circumstances when quality is most important. PIMS has found that high quality is most important in almost all situations, i.e. the importance of quality is unaffected by:

    the business sector,
    the degree of capital intensity,
    the degree of vertical integration,
    the growth rate of the market.*

*This is not entirely true, as PIMS[9] has found that businesses that sell high-quality products tend to gain market share in markets that are growing slowly and that quality differences are less important in determining market share in rapidly growing markets.

(d) How businesses become quality leaders. PIMS has found that quality leaders tend to have entered their markets early and have often been the pioneers in developing the markets. Furthermore, quality leaders have also frequently been innovators. The data for this conclusion is shown in Table 60.

Table 60. Product Quality and Market Entry[9]

Percentage who entered the market as:

		Pioneers	Early followers	Later entrants
	Lowest	46	33	21
		48	36	16
Relative quality level	Average	57	34	9
		66	26	8
	Highest	66	25	9

6. *Innovation/differentiation*. Extensive Research and Development will tend to have a positive effect upon the performance of a business which already occupies a strong market position and vice versa.

Some of the evidence that PIMS has advanced in support of this assertion is presented below.

Table 61. New Products Help Cope with the Profit Pressures of Inflation[2]

Rate of price increase

ROI		Low	4%	8%	High
New products (% of sales)	Low				
		26	23	20	
	1%				
		27	23	20	
	12%				
		16	20	18	
	High				

Table 62. Expensive Marketing of New Products Reduces ROI[2]

Marketing / Sales

ROI	Low	6%	11% High
Low			
	21	27	24
1%			
New products (% of sales)	29	19	21
12%			
	23	19	15
High			

Table 63. New Products Accentuate the Profit Damage of Low Quality[2]

Quality

ROI	Low	6%	36% High
Low			
	15	17	28
1%			
New products (% of sales)	14	18	25
12%			
	5	15	24
High			

Table 64. New Products Plus New Equipment Put a Strain on Profits[2]

Replacement value / original cost of P & E

ROI	Low	140%	197% High
Low			
	17	20	19
1%			
New products (% of sales)	17	18	21
12%			
	10	22	18
High			

7. *Vertical integration.* Generally businesses that are in mature and stable markets benefit from vertical integration. For businesses in other markets, the opposite tends to be true. Some of the evidence that PIMS has advanced to support this assertion is presented below.

Some of the evidence that PIMS has advanced to support this assertion is presented below.

Table 65. Low-integrated Businesses Need Product Quality the Most[2]

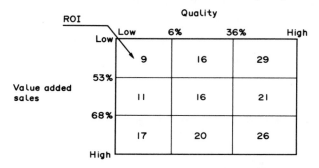

	Quality		
ROI	Low	6%	36% High
Low	9	16	29
Value added sales 53%	11	16	21
68%	17	20	26
High			

Table 66. Where the Degree of Integration is Low, High Inventories Damage Profits Severely[2]

	Inventory sales		
ROI	Low	15%	23% High
Low	25	15	9
Value added sales 53%	25	21	13
68%	28	24	14
High			

Table 67. Diverse Corporations Benefit Most from Vertical Integration[2]

	Corporate diversity	
ROI	Low	High
	19	8
Value added sales 53%	16	14
68%	20	30

Table 68. Low-integrated Businesses are Damaged Most by Low Employee Productivity[2]

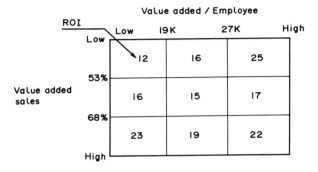

Value added / Employee

ROI

	Low	19K	27K	High
Low				
	12	16	25	
53%				
	16	15	17	
68%				
	23	19	22	
High				

Value added sales

Table 69. Low-integrated Businesses are Damaged by Having to Serve Too Many Customers[2]

Number of customers = 50% of sales

ROI

	Low	40	276	High
Low				
	22	15	12	
53%				
	15	16	17	
68%				
	22	21	21	
High				

Value added sales

8. *Cost push.* The rates of increase of wages, salaries and raw material prices, and the presence of a labour union, have complex impacts on profit and cash flow, depending on how the business is positioned to pass along the increase to its customers and/or to absorb the higher costs internally.

Some of the evidence that PIMS has advanced in support of this assertion is presented below.

9. *Current strategic effort.* A change in the direction of any of the above factors has effects on profit and cash flow that are frequently opposite to that of the factor itself. For example, having a strong market share tends to increase net cash flow, but striving to obtain market share may drain cash while the effort is being made.

Table 70. High Unionisation Reduces the Gains of High Market Share[2]

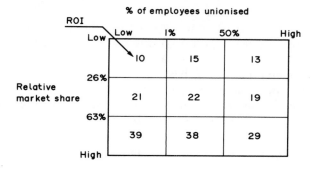

% of employees unionised

ROI	Low	1%	50%	High
Low	10	15	13
26%	21	22	19
63%	39	38	29
High			

Relative market share

Table 71. High Unionisation Depresses Harvesting Payoff[9]

% employees unionised

ROI	Low	1%	50%	High
Down	26	32	18
Steady	21	23	21
Up	24	25	21

Change in market share

Table 72. High Industry Concentration does Little to Offset the Effect of High Unionisation[2]

% employees unionised

ROI		41%	70%
	27	16	20
44%	25	20	20
71%	25	23	20

Industry concentration

V. The operation of the nine major strategic influences is complex

The operation of the influences is complex in that sometimes they can act in a reinforcing way upon each other and at other times they may have an offsetting effect. In other words, it may be highly misleading to make any judgements on the basis of the likely effects of changes in factors taken one at a time. The total cumulative effects should be considered, and this can really only be done through thorough comprehension of the realities lying behind the figures.

VI. Product characteristics do not matter

It does not matter what the actual product is, what is important is the characteristics of the business — i.e. the nine characteristics given above. If businesses have the same profile of characteristics, then they will tend to have the same operating results.

VII. The expected impact of strategic business characteristics tend to assert themselves over time

This really means two things:
  (a) When the fundamental of a business changes over time, then its profitability and cash flow tend to move in the direction of the norm for the new position.
  (b) If the actually realised performance of a business deviates from the expected norm, it will tend to move back towards that norm.

VIII. Business strategies are successful if their fundamentals are good, and are unsuccessful if they are unsound

The laws of the market place are a reliable source of confidence in estimating both the cost of undertaking a given strategy and the benefit of undertaking it. However, as noted above, the fundamentals do not always operate in a direct simplistic manner, so understanding the laws of the market place can be of immense help to the strategist.

IX. Most clear strategy signals are robust

When a particular strategy for a business is clearly indicated to be worthwhile, that signal is usually robust, i.e. moderate sized errors in the analysis — for example, an error in estimating the market growth rate — do not usually render the signal invalid.
  (e) The benefits of improving quality. Efforts to improve quality

generally lead to an increase in market share; however, there is a cost — short-term profitability is reduced.

Limitations of the PIMS Approach

Any critical evaluation of the PIMS program must be tempered with a recognition of the original and unique contribution which the program has already made to the development of strategic management. The program is still unique in that no other project has amassed (and analysed) such a vast pool of business experience. Furthermore, it seems likely, as more experience is accumulated, that the quality and accuracy of predictions will improve. In short, PIMS is the best business data base available. However, a number of criticisms of PIMS have arisen, some of which are given below.

Paradoxically, one of PIMS greatest strengths — the huge amount of data upon which it is built — may also be considered to be one of its weaknesses. Thus the 37 independent variables that explain 80% of the variation on ROI may not be genuinely independent, i.e. multicollinearity may exist, and this may preclude the isolation of the effects of an individual or pair of factors. This implies that the PIMS procedure of relating two variables to ROI (as shown in the 3 × 3 figures section "The PIMS Nine Basic Findings on Business Strategy" above) may be questionable. In other words, there may be errors in the model.

Similar to this criticism is the possibility that the, PIMS assumed, causal relationships in the regression model are not valid. PIMS does not supply strong theoretical or statistical evidence to support the claimed causal relationships. Perhaps the clearest unjustified example of unproven causality is the assumption that when a business fails to achieve its Par ROI (see the section "The Par Report" on page 185 above) that, automatically, this failure is due to managerial performance. Other possible causes could included environmental influences, especially in the context of the competitive environment. Thus Porter[11] has shown clearly that the PIMS assertion that there should be a strong positive correlation between relative market share and ROI does not always hold true and, indeed, in certain industries may be positively misleading. Porter suggests that, in certain industries, a U-shaped relationship between Market Share and ROI, as shown in Fig. 69, is more likely to be the correct one. In this situation it is claimed that firms which have a low market share but have a high degree of product differentiation earn above industry average returns and at the other end of the scale firms with a high market share also, for reasons of volume advantages, should earn above industry average returns. The middle of the curve contains firms who are "stuck in the middle" — i.e. they are neither large enough

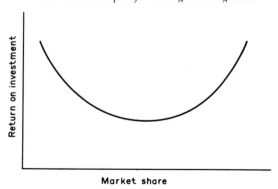

FIG. 69. *The U-shaped relationship between market share and return on investment (Ref (11), p. 43)*

to reap the benefits that accrue through size, nor are they small enough to reap the benefits which can accrue through product differentiation. In the motor industry, General Motors and Toyota are examples of companies who enjoy superior returns because of their high market share low cost positions, while Mercedes enjoys superior returns because it has very effectively differentiated its product. In the middle are companies such as British Leyland and Fiat, which both endure lower than average returns because they are neither sufficiently differentiated or are sufficiently large to generate above average returns. Such companies are said to be "stuck in the middle".

Additionally, there may be behavioural problems for users. Because the program is extremely complex, and also because it prints out specific quantitative results and recommendations, a misplaced managerial faith in the accuracy and validity of its findings may arise in spite of the following PIMS advice:

> "Don't ignore what the model says.
> Don't believe what the model says."[2]

The PIMS program considers each business on an individual basis and not on a portfolio basis. It could be argued that it is, today especially, important to assess a business not just in terms of its performance in isolation, but to assess its performance in relation to other businesses in the corporate portfolio. Thus, it is important to consider a business's position in the portfolio. For example, is it in, say a "cash generator" or, say, a "cash absorbing" location, or, is there synergy between this business and other businesses in the portfolio?

It could be argued that PIMS does not look sufficiently towards the future. Thus the strategic advice is based exclusively upon historical information and the models do not make sufficient provision for future environmental shocks, i.e. implicit in the PIMS approach is the view that the past is a good predictor of the future. Many business strategists (see, for example, Ref. (1)) would argue that today this is not so.

There is considerable emphasis in strategic management literature of the importance of goals in determining what strategy a business adopts and in measuring the performance of the business. PIMS assumes a goal of maximisation of ROI, and also assumes that ROI is the best measure of performance. This may be too narrow a view of business performance — many businesses aspire to other goals or indeed multiple goals (see Ref. (8)). It may be, then, that this may be an unrealistically simple way to treat the strategically crucial element of objectives.

Finally, it could be claimed that the PIMS studies are too concerned with U.S. big business to be of real value to smaller businesses operating in Europe. While the bulk of the research effort has, indeed, been seeded in U.S. big businesses, nonetheless, at one level, it seems reasonable to investigate European business along the same lines as PIMS to see if similar relationships exist, and, at a lower level, the PIMS studies can provide the smallest business with a stimulating way of analysing itself. Thus the PIMS measures can be plotted by planners in small businesses and used to monitor their own progress in an insightful way. For example, even the smallest business can plot, over a number of years, using the PIMS methodology, its "Investment Intensity" against its "Return on Investment" and predict the effect that "Investment Intensity" will have upon it.

References

1. Ansoff, H. I. *Strategic Management*, MacMillan, 1979.
2. *Basic Principles of Business Strategy*, The Strategic Planning Institute, Cambridge, Mass., 1981.
3. Buzzell, R. D. "Product Quality", *PIMSLetter*, No. 4, The Strategic Planning Institute, 1980.
4. Buzzell, R. D., B. Gale and R. G. M. Sultan, "Market Share — A Key to Profitability", *Harvard Business Review*, Jan./Feb. 1975.
5. Gale, B. T. "Selected Findings from the PIMS Project: Market Strategy Impacts on Profitability", *American Marketing Association Combined Proceedings*, Series 36, 1974, pp. 471–474.
6. Gale, B. T. and B. Branch, "Strategic Marketing: The Dispute About High-Share Businesses", *Journal of Business Strategy*, Vol. 1, No. 1, Summer 1980, pp. 71–71.
7. Griffiths, J. "The Crisis Facing Japan", *Financial Times*, 21 March 1983, p. 14.
8. McNamee, P. B. "Multiple Objectives in Accounting and Finance", *Journal of Business Finance and Accounting*, Vol. 10, No. 4, Winter 1983, pp. 595–621.
9. *PIMS, Some Research Findings*, 1977 revised edition, The Strategic Planning Institute, Cambridge, Mass., 1977.
10. *PIMS: The PIMS Program*, SPI, The Strategic Planning Institute, Cambridge, Mass.

11. Porter, M. E. *Competitive Strategy*, The Free Press, 1980.
12. Schoeffler, S. "Nine Basic Findings on Business Strategy", *The PIMSLetter*, No. 1, 1980.
13. Schoeffler, S. "The Unprofitability of Modern Technology And What To Do About It", *PIMSLetter*, No. 2, 1980.

Bibliography

Anderson, C. and Paine, F. "PIMS: A Re-examination", *Academy of Management Review*, July 1978, pp. 602–612.

Anonymous. "Strategic Planning Institute Computerises Business Basics", *Chain Store Age Executive*, Vol. 55, No. 10, Oct. 1979, pp. 43–44.

Bucatinski, J. "Management Science Roundup — What is PIMS?", *Interfaces*, Vol. 6, No. 3, May 1976, pp. 95–100.

Burgess, A. R. "The Modelling of Business Profitability: A New Approach", *Strategic Management Journal*, Vol. 3, No. 1, Jan./Mar. 1982, pp. 53–65.

Buzzell, R. D. "Are There 'Natural' Market Structures?", *Journal of Marketing*, Vol. 45, No. 1, Winter 1981, pp. 42–51.

Buzzell, R. D. and Wiersema, F. D. "Successful Share Building Strategies", *Harvard Business Review*, Jan./Feb. 1981, pp. 135–144.

Capon, N. and Spogli, J. R. "Strategic Market Planning: A Comparison and Critical Examination of Two Contemporary Approaches", *American Marketing Association Proceedings*, No. 41, 1977, pp. 219–223.

Cook, C. J. Jr. "Marketing Strategy and Differential Advantage", *Journal of Marketing*, Vol. 47, No. 2, Spring 1983, pp. 68–75.

Cooper, J. R. "How Does Business Analysis Impact the Planning for Marketing of Existing Products", *American Marketing Association, Business Proceedings*, Series 40, 1977, pp. 60–62.

Day, G. "Gaining Insights Through Strategy Analysis", *Journal of Business Strategy*, Vol. 4, No. 1, Summer 1983, pp. 51–58.

Donath, R. "Measuring Bang in the Marketing Buck: How General Electric Predicts Marketing Productivity", *Industrial Marketing*, Vol. 67, No. 7, July 1982, pp. 60–64.

Enis, B. M. "G.E., PIMS, BCG and the PCL", *Business*, Vol. 30, No. 3, May/June 1980, pp. 10–13.

Ham, M. J. "The Profit Impact of Market Strategy in the Insurance Industry", *Best's Review*, Vol. 79, No. 8, Dec. 1978, pp. 22–26.

Hambrick, H. J. "An Empirical Typology of Mature Industrial-Product Environments", *Academy of Management Journal*, Vol. 26, No. 2, June 1983, pp. 213–230.

Hambrick, H. J., MacMillan, I. C. and Barbosa, R. R. "Business Unit Strategy and Changes in the Product R and D Budget", *Management Science*, Vol. 28, No. 7, July 1983, pp. 757–769.

Hambrick, D. G., MacMillan, I. C. and Day, D. L. "Strategic Attributes and Performance in the BCG Matrix — A PIMS based Analysis of Industrial Product Businesses", *Academy of Management Journal*, Vol. 25, No. 3, Sept. 1982, Series 36, 1974, pp. 471–474.

Herbert, P. J. and Boss, E. W. "Corporate Strategy and Acquisitions Policy", *Journal of General Management*, Vol. 6, No. 3, Spring 1981, pp. 18–30.

Kane, R. W. "Quality Costs and Product Integrity", *American Institute of Industrial Engineering, Inc.*, 1975, pp. 361–364.

Kehoe, W. J. "Strategic Market Planning: The PIMS Model", *SA M Advanced Management Journal*, Vol. 48, No. 2, Spring 1982, pp. 45–49.

Kilgore, K. "New Game Plans for Corporate Teams", *The New Englander*, Vol. 2, No. 8, Dec. 1977, pp. 38–40, 45.

Leontiades, M. "Rationalizing the Unrelated Acquisition", *California Management Review*, Vol. 24, No. 3, Spring 1982, pp. 5–14.

Loughridge, R. F. "How to Assure Failure in Strategic Planning: Ten Sure-Fine Rules", *Managerial Planning*, Vol. 30, No. 5, Mar./Apr. 1982, p. 26.

Lubatkin, M. and Pitts, M. "PIMS: Fact or Folklore?", *Journal of Business Strategy*, Vol. 3, No. 3, Winter 1983, pp. 38–43.

Mitroff, I. I., Mason, R. O. and Barbara, V. P. "Comparing Apples and Oranges: Relating Approaches to Business Policy", *Journal of Enterprise Management*, Vol. 3, No. 2, 1981, pp. 91–101.

Murphy, L. "How They Monitor Planning at Greer Hydraulics", *Sales and Marketing Management*, Vol. 12, No. 8, 7 Dec. 1981, pp. 51–53.

Naylor, T. H. "Strategic Planning Model", *Managerial Planning*, Vol. 30, No. 1, July/Aug. 1981, pp. 3–11.

Naylor, T. H. "PIMS: Through a Different Looking Glass", *Planning Review*, Vol. 6, No. 2, March 1978, pp. 15–16.

Newton, J. K. "Market Share — Key to Higher Profitability?", *Long Range Planning*, Vol. 16, No. 1, 1983, pp. 37–41.

Page, A. L. "A Test of the Share/Price Market Planning Relationship in One Retail Environment", *Journal of the Academy of Marketing Science*, Vol. 7, No. 1, Winter/ Spring 1979, pp. 25–39.

Schoeffler, S. "Cope Team Tells how PIMS Academic-Business Search for Basic Principles Can Get Line Managers into Strategic Planning", *Marketing News*, Vol. 10, No. 2, 16 July, 1976, pp. 6–7.

Schoeffler, S., Buzzell, R. and Heany, D. F. "Impact of Strategic Planning on Profit Performance", *Harvard Business Review*, March/April 1974, pp 137–145.

Schneewies, T. "Determinant of Profitability", *Journal of Business Strategy*, Vol. 23, No. 2, 1983, pp. 15–21.

Smith, P. "Unique Tool for Marketeers: PIMS", *Dun's Review*, Vol. 103, No. 4, Oct. 1976, pp. 95–100.

Thorelli, H. B. and Burnett, S. C. "The Nature of Product Life Cycles for Industrial Goods Businesses", *Journal of Marketing*, Vol. 45, No. 4, Fall 1981, pp. 97–108.

Wensley, R. "PIMS and BCG: New Horizons or False Dawn?", *Strategic Management Journal*, Vol. 3, No. 2, Apr./June 1982, pp. 147–158.

Woo, C. Y. and Cooper, A. C. "Strategies of Effective Low Share Businesses", *Strategic Management Journal*, Vol. 2, No. 3, July/Sept. 1981, pp. 301–318.

CHAPTER 7

Scenario Planning

Introduction

Table 73 shows some of the operating and financial data for a large European company over the period 1970–74. On the basis of this limited information, what plans should have been made for the next two years?

Table 73. Selected Data from a Large European Company (all figures are in million DM)

Year	1970	1971	1972	1973	1974
Sales	10,373	11,144	12,086	13,904	18,879
Income after tax	358	315	448	541	621

"Common sense" and "logic" indicate that it might be reasonable to commence by arguing that plans for the future should be made on the basis of best estimates of what the future will be and that best estimates can be obtained by forecasting. In this case the growth of the company has been so smooth that forecasting the next two years should be easily achieved through simple forecasts. Three such forecasts* and the actual results which were achieved are shown in Table 74.

As can be seen, the differences between the forecast results and the actual results were quite significant. The company from which this data was taken was the Bayer Company of Germany and the actual effects of this "shortfall of demand" were perceived by the company itself to be relatively severe. Thus, the then chairman of the Board of Bayer, Dr. H. Grunewald, in his 1975 annual statement wrote:

"In 1975 the world economy suffered a serious setback which — unlike those of former years — hit almost all the industrial countries simultaneously. In the chemical industry, the slump was especially strong during the first three quarters of the year. The oil crisis had far-reaching, prolonged effects.

*The workings to support these forecasts are given in Appendix I of this chapter.

Table 74. A Comparison of Extrapolated Forecasts with Actual Results for a Large European Company (all figures are in million DM)

Type of forecast and actual results	Year 1975	1976
Graphical extrapolation		
Sales	20,100	22,400
Income after tax	700	780
Linear regression		
Sales	19,209	21,186
Income after tax	682	757
Logarithmic trend		
Sales	20,610	24,040
Income after tax	723	853
Actual results		
Sales	17,734	20,880
Income after tax	336	523

These developments put our company to a hard endurance test. The sales decline which commenced toward the end of 1974 became more acute well into the summer of 1975, due to intensive inventory reductions made by customers at all stages of production and distribution. Our export business, which in the past had often compensated for weaker domestic business, was particularly affected.

. . . Because of the decline in sales we were forced to cut back production drastically, especially during the summer months. The individual divisions were affected to a varied extent. . . . Short time work was unavoidable for lines with particularly low capacity utilization. The staff was reduced through normal fluctuations; employees who left were not replaced. Our employees showed understanding for the measures necessary to overcome the difficulties and to secure their jobs." (Ref. (1), p. 11)

What happened to Bayer also happened to many other companies at that time, and indeed the trauma that the oil crisis provoked caused a general questioning of the value of traditional forecasting methods in a world which had, apparently, become subject to extreme and uncontrollable change.

Perhaps the clearest public case of disillusionment with formal forecasting methods, as a basis for strategic planning, was provided by Ciba-Geigy. Figure 70 shows the discrepancy between Ciba-Geigy's forecast group sales over the period 1969–80 and its actual sales. At a

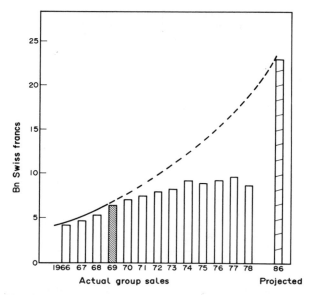

Fig. 70. *Ciba-Geigy's actual and predicted group sales for the period 1970–1980 (prediction made in 1969)*[9]

more specific level, in 1969 the company engaged in forecasting to an accuracy of one decimal point for the following decade. At that time they forecast that by 1980 "chemicals and dyestuffs" and "plastics and additives" would contribute 27.2% and 9.8% of group sales respectively. The actual shares of "chemicals and dyestuffs" and "plastics and additives" were 17% and 20% respectively in 1980.[3] Clearly, under certain circumstances, traditional forecasting methods can prove to be highly inaccurate.

Further evidence of the inadequacy of these types of methods is provided by Spivey and Wrobleski,[11] who examined past studies of econometric models used in the U.S. Government and for industry planning. They found that non-econometric forecasts were as good, or better, and that in the period 1970–75 U.S. econometric models were unreliable for three or more quarters into the future.

Similarly, in 1978, Franssen[4] found that energy forecasting had not been very good and that "the track record of judgemental forecasts had been more accurate than most of the available mathematical models".

Why is Forecasting So Difficult Today?

The fundamental cause of the difficulty in forecasting today is that the environment has become more turbulent. The sources of this increase in turbulence have already been discussed in Chapter 1. Three additional elements which now contribute to the high level of unpredictability obtaining today are:

(a) *An Increase in the Complexity and Mutual Interdependences of the Environment*

A natural consequence of technological development has been a globalisation of business and society and a changing relationship between business and society. The traditionally distinct technological, geographical, economic, social and political forces that, in the past, defined separate businesses have increasingly tended to overlap and the boundaries between them have been increasingly fuzzy. This ill-structured integration has added greatly to complexity in the environment. An industry which currently illustrates this phenomenon well is the world shipbuilding industry. In this industry, since the 1950s especially, the following are among the more significant interrelated strategic developments that have occurred.

major technological developments in types of vessels and methods of construction;

ship purchasers have become more global in their perspectives;

societal pressures have increased — the pressure to preserve jobs and the pressure to build safe non-polluting ships;

international political events have become more influential: for example, the uncertainty about military/political developments in the Middle East has ramifications for the type of oil tanker constructed;

perhaps, most importantly, home government support for native shipbuilding industries, as shown in Table 75, has distorted "the market".

All of the above factors have contributed to the complexities which planners in the shipbuilding industry now face. Similar overlapping and unpredictable forces now face many industries.

(b) *Growth in Competitive Pressure*

Today firms are meeting unprecedented competitive pressures. These pressures have been caused by a large number of factors, chief among them being:

(i) *Supply factors*: there have been major structural changes in industries and the "rules of the game" are constantly changing. Among the more important of these changes that have occurred

Table 75. Summary of Government Supports to Maritime Industry (Ref. (10), p. 72)

	Japan	Sweden	United Kingdom
Construction subsidy	None.	None. However, interest-free loans to yards in financial difficulties are made. Additionally, major price increases recently accepted by numerous customers on orders firmly under control.	None.
Loans & interest, domestic sales	Government-backed. 70% maximum 10 years–interest moratorium years. Interest rates subsidised.	Loans guaranteed to 50% of ship value. Credit period 15 years. Interest as of current bond markets.	None unique.
Loans & interest, foreign sales	Conform with OECD understanding on export credit for ships. Essentially, 8 year term. 7.5% interest rate; 20% of price paid on delivery, 70% of value covered.	Loans available from Export Credit Association. Terms in accord with OECD agreements.	None special. Certain circumstances of unconditionally guaranteed loans result in lower interest rates.
Depreciation	For domestic trade, 16-year maximum rate, 13.4% annually — for foreign trade, complex formula, resulting in less than 16 years.	Flexible and liberal. 30% per year or complete writeoff on 5 years. Ships recently delivered qualify for special investment allowance in addition to 100% depreciation allowance.	"Free," i.e. may be taken at any rate up to 100% first year.
Tax aids	Complex — corporate tax minimised for operators who continue fleet improvement. Credits against foreign trade earnings. Deferred capital gains tax on ship sales.	40% of pre-tax net income to tax-free future investment, with 54% of this available to current working capital. Tax free capital gains from ship sales.	2% relief from taxes on ship-building costs. Imported materials exempt from customs duty.
Replacement program	"Scrap and build." Government-backed favourable loans.	None formal.	None formal.
Operating subsidies	Annual and varied — first 5 years service on cross trades and special ones — up to 8% on revenue.	None on foreign trade.	None on foreign trade.

are: the globalisation of industries, the entry of new, geographically distant, competitors who play by different rules, lumpy augmentation of capacity, leading to overcapacity in the industry, and the influence of government in the form of support for favoured industries.

(ii) *Demand factors*: since the oil crisis of 1973 there has been, at the least, a less intensive rate of growth in many industries and this, combined with the twin forces of growth of existing competitors and the entry of new competitors, has caused chronic overcapacity to develop in many industries.

(c) *The Importance of Size**

For many businesses globalisation has meant that survival has become increasingly dependent upon size, and today, in many businesses, this minimum size required for survival would have been undreamt of 20 years ago. Industries which are particularly prone to this are those which are in high technology, are capital intensive, have long lead times and sell on a global basis. The problems which size brings are manifested not just in the scales of operations, but, perhaps more importantly, in the risks attached to introducing new products.

The influence of size can be clearly seen in the commercial aircraft industry. In this industry each time a major new product is developed it places at risk the survival of the company (or consortium of companies) developing the product. Thus in order to be of a size capable of competing with Boeing in the late 1980s, European aircraft manufacturers have had to form a consortium. Aerospatiale, British Aerospace, Messerchmidtt-Boelkow-Blohm and CASA have, though, Airbus Industrie, formed a consortium to develop a new European Airbus, the 150 seat A-320 which, they hope, will be capable of competing with Boeing. At stake, according to Sir Austin Pearce, the Chairman of British Aerospace, is "the fundamental question — does Europe want an aircraft industry of its own capable of being competitive, or does it want to become merely a subcontractor to the U.S.?"[5]

A consequence of all the above broad trends is that there has been a severe reduction in the predictability of the environment and that to prosper firms must increasingly develop their anticipatory ability and also their organisational flexibility. Scenario planning is suggested here as a methodology for improving a firm's anticipatory ability.

It could be argued, of course, that size is simply one aspect of competitive pressure. While this is true, the factor of size has been made separate and explicit here in order to emphasise its importance.

An Approach to Scenario Planning

The nature of scenario planning is in the eye of the beholder: it can be quantitative and precise (the hard approach), or it can be qualitative and descriptive (the soft approach); it can comprise a single scenario, or it can comprise multiple scenarios; its time span can vary from the fairly near future — three years up to and beyond twenty years.

In this book a scenario is considered to be a self-contained envelope of consistent possibilities which describes the future. This picture of the future is evolved through a group decision-making iterative process and is based upon the group's qualitative judgements supported by quantitative data. (The process is described in detail in the next section of this chapter: A Practical Approach to Scenario Planning.) This is somewhat different from a forecast in that it is not a definite and quantitative prediction about the future, relying for its authority upon information from the past and the skill of the forecaster. Rather, in developing a scenario, the view is that the past is *not* a good guide to the future and that there can be considerable benefit from examining an organisation's plans in the context of the more qualitative and open-ended future picture (or "Leitbild"*).

Scenario planning involves building a number of scenarios, each taking a different view of the future, and then testing the organisation's plans against each scenario that is built. The scenarios are built by planners and managers from the organisation plus, as required, outside experts. The scenarios must be internally consistent. For example, if in an energy scenario it is postulated that the power of OPEC is going to increase, that alternative sources of energy will not be discovered or developed and that demand for energy will continue to grow, then the view that the price of energy will remain constant is internally inconsistent.

The Shell Company, which has been a leading advocate of scenario planning, suggests that the fewer the number of scenarios built the better, and they suggest that scenario builders "try to distil the range of possible futures into two broad archetypes"[2] and that these two contrasting scenarios be extreme situations — i.e. situations where that which is postulated is not likely, but nonetheless possible. Plans can then be examined to see how robust and flexible they are under the extreme conditions postulated in each scenario. This is the approach advocated here and is shown schematically in Fig. 71. How this approach is implemented in practice is now considered.

---

*This is the term used by Ciba-Geigy (see Ref. (3)).

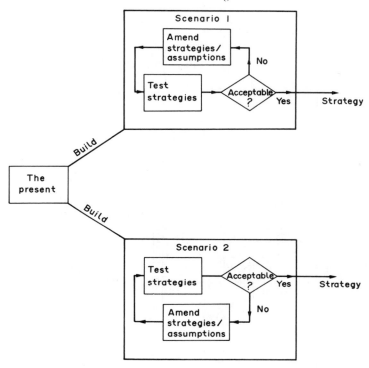

FIG. 71. *Evaluating strategies in two scenarios*

A Practical Approach to Scenario Planning

A methodology for practical scenario planning is shown schematically in Fig. 72 and is described below. The method is set out in a series of discrete steps.

STEP 1. DEVELOP A DATA BASE

The purpose of the data base is to provide a readily accessible reservoir of information so that the scenario builders can be provided, quickly, with the information they require.

The data base comprises two major overlapping sections: a section containing information relevant to the operation of the organisation and a section containing information on the environment within which the organisation is operating. For both sections the historical period of time for which data is collected really depends upon the industry being analysed. A rough rule of thumb which is frequently given (see Ref. (6)) is that the forecast should be for no more years into the future than the

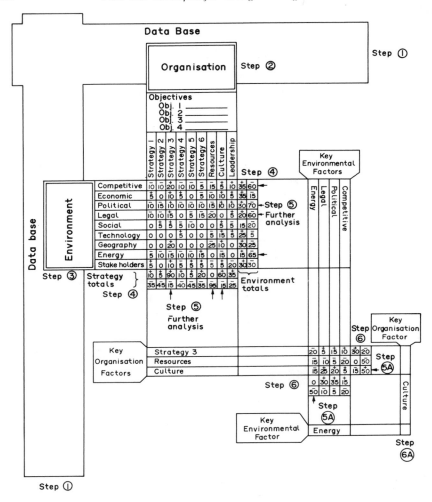

FIG. 72. *A schematic representation of a practical approach to scenario planning*

number of years for which historical data is available. The wisdom of this advice in today's turbulent environment may, however, be somewhat questionable.

Finally, the data base should be stored in a fashion that makes it easy to update and easy to access. The method recommended is that one of the proprietary spread sheet or data base programs available for microcomputers be used. Details of how this can be done are given in Chapter 8.

The Data Base for the Organisation

The objective of this data base is to provide planners with a record of the company's performance over the historical period selected. Performance can, of course, be evaluated along many dimensions. Here it is suggested that data on the performance of each of the functional areas be assembled. In addition to recording this data in traditional form (for example, in assessing the financial performance of a firm, a traditional measure is Earnings per Share), it is also suggested that some of the PIMS measures of performance given in Chapter 6 could also be used. The type of data that is stored on this data base could include the following annual statistics.

Financial performance data
Size: total assets, total debts, total shareholders' funds.
Profitability: return on investment, gross profit, net profit, return on equity, stock price, dividend rates, earnings per share.
Liquidity: current ratio, quick ratio, size of current assets, size of cash balances, cash flow.
Leverage: debt to equity ratio, debt coverage, cost of capital.
Control: accounts receivable turnover ratio, average collection period.
Investment intensity.*

Marketing performance data
Total sales: including information by product line, by volume and by value.
Growth in sales.
Market shares and relative market shares.*
Number of products, width of product lines,* geographical coverage.
Marketing costs, sales per employee.*
Number of customers.*
Rate of new product introduction,* research and development expenditure as a proportion of sales.
Quality of products.*
Patent protection.

Production and operations performance data

Total operations costs in relation to competitors.
Output per person, per unit of capital, etc.
Inventory levels.

All performance measures on this and the immediately following pages which have an asterisk are measures which are used by PIMS. See Chapter 6 for details on these measures.

Degree of vertical integration — i.e. the amount of value added, value added per employee.*
Level of capacity utilisation.*
Age of equipment.*

Personnel performance data

Cost of labour.
Levels of: absenteeism, labour turnover, days lost through strikes and stoppages.
Balanced functional expertise.
Quality of employees.
Degree of unionisation.*

The Data Base for the Environment

The construction of the data base for the environment in which the organisation is operating is a more daunting task. This is because of the all-embracing nature of the environment and the infinite number of interrelating factors and forces that may have some influence upon the organisation. In order to place the task within manageable proportions it is suggested here that, as with the organisation data base, the environment be divided into the traditional component areas and that data be assembled for each of these areas. The type of data to be stored on the data base could include the following.

Competitive data

Threat of new entrants.†
Threats from substitutes.†
Power of buyers.†
Power of suppliers.†
Intensity of competition.†

Economic data

Actual levels and rates of growth of: gross domestic product, disposable income, imports, exports, unemployment.
Inflation.

---

†*Further details on the type of data that could be held on each of these factors is given in Chapter 1. For example, data on "the intensity of competition" could include information on: the number of competitors, the rate of industry growth, the degree of differentiation, the scale of operations, the level of exit barriers, etc.*

Monetary policies.
Fiscal policies including tax rates.
Stage in the business cycle.
Economic activity in other major trading blocs.

Political

The role of the government in regulating the economy.
Government attitudes towards business.
Government regulation in such areas as monopolies, free trade, protection of domestic businesses, promotion of exports.
The influence of foreign governments towards the domestic country and its products.

Legal

Complying with national legislation on health and safety at work, minimum wage levels, consumer protection, environmental protection and conservation.
The influence of supra-national legal systems such as the European Community and the United Nations.

Social

Attitudes towards business in general and this industry in particular.
Attitudes towards such social issues as pollution, ecology and energy conservation.
Attitudes towards discrimination, trade with "unapproved of" countries.
The influence of education and travel.
The spending power and characteristics of the different groups comprising society in general and industry customers in particular.

Technological

The speed of technological change in this and potentially impacting industries.
The costs of keeping up with technological change.
The geographical areas where there is dedication to and success in achieving technological leadership.

Geographical data

The location of the industry leadership.
The mobility of the industry.
How old markets have decayed and what new ones have been born.
The factors that confer advantage through location — nearness to

technology, nearness to suppliers, nearness to markets, cheap labour, government incentives, etc.

Energy

The importance to the industry of cheap and plentiful supplies of energy.
The world energy situation and its affects on the world economy.

Stakeholders

The main stakeholders in the industry and the influence they exert. For example: trade unions, social pressure groups, shareholders, etc.
The roles these stakeholders play.

This data should always be available to the scenario builders so that at any time in their analysis the information they require can be provided.

STEP 2. DEVELOP A STRATEGIC PROFILE OF THE ORGANISATION

The objective of this step is to develop a succinct and comprehensive profile of the organisation: the major elements of this profile are assumed to be its objectives, its resources, culture and leadership and the strategies it is following.

The starting point in developing the profile is determining the organisation's objectives. Here it is assumed that the organisation's objectives,* whether formally recorded or implicit, set its fundamental directions and are standards against which performance can be measured.

The resources of the organisation are considered to be the sums of all the resources of the functional areas plus corporate resources. These resources can be measured quantitatively using a variety of units. However, the principlf units used will be the financial value, the physical size and the number of personnel. The resources can also, of course, be assessed, qualitatively, by making judgements about such resources as: the quality of the Research and Development personnel; the depth of skills of the employees, the functional balance of the board, etc. The nature and importance of culture† and leadership have already been discussed in Chapter 1. The organisation's historic and current levels of

*It is important to distinguish between those objectives and strategies which remain as verbal or written aspirations and those which are actually being followed, irrespective of what is written. The reality of an objective or a strategy is manifested in action.
†In Chapter 1, the role of power was also considered. Here it is subsumed within the broader context of culture.

"performance" in each of these areas should be included. Much of this information will be provided by the data base.

Finally, the strategies are considered to be those longer term, frequently irreversible, policies which the organisation is following and are crucial for its survival. The number of strategies which should be included in the matrix in Fig. 72 depends upon the circumstances. However, irrespective of the circumstances, the current major strategies which are actually being followed must be included.

A summary of all the above information can be recorded on a chart such as is shown in Table 76.

STEP 3. DEVELOP A PROFILE OF THE ENVIRONMENT

The objective of this step is to develop a profile of those sections of the environment that impact upon the organisation or will be influenced by it. The process of selection of which environmental elements are relevant and the assessment of their natures and likely influence should be undertaken in a "free thinking" fashion, perhaps using Delphi.*

An illustration of one environmental influence — the energy situation — is given below. Here it is assumed that there is a hypothetical U.K. company which is extremely susceptible to changes in the supply of, demand for and cost of energy. The company wishes to assess its environment for the next planning period with particular reference to the energy environment. It plans to have just two scenarios: a worst case, one in which the energy environment develops a Doomsday hue — the Doomsday scenario — and a best case scenario, in which energy is no longer a serious environmental threat — the Good-day scenario. How the Doomsday scenario is constructed is set out below. The Good-day scenario would be constructed in exactly the same manner. The environment is assessed in two main sections: quantitative data on energy and qualitative judgements about energy.

Assessing the Energy Environment for the Next Planning Period

Section I. Quantitative Data on Energy

The information for this section has been taken exclusively from Ray, G., "Energy and Primary Materials", Chapter 5 in *Long Range Planning*, Special Issue: *British Planning Databook*, Vol. 15, No. 5, Oct. 1982, pp. 95–130.

---

*An explanation of how Delphi can be used is given in Appendix II to this chapter.

Table 76. A Chart for Summarising the Strategic Profile of an Organisation

Organisation:								Year:			

Objectives:
1.

2.

3.

4.

5.

Culture:

Leadership:

Any other relevant information:

Resources											
Finance		Marketing		Production		Personnel		Corporate		R & D	
Budget*	Pers†	Budget	Pers	Budget	Pers	Budget	Pers	Budget	Pers	Budget	Pers

Other	Other	Other	Other	Other	Other

Strategies

1.

2.

3.

4.

5.

Special strengths:

Special weaknesses:

*Size of departmental budget.
†Number of personnel in the department.

(a) *The production of energy.* Tables 77 to 85 show selected statistics which give overall production of energy patterns.

Table 77. Percent Contribution to World Energy Supplies

Year	1950	1973	1978	1980
Coal and lignite	59	29	30	30
Crude petroleum	30	50	49	47
Natural gas	9	19	18	20
Primary (hydro and nuclear)	2	2	3	3

Table 78. Growth Rates for Primary Energy (average annual (compound) rate of growth, percent)

	1950–1973	1973–1977	1977–1980
Total primary energy	4.9	2.3	1.3
Coal	1.9	3.0	2.1
Crude oil	7.2	1.5	−0.3
Natural gas	8.0	2.5	4.2
Primary (hydro and nuclear)	6.4	7.8	2.9

Table 79. World Production of Primary Energy 1970–1980 (millions tonnes of coal equivalent)

Year	Total	Coal	Crude oil	Natural gas	Hydro & nuclear electricity
1970	7350	2399	3473	1323	154
1971	7656	2395	3681	1415	165
1972	7980	2426	3888	1489	177
1973	8448	2470	4239	1554	185
1974	8537	2503	4251	1576	207
1975	8482	2633	4043	1585	222
1976	8951	2702	4359	1662	228
1977	9254	2763	4569	1671	250
1978	9332	2784	4557	1735	257
1979	9693	2844	4750	1836	263
1980	9635	2945	4527	1891	272

Table 80. Production of Nuclear Electricity 1976–1980 (thousand million kWh)

	World	U.S.A.	Canada	Japan	France	Germany	U.K.	U.S.S.R.	Others
1976	397.8	191.1	16.4	34.1	15.8	24.3	36.2	14.0	65.9
1977	498.0	251.0	27.6	26.2	19.7	36.0	40.0	18.7	78.8
1978	571.0	279.5	34.0	47.4	24.7	35.6	37.6	19.2	93.0
1979	589.0	255.5	34.0	55.6	32.0	39.8	38.3	21.8	112.0
1980	637.0	251.1	36.8	75.4	49.3	39.5	36.9	23.5	124.5

1980: Nuclear as percentage of total electricity generation by country.

	8.2	10.2	10.0	14.0	20.3	10.7	12.9	1.8	—

(b) *The consumption of energy*

Table 81. *Per capita* Energy Consumption 1970–1980 (kg of coal equivalent)

	1970	1976	1978
World	1,004	2,032	2,074
North America	10,748	11,349	11,231
W. Europe	3,813	4,238	4,245
Soviet Bloc	4,214	5,256	5,477
China	548	675	837
Japan	3,342	3,775	3,825
All LDCs	314	414	449

Table 82. World Consumption of Energy: Shares of Total Consumption of Primary Energy 1970–1980 (percent)

	Solid fuels	Liquid fuels	Natural gas	Hydro & nuclear electricity
1970	35.5	43.0	19.2	2.3
1975	33.0	44.4	19.8	2.8
1978	32.0	45.2	19.8	3.0
1980	33.7	42.9	20.4	3.0

Table 83. Dependence on Imported Energy 1950–1980 (net imports in % of consumption)

	1950	1970	1976	1978
Western Europe	16	70	67	62
U.S.A.	2	9	21	23
Brazil	77	56	76	73
Japan	6	85	92	94
India	7	18	18	21
S. Korea	44	50	68	76

(c) *The price of energy*

Table 84. Crude Oil Prices 1970–1981

Year	OPEC average $/barrel	Index 1975=100
1970	1.60	54
1971	1.95	57
1972	2.15	62
1973	2.60	73
1974	9.90	89
1975	10.90	100
1976	11.90	100
1977	12.80	109
1978	13.09	125
1979	19.01	143
1980	31.89	158
1981	35.88	152

Table 85. Relative Prices of Fuels in the U.K. 1974–1980 (15 Jan. 1974 = 100)

	1974	1975	1976	1977	1978	1979	1980
Coal	106	142	175	204	226	268	343
Gas	104	120	147	171	176	183	213
Electricity	141	152	194	241	245	310	415
Petrol and oil	127	173	184	197	187	246	315

Section II. Qualitative Judgements About the Energy Future

In this section the opinions given below have been evolved as a result of discussion of the scenario building group and the use of expert outside witnesses. In addition, material such as Zentner, R. D., "Scenarios, Past, Present and Future", *Long Range Planning*, Special Issue: *Progress in Planning: An International Review*, Vol. 15, No. 3, June 1982, pp. 12–20, has been used. It is assumed that the major trends over the next planning period will be:

Social trends

Minor support is given to solving the energy problem; no real effort is made to lower demand.

The need for alternative energy sources, although discussed, is never translated into action as short-term problems command governments' attention. Consequently, oil prices continue to rise rapidly with a knock-on effect on other fuels throughout the period of analysis.

Policy trends

Restrictive environmental regulations slow energy development.

Energy policy places extremely heavy tax burdens on energy companies.

International trends

World economies weaken, keeping demand levels low.

Oil prices escalate.

International borrowing increases and currencies become subject to wild fluctuations.

OPEC becomes stronger.

These quantitative and qualitative sections together form the foundations upon which the free thinking and open-ended discussion of the energy environment is based.

In a similar fashion to the above, a view of each of the other relevant constituent elements of the environment is constructed. These results are then assembled together to provide the Doomsday situation scenario. Next the Good-day scenario is built in exactly the same manner.

STEP 4. TESTING THE LIKELY IMPACT OF EACH ENVIRONMENTAL ELEMENT UPON EACH ORGANISATIONAL ELEMENT

The objective of this step is to assess what impact each environmental element is likely to have upon each organisational element and to quantify the magnitude of each impact. This is illustrated in Fig. 72 for the "Doomsday" scenario. The methodology for doing this is similar to that advocated by Neubauer and Solomon.[8]

The type and strength of each environmental element is quantified in the same way as the "Business Sector Prospects" and the "Business Position" were quantified in Chapter 5. The description of the method is repeated here. The *importance* of each factor is ranked on an ordinal scale of 0 to 5. Thus if a factor is of no importance at all, it scores zero; if it is of only minor importance, it scores 1; if it is of average importance, it scores 3, and finally if the factor is of crucial importance, it scores 5.

The *strength* of each factor is ranked on an ordinal scale from −5 to +5: −5 indicates that this factor has the strongest possible negative effect, +5 indicates that the factor has the strongest possible positive influence, and finally 0 indicates that the factor has no impact on the organisation. Once the importance and the strength of each factor have been ascertained, they are multiplied together to give an overall ranking for each factor. The assessment proceeds, using the large matrix in Fig. 72, to record the results of the analysis. Consensus on the score to be given to each element in the matrix can be achieved using a Delphi approach.

When the matrix has been completed, the positive numbers in each column are summed and the totals entered in the "Strategy Totals" row. The negative numbers in each column are similarly summed and also entered in the "Strategy Totals" row. The "Strategy Totals" rows then show which strategies are likely to present the organisation with strong positive opportunities and which strategies are likely to pose major threats. These are the key organisation factors. In Fig. 72 these are: strategy 3, resources and culture.

In a similar fashion, the positive and negative numbers in each row are separately summed and their totals entered in the "Environment Totals" column. This enables those elements in the environment which are likely to have the strongest negative and positive impacts to be identified quickly. These are the key environmental factors. In Fig. 72 these are: competitive, legal, political and energy.

STEP 5. FURTHER ANALYSIS OF THE KEY ORGANISATION AND KEY ENVIRONMENTAL FACTORS IDENTIFIED ON THE FIRST PASS

Although step 4 should identify the key organisation and the key environmental factors, the degree of resolution is low — they are simply flagged numerically for attention. These key factors now require further and deeper analysis to flesh out the realities behind the numbers. This can be done through discussion and further research using the data base and any other relevant sources of information.

STEP 6. TESTING THE LIKELY IMPACT OF THE KEY ENVIRONMENTAL
FACTORS ON KEY ORGANISATION FACTORS THAT WERE IDENTIFIED ON THE
FIRST PASS

The result of step 5 should be that the key factors are reconsidered
and their likely cross-impact is recomputed. This is shown by the smaller
matrix in Fig. 72. The same procedure as for step 4 is followed here, and
a further set of key environmental (in this case energy) and organisation
factors (in this case culture) is developed.

This step may end the process, in which case a scenario is agreed. If,
however, the group feels that further analysis and discussion of the key
factors considered in the second pass is required, then steps 5 and 6 are
repeated. This procedure is shown as steps 5A and 6A in Fig. 72.

A scenario analysis for the "Good-day" scenario is carried out in
exactly the same fashion as the above.

STEP 7. IMPLEMENTATION OF THE CHOSEN STRATEGY

With the completion of step 6 the effects of the various strategies
under starkly different scenarios will have been appraised. The final
step is to consider how the strategies ought, if necessary, to be amended
after their testing, how the organisation ought to change, if necessary, to
make the chosen strategies successful, and finally to decide which
strategies should be followed.

Implementing Scenario Planning

Scenario planning is more appropriate to some industries than to
others. Figure 73 relates the types of industries to methods of looking at

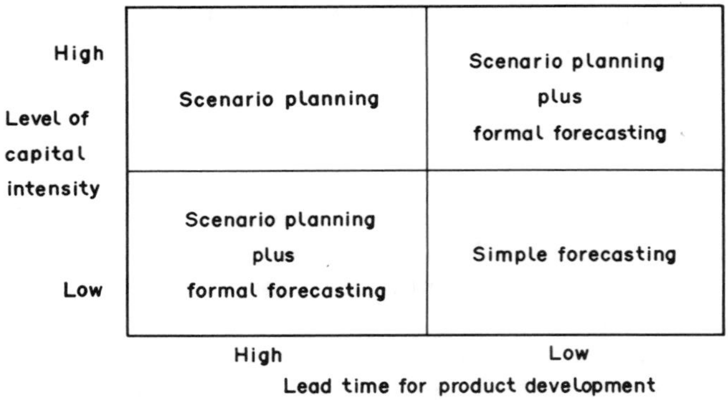

	High lead time	Low lead time
High capital intensity	Scenario planning	Scenario planning plus formal forecasting
Low capital intensity	Scenario planning plus formal forecasting	Simple forecasting

Level of capital intensity (vertical axis: High / Low)

Lead time for product development (horizontal axis: High / Low)

FIG. 73. *The relationship between the type of industry and methods of looking at the future*

the future. It is not by accident, but through necessity, that multinational oil companies, mining companies and chemical companies (all of which have high levels of capital intensity and long lead times for product development) have devoted such efforts to develop scenario planning. In contrast, industries such as home video rentals and small-scale builders, both of which have low mobility barriers, are not capital-intensive and have short lead times, for the introduction of new products has little need of this approach.

A major problem in establishing the process of scenario planning, even in an industry to which it is suited, is achieving management's commitment to it. Culture and tradition have inculcated in management and planners a (frequently misplaced) faith in the power of sophisticated mathematical forecasting techniques. There is a strong level of emotional comfort to be derived from viewing the future as an extension of the past and having the added security that exact numbers can provide. Weaning management from such traditions on to the more free thinking qualitative methodology of scenario planning is an extremely difficult task. Zentner[12] points out that even in Shell "it has taken nearly 8 years to convince all the main business divisions that in today's uncertain world the scenario approach affords an invaluable tool on which to base corporate planning".[12]

Perhaps the approach should be to, firstly, convince top management of the shortcomings of traditional forecasting methods and then to illustrate the benefits that the scenario approach can bring through examination of success it has enjoyed in firms such as Ciba-Geigy and Shell.

References

1. Bayer, Annual Report, 1975.
2. Beck, P. W. "Corporate Planning for an Uncertain Future", *Long Range Planning*, Vol. 15, No. 4, August 1982.
3. Ciba-Geigy, Annual Report 1981.
4. Franssen, H. "Energy: An Uncertain Future", U.S. Senate Publication, Dec. 1978, pp. 95–157.
5. Marsh, D. "The Dilemma that Faces Europe", *The Financial Times*, 31 Oct. 1983, p. 16.
6. McNulty, C. "Scenario Development for Corporate Planning", *Futures*, Vol. 9, Apr. 1977, pp. 128–138.
7. Moyer, R. "The Futility of Forecasting", *Long Range Planning*, Vol. 17, No. 1, pp. 65–72.
8. Neubauer, F. F. and Solomon, N. B. "A Management Approach to Environmental Assessment", *Long Range Planning*, Vol. 10, Apr. 1977, pp. 14–20.
9. "Planning in an Uncertain World", a series published by *The Financial Times*, 1980.
10. Porter, M. E. *Cases in Competitive Strategy*, The Free Press, Collier Macmillan, London, 1983, p. 72.

11.   Spivey, A. W. and Wrobleski, W. J. "Surveying Recent Econometric Forecasting Performance", Reprint 106, American Enterprise Institute, Feb. 1980.
12.   Zentner, R. D. "Scenarios Past, Present and Future", *Long Range Planning*, Vol. 15, No. 3, June 1982, pp. 12–20.

Bibliography

Anonymous, "Background on Energy — 'Scenario for a Productive Society' ", *Journal of Industrial Management*, Vol. 22, No. 2, Mar./Apr. 1980, pp. 20–25.

Anonymous, "Scenario Calls for Pacific Rim to Flex its Economic Muscle by the Year 2010", *Marketing News*, Vol. 17, No. 15, 22 July 1983, p. 16.

Anonymous, " 'Shell's Multiple Scenario Planning': A Realistic Alternative to the Crystal Ball", *World Business Weekly*, Vol. 3, No. 13, Apr. 1980, pp. 14–15.

Ascher, W. "Political Forecasting: The Missing Link", *Journal of Forecasting*, Vol. 1, No. 3, July–Sept. 1982, pp. 227–239.

Barney, G. O. *The Global 2000, Report to the President*, Greno, GmbH, West Germany, 1981.

Brown, R. G. "The Balance of Effort in Forecasting", *Journal of Forecasting*, Vol. 1, No. 1, Jan.–Mar. 1982, pp. 49–53.

Chandler, J. and Cockle, P. *Techniques of Scenario Planning*, McGraw-Hill, 1983.

Crabill, T. B. and Nilsen, K. D. "What If? — Planning Models for Plotting Future Scenarios", *Management Focus*, Vol. 26, No. 1, Jan./Feb. 1979, pp. 32–35.

Czinkota, M. R. "Scenarios: Key to Strategic Plans of International Marketing Managers", *Marketing News*, Vol. 13, No. 24, May 1980, p. 13.

Dakin, A. J. *Feedback from Tomorrow*, Pion and Methuen, London, 1979.

De Kluyver, C. A. "Bottom-Up Sales Forecasting Through Scenario Analysis , *Industrial Marketing Management*, Vol. 9, No. 2, Apr. 1980, pp. 167–170.

Dino, R. N., Riley, D. E. and Yatrakis, P. G. "The Role of Forecasting in Corporate Strategy: the Xerox Experience", *Journal of Forecasting*, Vol. 1, No. 4, Oct. 1982, pp. 335–348.

Drucker, P. *Managing in Turbulent Times*, Heinemann, 1980.

Dutta, B. K. and King, W. R. "A Competitive Scenario Modelling System", *Management Science*, Vol. 26, No. 3, Mar. 1980, pp. 261–273.

Edmunds, W. W. "The Role of Futures Studies in Business Strategic Planning", *Journal of Business Studies*, Vol. 2, No. 2, Fall 1982, pp. 40–46.

El-Hinnawi, E. and Hashmi, M. H. *Global Environmental Issues*, Tycooly, International, Dublin, 1982.

Evans, J. S. and Evans, B. T. "Psychological Pitfalls in Forecasting", *Futures*, Vol. 14, No. 4, Aug. 1982, pp. 258–265.

Fitzgerald, J. "Developing and Ranking Threat Scenarios", *EDPACS (EDP Audit, Control and Sec.) Newsletter*, Vol. 6, No. 3, Sept. 1978, pp. 1–5.

Galer, G. and Kaspar, W. "Scenario Planning for Australia", *Long Range Planning*, Vol. 15, No. 4, Aug. 1982.

Ghosh, A. and McLafferty, S. L. "Locating Stores in Uncertain Environments: A Scenario Planning Approach", *Journal of Retailing*, Vol. 58, No. 4, Winter 1982, pp. 5–22.

Ghosh, B. C. and Nee, A. Y. C. "Strategic Planning — A Contingency Approach — Part 1. The Strategic Analysis", *Long Range Planning*, Vol. 16, No. 4, Aug. 1983, pp. 93–103.

Ghosh, B. C. and Nee, A. Y. C. "Strategic Planning — A Contingency Approach — Part 2. The Plan", *Long Range Planning*, Vol. 16, No. 6, Dec. 1983, pp. 46–58.

Godet, M. "From Forecasting to 'La Prospective'. A New Way of Looking at Futures", *Journal of Forecasting*, Vol. 1, No. 3, July–Sept. 1983, pp. 293–301.

Haehling, von Lanzenauer, C. and Sprung, M. R. "Developing Inflation Scenarios", *Long Range Planning*, Vol. 15, No. 4, Aug. 1982, pp. 37–44.

Hamilton, H. R. "Scenarios in Corporate Planning", *Journal of Business Strategy*, Vol. 2, No. 1, Summer 1981, pp. 82–87.

Harris, P. R., "HRD Scenario for the Year 2000", *Training and Development Journal*, Vol. 36, No. 3, March 1982, pp. 68–70.

Hirschhorn, L. "Scenario Writing: A Developmental Approach", *Journal of The American Planning Association*, Vol. 46, No. 2, Apr. 1980, pp. 172–183.

Hohn, S. "The European Automobile Industry — Three Possible Scenarios", *Long Range Planning*, Vol. 13, No. 4, Aug. 1980, pp. 12–17.

Hohn, S. "Economic Development and Ecological Equilibrium — A Target Conflict in Modern Industrial Enterprise", *Long Range Planning*, Vol. 15, No. 4, Aug. 1982, pp. 22–36.

Holloway, C. and Pearce II, J. A. "Computer Assisted Strategic Planning", *Long Range Planning*, Vol. 15, No. 4, Aug. 1982, pp. 56–63.

Hopkins, M. and van der Hoeven, R. "Basic Needs Planning and Forecasting: Policy and Scenario Analysis in Four Countries", *International Labour Review (Switzerland)*, Vol. 121, No. 6, Nov./Dec. 1982, pp. 689–711.

Hussey, D. *Strategic Management Analysis: A Handbook*, Harbridge House, Europe, 1982.

Jones, R. *Readings from 'Futures'*, IPC, Science and Technology Press, Guildford, 1981.

Jonsson, S. and Petzall, I. "Forecasting Political Decisions and their Impact on Business, *Long Range Planning*, Vol. 15, No. 4, Aug. 1982, pp. 98–104.

Kahn, H. "Three Scenarios for Japan's Role in the '80s.", *Dun's Review*, Vol. 114, No. 1, July 1979, pp. 70–72.

Kahn, H. and Weiner, A. *The Year 2000*, Macmillan, 1967.

Keegan, W. J. "The Future" of the Multinational Manufacturing Corporation: Five Scenarios", *Journal of International Business Studies*, Vol. 10, No. 1, Spring/Summer 1979, pp. 93–104.

King, W. R. "Using Strategic Issue Analysis", *Long Range Planning*, Vol. 15, No. 4, Aug. 1982, pp. 45–49.

Kirkwood, C. W. and Pollock, S. M. "Multiple Attribute Scenarios, Bounded Probabilities, and Threats of Nuclear Theft", *Futures*, Vol. 16, No. 6, Dec. 1982, pp. 545–553.

Korhonen, P. and Soismaa, M. "An Interactive Multiple Criteria Approach to Ranking Alternatives", *O.R.*, Vol. 32, No. 7, July 1981, pp. 577–585.

Linneman, R. E. and Klein, H. "The Use of Multiple Scenarios by U.S. Industrial Companies: A Comparison Study, 1977–1981", *Long Range Planning*, Vol. 16, No. 6, Dec. 1983, pp. 94–101.

Linneman, R. E., Klein, H. E. and Stanton, J. L. Jr., "Using Multiple Scenarios for Strategic Environmental Assessment: Implications for Marketing Management", *Marketing Intelligence and Planning*, Vol. 1, No. 1, 1983, pp. 67–76.

Loomis, C. J. "How International Paper Spurned Scenario A, Chose B and is Getting C", *Fortune*, Vol. 97, No. 2, Jan. 1980, pp. 102–108.

Lyons, H. "The Delphi Technique for Problem Solving", *Personnel Management*, Jan. 1982, pp. 42–45.

MacKenzie, I. "Two Scenarios Offered for the Full Financial Future", *National Underwriter (Life/Health)*, Vol. 87, No. 7, Feb. 1983, pp. 2–14.

Mandel, T. F. "Scenarios and Corporate Strategy: Planning in Uncertain Times", S.R.I. Research Report 669, Nov. 1982.

Matthews, M. B. "The Use of Scenario Generation for Examining Future Hospital Utilization", *Health Care Management Review*, Vol. 8, No. 3, Summer 1983, pp. 57–60.

May, G. "The Argument for More Future-Orientated Planning", *Futures*, Vol. 14, No. 4, Aug. 1982, pp. 313–318.

Meadows, D., Richardson, J. and Bruckman, G. *Groping in the Dark: The First Decade of Global Modelling*, Wiley, Chichester, 1982.

Nagan, P. S. and Kaufman, K. A. "Two Credible Scenarios Dominate Thinking About Interest Rates", *ABA Banking Journal*, Vol. 74, No. 8, Aug. 1982, pp. 10–12.

Nair, K. and Sarin, R. K. "Generating Future Scenarios — Their Use in Strategic Planning", *Long Range Planning*, Vol. 12, No. 3, June 1979, pp. 57–61.

Nanus, B., "QUEST — Quick Environmental Scanning Technique", *Long Range Planning*, Vol. 15, No. 2, Apr. 1982, pp. 39–45.

Neubauer, F. and Solomon, N. B. "A Managerial Approach to Environmental Assessment", *Long Range Planning*, Vol. 10, Apr. 1977, pp. 13–20.

Prebble, J. F. "Future Forecasting with LEAP", *Long Range Planning*, Vol. 15, No. 4, Aug. 1982, pp. 64–69.

Sathaye, J. and Rukderman, H. "Direct and Indirect Economic Impacts of a National Energy Plan Scenario", *Energy Systems and Policy*, Vol. 3, No. 4, 1980, pp. 309–336.

Schwartz, B., Svedin, H. and Wittrock, B. *Methods in Future Studies*, Westview, Colorado, 1982.

Twiss, B. *Social Forecasting for Company Planning*, The Macmillan Press, 1982.

Steiner, G. A. "Formal Strategic Planning in the U.S. Today", *Long Range Planning*, Vol. 16, No. 3, 1983, pp. 12–17.

van Dam, A. "How to Adjust to the Uncertain 1980s", *MP*, Nov./Dec. 1981, pp. 7 etc.

Wheelwright, S. C. and Makridakis, S. *A Handbook of Forecasting: A Manager's Guide*, Wiley, Chichester, 1982.

Williams, T. A., *Learning to Manage Our Futures*, Wiley, Chichester, 1982.

Wissema, J. G. "The Modern Prophets — How Can They Help Us?", *Long Range Planning*, Vol. 15, No. 4, Aug. 1982, pp. 126–134.

Wright, P., Townsend, D., Kinard, J. and Iverstine, J. "The Developing World to 1990: Trends and Implications for Multinational Business", *Long Range Planning*, Vol. 15, No. 4, Aug. 1982, pp. 116–125.

Appendix I
Forecasts for the Introduction to Chapter 7

The forecasts given in the introduction are calculated below, either graphically or manually. Where appropriate, the computer solution is given in Chapter 8.

Forecast Number 1

This forecast was made on the basis of simple straight line graphical extrapolation by eye. Figure 74 shows the graphs of the actual data and the extrapolations. As can be seen, the forecast for sales in 1975 and 1976 were DM 20,100 million and DM 22,400 million respectively, while the forecast income after tax for each of these years was DM 700 million and DM 780 million respectively.

Forecast Number 2

This forecast was made using an Ordinary Least Squares model. The workings are given below.

(a) *Forecast for sales*

Year	X	Y	X^2	XY
1970	1	10,373	1	10,373
1971	2	11,144	4	22,288
1972	3	12,086	9	36,258
1973	4	13,904	16	55,616
1974	5	18,879	25	94,395
	15	66,386	55	218,930
	$= \Sigma X$	$= \Sigma XY$	$= \Sigma X^2$	$= \Sigma XY$

The normal equations are:

$$. \Sigma Y = nA + b\Sigma X$$
$$\Sigma XY = a\Sigma X + b\Sigma X^2$$

237

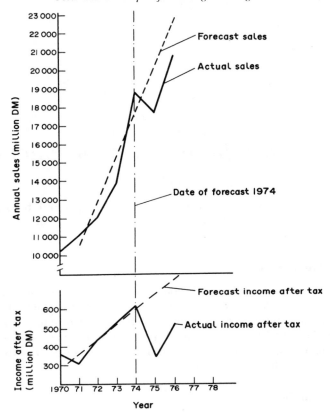

FIG. 74. *Forecast Number 1: straight line extrapolation by eye*

In this case:

$$66,386 = 5a + 15b$$
$$218,930 = 15a + 55b$$

Solving for a and b yields:

$$a = 7345.6$$
$$b = 1977.2$$

Therefore the Ordinary Least Squares equation is:

$$Y = 7345.6 + 1977.2 \ (X)$$

To make forecasts for the years 1975 and 1976 X will take the values 6 and 7 respectively.

Thus forecast sales in 1975 were:

$Y = 7345.6 + 1977.2 \ (6)$
$Y = 19{,}208.8$

Similarly, forecast sales in 1976 were:

$Y = 7345.6 + 1977.2 \ (7)$
$Y = 21{,}186$

(b) *Forecast for income after tax*

Year	X	Y	X^2	XY
1970	1	358	1	358
1971	2	315	4	630
1972	3	448	9	1344
1973	4	541	16	2164
1974	5	621	25	3105
	15 $=\Sigma X$	2283 $=\Sigma XY$	55 $=\Sigma X^2$	7601 $=\Sigma XY$

Again, the normal equations are:

$\Sigma Y = nA + b\Sigma X$
$\Sigma XY = a\Sigma X + b\Sigma X^2$

In this case:

$2283 = 5a + 15b$
$7601 = 15a + 55b$

Solving for a and b yields:

$a = 231$
$b = 75.2$

Therefore the Ordinary Least squares equation is:

$Y = 231 + 75.2 \ (X)$

To make forecasts for the years 1975 and 1976 X will take the values 6 and 7 respectively.

Thus forecast income after tax in 1975 was:

$Y = 231 + 75.2 \ (6)$
$Y = 682.2$

Similarly, forecast sales in 1976 were:

$$Y = 231 + 75.2 \ (7)$$
$$Y = 757.4$$

Thus the forecast for sales in 1975 and 1976 were DM 19,208.8 million and DM 21,186 million respectively, while the forecast income after tax for each of these years was DM 682.2 million and DM 757.4 million respectively.

Forecast Number 3

This forecast was made using a Logarithmic Straight Line Trend model. The workings are given below.

(a) *Forecast for sales*

Year	X	Y	X^2	log Y	X log$Y$
1970	1	10,373	1	4.0158	4.0158
1971	2	11,144	4	4.0469	8.0938
1972	3	12,086	9	4.0824	12.2472
1973	4	13,904	16	4.1430	16.5720
1974	5	18,879	25	4.2760	21.3800
	15 $=\Sigma X$	66,386	55 $=\Sigma X^2$	20.5641 $=\Sigma \log Y$	62.3088 $=\Sigma X \ log Y$

The normal equations for the logarithmic straight line trend are:

$$\Sigma \log Y = n \ \log A + \log b \Sigma X$$
$$\Sigma X \ \log Y = \log a \Sigma X + \Sigma \log b \ X^2$$

In this case:

$$20.5641 = 5 \ \log a + 15 \ \log b$$
$$62.3088 = 15 \ \log a + 55 \ \log b$$

Solving for log$a$ and log$b$ yields:

$$\log a = 3.928$$
$$\log b = 0.0616$$

Therefore the logarithmic trend equation is:

$$\log Y = 3.928 + 0.0616 \ (X)$$

To make forecasts for the years 1975 and 1976 X will take the values 6 and 7 respectively.

Thus forecast sales in 1975 were:

$$\log Y = 3.928 + 0.0616 \ (6)$$
$$\log Y = 4.2976$$
$$Y = 19,850$$

Similarly, forecast sales in 1976 were:

$$\log Y = 3.928 + 0.0616 \ (7)$$
$$\log Y = 4.3592$$
$$Y = 22,870$$

(b) *Forecast for income after tax*

Year	X	Y	X^2	$\log Y$	$X \log Y$
1970	1	358	1	2.5539	2.5539
1971	2	315	4	2.4983	4.9966
1972	3	448	9	2.6513	7.9539
1973	4	541	16	2.7332	10.9328
1974	5	621	25	2.7931	13.9655
	15	2283	55	13.2298	40.4027
	$=\Sigma X$	$=\Sigma XY$	$=\Sigma X^2$	$=\Sigma \log Y$	$=\Sigma X \log Y$

Again the normal equations for the logarithmic straight line trend are:

$$\Sigma \log Y = n \ \log a + \log b \Sigma X$$
$$\Sigma X \ \log Y = \log a \Sigma X + \log b \Sigma X^2$$

In this case:

$$13.2298 = 5 \ \log a + 15 \ \log b$$
$$39.6894 = 15 \ \log a + 55 \ \log b$$

Solving for $\log a$ and $\log b$ yields:

$$\log a = 2.432$$
$$\log b = 0.07133$$

Therefore the logarithmic trend equation is:

$$\log Y = 2.432 + 0.0713 \ (X)$$

To make forecasts for the years 1975 and 1976 X will take the values 6 and 7 respectively.
Thus income after tax in 1975 was:

$$\log Y = 2.432 + 0.0713 \ (6)$$
$$\log Y = 2.8598$$
$$Y = 724.3$$

Similarly, forecast income after tax in 1976 was:

$$\log Y = 2.432 + 0.0713 \quad (7)$$
$$\log Y = 2.9311$$
$$Y = 853.1$$

Thus the forecast for sales in 1975 and 1976 were DM 19,850 million and DM 22,870 million respectively, while the forecast income after tax for each of these years was DM 724.3 million and DM 853.1 million respectively.

Note on references

Almost any first year university statistics textbook will provide further details on the above and other approaches to forecasting. An excellent reference, because of its clarity, is Mason, R. D., *Statistical Techniques in Business and Economics*, R. D. Irwin, 1974.

Appendix II
A Short Note on the Delphi Method

By a Delphi method is meant an interactive and a personality-free team approach to decision-making. In the context of the energy scenario used in this chapter, the approach could proceed as follows.

Firstly, a team of planners and managers are assembled together. Secondly, these planners are asked by an independent Delphi administrator to make a private written judgement about some aspect of the scenario under consideration, say the expected price of coal over the next 5 years. The administrator has the crucial task of ensuring that none of the participants knows the answers given by other participants. (This is a most important aspect of Delphi — unless there is confidentiality, then one participant may influence others through personality, status, emotion, etc., and a "bandwagon of agreement" may result.)

When the participants have completed their estimates, the results are collected and tabulated by the administrator. This tabulated information is then given to each participant and each is again asked to, confidentially, "rethink" his estimate. If on his second selection a participant selects an estimate which is in the bottom quartile or top quartile of the previous tabulated set of estimates, then he must provide a short written explanation of why he thinks his estimate is correct. These explanations are then made available to all the planners in the next round. This may, of course, have the effect of causing the participants to alter their views drastically, and changing the estimate have arrived at a consensus by the fourth or fifth round.

Although the approach lacks scientific rigour, the Rand Corporations of U.S.A. has validated its use through controlled experimentation and it has gained considerable currency as an aid to good managerial decision-making in the United States. For more evidence of its effectiveness, consult the reference given below.

Tools and Techniques for Strategic Management

References for the Delphi method

Baldwin, G. H. "The Delphi Technique and the Forecasting of Specific Fringe Benefits", *Futures*, Vol. 14, No. 4, Aug. 1982, pp. 319–325.

Campbell, R. M. and Hitchin, D. "The Delphi Technique: Implementation in the Corporate Environment", *Management Services*, Nov./Dec. 1968, pp. 37–42.

Hodgetts, R. M. "Applying the Delphi Technique to Management Gaming", *(SCS) Simulation*, Vol. 29, No. 1, July 1977, pp. 209–212.

Lyons, H., "The Delphi Technique for Problem Solving", *Personnel Management*, Jan. 1982, pp. 42–45.

CHAPTER 8

Computer Programs for Strategic Management

Introduction

Of all today's businesses perhaps the most turbulent, changeable and exciting is that of computers, especially microcomputers. This industry is a fast moving, unstable revolutionary whose rules have not yet emerged and whose ultimate structure has yet to be decided. One trend, however, that appears to be fairly certain is that microcomputers will, in the future, be as indispensable to strategic management as an electronic calculator is today. There are a number of reasons for taking this view, the main ones being as follow.

Price. There have been dramatic price reductions in the cost of microcomputers. Today it is possible to purchase a computer system, capable of handling much of the data normally used by businesses (including modelling for strategic management), for less than £1000. Two immediate consequences of this are: the purchase of a microcomputer is no longer a financially risky business decision and, secondly, that outright purchase has become, for many businesses, cheaper than using a computer bureau. Consequently there will be a great expansion in the use of microcomputers.

Power and size. As computer manufacturers have dramatically added to the power of their machines, they have simultaneously reduced their size. For example, today a microcomputer no larger than a typewriter and weighing 30–60 lb can be as powerful as the IBM 360/20 computer introduced in 1964 and weighing 2½ tons. This trend seems likely to accelerate, as within the next two years it is anticipated that 16- and 32-bit microcomputers will be introduced which will be comparable in power to today's 2½-ton computers.[2]

Portability. Unlike mainframe computers, microcomputers are extremely portable and do not require a specially designed room environment and a specialised data processing staff. They can be used almost anywhere by people without any formal computer training.

Software. There has been an explosive growth in the volume of software available and also a dramatic increase in terms of its sophistication and its user friendliness. Today there are many proven sophisticated easy to use business programs available at prices of less than £100.

Education. Through formal and informal channels there has been, worldwide, a great increase in the level of people's understanding of computer hardware and software. This higher educational base will further propel people towards greater computer usage.

It seems appropriate, therefore, to include in this book computer programs which will assist readers in their strategic planning. The programs included are small, are written in BASIC and can, with appropriate amendments, be run on most micro systems. These programs were written to support teaching on various courses held at the University of Ulster. The programs were written for, and currently operate on, the Apple II Europlus computer and the Apple IIe computer.

Notes on the Programs

(1) Readers may avail themselves of the programs either by purchasing the disk BASIC Programs for Tools and Techniques for Strategic Management, or, alternatively, by typing in the program listings given in this chapter. Note that the programs are constantly being updated and being made available for a greater range of computers.

(2) All the programs are written so that they may be run, with appropriate amendments, on most home computers. This feature has meant that the input and the output have been formatted to have a maximum width of 40 characters. This has imposed limitations on the style of the layout.

(3) Readers are encouraged to use these programs as building blocks to develop their own programs suited to their own particular circumstances. The author will be pleased to receive comments on the programs and will incorporate, in future releases, any improvements suggested by readers.

The Suites of Programs

The suites of programs included are:

FINA: Finance for strategic management: linked to Chapter 2.
EXCU: Experience curve analysis: linked to Chapter 3.
PROM: Product Market Portfolio analysis: linked to Chapter 4.
SCEN: Scenario planning programs: linked to Chapter 7.

Each suite of programs is set out in the following format:

Description of the suite and the functions it will perform.

A print-out of the program for the data given in the relevant chapter.

Additionally, a source listing of all the programs on the disk is given at the end of this chapter. This will enable those readers who have a computer, other than the ones for which commercial disks have been prepared, to set up the program on their own computers.

Suite FINA

Description

This suite of programs is called FINA and carries out the financial analyses considered in Chapter 2. Given a set of input data comprising:

a firm's Balance Sheet and Income Statement for one or two years,

FINA will carry out the following functions:

1. Ratio analysis for each year specified.
2. Sources and Applications of Funds Statement.

Given a set of input data comprising:

the rate of return on assets, the total assets, the rate of interest, the amount of debt, the amount of equity and the proportion of earnings retained,

FINA will calculate

the maximum sustainable rate of growth.

Given a set of input data comprising:

fixed costs, variable costs, price per unit and sales forecast,

FINA will calculate the following:

(a) The break-even point.
(b) Different profit before interest and tax levels for different sales forecasts.

Print-out of FINA

Below is given a print-out of the input data and also each of the three options in FINA. Where appropriate, the data is taken from Chapter 2.

```
*******************************************
*                                         *
*      TOOLS AND TECHNIQUES FOR           *
*         STRATEGIC MANAGEMENT            *
*                                         *
*******************************************
```

```
********************************
*  BASIC COMPUTER PROGRAMS  *
********************************
```

THIS DISK CONTAINS A SET OF SMALL
COMPUTER PROGRAMS WRITTEN IN BASIC
WHICH SUPPORT THE BOOK..

TOOLS AND TECHNIQUES FOR
  STRATEGIC MANAGEMENT
      BY P.B. MC NAMEE

PRESS (RETURN) TO CONTINUE

THERE ARE 4 SUITES ON THE DISK.
THESE ARE...

1 FINA: A SUITE OF PROGRAMS THAT CARRY
        OUT VARIOUS STRATEGIC FINANCIAL
        ANALYSIS
2 EXCU: A SUITE OF PROGRAMS FOR
        EXPERIENCE CURVE CALCULATIONS
3 PROM: A SUITE OF PROGRAMS THAT CARRY
        OUT VARIOUS PRODUCT MARKET
        PORTFOLIO CALCULATIONS
4 SCEN: A SUITE OF PROGRAMS TO AID
        SCENARIO PLANNING

SELECT OPTION (1-4)1

```
******************
* OPTION 1 : FINA *
******************
```

THIS PROGRAM CARRIES OUT VARIOUS
FINANCIAL ANALYSIS AND SHOULD BE
USED IN CONJUNCTION WITH...
          CHAPTER 2
          FINANCE FOR
    STRATEGIC MANAGEMENT

OPTIONS AVAILABLE ARE...
  0 TERMINATE CURRENT RUN
  1 RATIO ANALYSIS
  2 SOURCES AND USES OF
    FUNDS STATEMENTS
  3 FOR FUTURE DEVELOPMENT
  4 CALCULATION OF THE MAXIMUM
    SUSTAINABLE RATE OF GROWTH
  5 BREAK EVEN ANALYSIS
  6 INPUT NEW COMPANY BALANCE
    SHEET AND INCOME STATEMENT
SELECT AN OPTION (0-6)1


```
***************************************
*BALANCE SHEET DATA INPUT SECTION*
***************************************
```

YOU ARE REQUIRED TO INPUT ANNUAL BALANCE
SHEET FIGURES FOR THE COMPANY UNDER
CONSIDERATION. YOU MAY INPUT FIGURES FOR
UP TO TWO YEARS TRADING

PLEASE GIVE COMPANY NAME:X

NUMBER OF YEARS (1 OR 2):2

YEAR 1 IS?1982
YEAR 2 IS?1983
FIXED ASSETS(COST) FOR YEAR   1982

```
    LAND                      4
    BUILDINGS                48
    EQUIPMENT               100
    DEPRECIATION            60

NET FIXED ASSETS            92
```

IS THIS CORRECT (Y/N):Y

```
INVESTMENTS AND OTHER ASSETS   8

CURRENT ASSETS FOR YEAR        1982

    INVENTORY                  150
    ACCS RECEIVABLE            100
    SHORT TERM INVESTMENTS       0
    PREPAID EXPENSES             2
    CASH                        16

TOTAL CURRENT ASSETS           268

IS THIS CORRECT (Y/N):Y


TOTAL ASSETS                   368

FINANCED BY:
  SHAREHOLDERS EQUITY
      COMMON STOCK             161
      RETAINED EARNINGS         40

      TOTAL EQUITY             201

IS THIS CORRECT (Y/N):Y

LONG TERM DEBT                  59
OTHER NONCURRENT LIABILITIES    15

CURRENT LIABILITIES

    ACCOUNTS PAYABLE             6
    NOTES PAYABLE               29
    ACCRUED EXPENSES            44
    TAXES                       14

      TOTAL CURRENT LIABILITIES  93

IS THIS CORRECT (Y/N):Y


      TOTAL LIABILITIES        368

AVG. NUM. SHARES OUTSTANDING   55000
```

```
FIXED ASSETS(COST) FOR YEAR    1983

    LAND                       4
    BUILDINGS                  50
    EQUIPMENT                  120
    DEPRECIATION               70

NET FIXED ASSETS               104

IS THIS CORRECT (Y/N):Y

INVESTMENTS AND OTHER ASSETS   8

CURRENT ASSETS FOR YEAR        1983

    INVENTORY                  140
    ACCS RECEIVABLE            110
    SHORT TERM INVESTMENTS     11
    PREPAID EXPENSES           2
    CASH                       39

TOTAL CURRENT ASSETS           302

IS THIS CORRECT (Y/N):Y


TOTAL ASSETS                   414

FINANCED BY:
 SHAREHOLDERS EQUITY
      COMMON STOCK             170
      RETAINED EARNINGS        64

      TOTAL EQUITY             234

IS THIS CORRECT (Y/N):Y

LONG TERM DEBT                 44
OTHER NONCURRENT LIABILITIES   15

CURRENT LIABILITIES

    ACCOUNTS PAYABLE           12
    NOTES PAYABLE              31
    ACCRUED EXPENSES           60
    TAXES                      18

      TOTAL CURRENT LIABILITIES 121

IS THIS CORRECT (Y/N):Y


      TOTAL LIABILITIES        414

AVG. NUM. SHARES OUTSTANDING  57800
```

```
**************************************
*INCOME STATEMENT INPUT SECTION*
**************************************

YOU ARE REQUIRED TO INPUT THE INCOME
STATEMENT FOR COMPANY X
 FOR THE YEAR(S) SPECIFIED PREVIOUSLY

INCOME STATEMENT FOR YEAR   1982

NET SALES                   550
COST OF SALES               400
GROSS PROFIT                150

EXPENSES

 SELLING GEN AND ADMIN       95
 INTEREST                     6
 DEPRECIATION                 5
TOTAL EXPENSES              106
PROFIT BEFORE TAX           44
PROVISIONS FOR TAX          22
NET EARNINGS                 22
CASH DIVIDENDS               6
RETAINED EARNINGS            16

INCOME STATEMENT CORRECT (Y/N):Y

INCOME STATEMENT FOR YEAR   1983

NET SALES                   620
COST OF SALES               440
GROSS PROFIT                180

EXPENSES

 SELLING GEN AND ADMIN      105
 INTEREST                     4
 DEPRECIATION               10
TOTAL EXPENSES              119
PROFIT BEFORE TAX           61
PROVISIONS FOR TAX          30
NET EARNINGS                 31
CASH DIVIDENDS               7
RETAINED EARNINGS            24

INCOME STATEMENT CORRECT (Y/N):Y

PLEASE GIVE INVENTORY LEVEL OR AN
ESTIMATE FOR YEAR 1981
?148
```

```
*********************************
*  RATIO ANALYSIS RESULTS*
*********************************
COMPANY: X
                    1982        1983
*LIQUIDITY RATIOS*
CURRENT RATIO        2.88       2.5
QUICK RATIO          1.28       1.3
*PROFITABILITY RATIOS*
GROSS PROFIT MARGIN 27.27      29.03
NET PROFIT MARGIN    4          5
RETURN ON INVSTMNTS 5.98        7.49
RETURN ON EQUITY    10.95      13.25
EARNINGS PER SHARE  .04         .05
PAYOUT RATIO        27.27      22.58
*LEVERAGE RATIOS*
DEBT - EQUITY       29.35      18.8
DEBT COVERAGE        8.33      16.25
*ACTIVITY RATIOS*
FIXED ASSET TURNOVER5.98        5.96
INVENTORY TURNOVER   3.67       4.43
ACCTS RECEV TURNOVER5.5         5.64
AVG CLLCTN PRD(DAYS)65.45      63.87


PRESS (RETURN) TO CONTINUE
OPTIONS AVAILABLE ARE...
  0 TERMINATE CURRENT RUN
  1 RATIO ANALYSIS
  2 SOURCES AND USES OF
    FUNDS STATEMENTS
  3 FOR FUTURE DEVELOPMENT
  4 CALCULATION OF THE MAXIMUM
    SUSTAINABLE RATE OF GROWTH
  5 BREAK EVEN ANALYSIS
  6 INPUT NEW COMPANY BALANCE
    SHEET AND INCOME STATEMENT
SELECT AN OPTION (0-6)2
```

```
                  COMPANY: X
             SOURCES AND USES OF FUNDS

SOURCES OF FUNDS                     1983
PROFIT BEFORE TAX                     61
ADJMTS FOR ITEMS NOT INVOLVING
FUND MOVEMENTS:
   DEPRECIATION                       10
TOTAL GENERATED                       71
FUNDS FROM OTHER SOURCES:
   ISSUE OF SHARES FOR CASH            9
                                      80
APPLICATION OF FUNDS:
   PURCHASE OF FIXED ASSETS          -22
   REDEMPTN OF LONG TERM DEBT        -15
   DIVIDENDS PAID                     -7
   TAX PAID                          -26
                                     -70
                                      10


PRESS <RETURN> TO CONTINUE

INCREASE IN WORKING CAPITAL:
   INVENTORY                         -10
   ACCOUNTS RECEIVABLE                10
   PREPAYMENTS                         0
   ACCOUNTS PAYABLE                   -6
   NOTES PAYABLE                      -2
   ACCRUED EXPENSES                  -16
MOVEMENT IN NET LIQUID FUNDS:
   INCREASE IN CASH                   23
   SHORT TERM INVSTMNT INCREASE11
                                      10
```

```
*************************
*BREAK-EVEN ANALYSIS*
*************************
```

THIS OPTION CALCULATES THE LINEAR
BREAKEVEN POINT AND OPTIONALLY
ALLOWS YOU TO LINK THIS TO SALES
FORECASTS FOR VARIOUS PRICES

```
COMPANY NAME          Z
PRODUCT NAME          Y
DATE (YEAR)           1983
FIXED COSTS           10000
VARIABLE UNIT COSTS   3
UNIT SELLING PRICE    5
```

COMPANY: Z
BREAKEVEN POINT FOR PRODUCT: Y
FOR 1983 AT A PRICE OF 5 IS

```
             ********************
             5000 UNITS
             ********************
```

PRESS (RETURN) TO CONTINUE
    +   REVENUE
    X   VARIABLE COSTS
    -    FIXED COSTS
PRESS (RETURN) TO CONTINUE

DO YOU WISH TO LINK THIS TO
SALES FORECASTS TO CALCULATE THE
OPTIMAL INTEREST BEFORE TAX (BIT)
(Y/N)Y
HOW MANY SALES FORECASTS 6
1 FORECAST PRICE?5
1 FORECAST SALES?10000
2 FORECAST PRICE?4.5
2 FORECAST SALES?14000
3 FORECAST PRICE?4
3 FORECAST SALES?22000
4 FORECAST PRICE?3.7
4 FORECAST SALES?29000
5 FORECAST PRICE?3.4
5 FORECAST SALES?30000
6 FORECAST PRICE?3.25
6 FORECAST SALES?32000
```

| PRICE | SALES FORECAST | BREAKEVEN POINT | PROFIT B.I.T. |
|-------|----------------|-----------------|---------------|
| 5 | 10000 | 5000 | 10000 |
| 4.5 | 14000 | 6667 | 10999.5 |
| 4 | 22000 | 10000 | 12000 |
| 3.7 | 29000 | 14286 | 10299.8 |
| 3.4 | 30000 | 25000 | 2000 |
| 3.25 | 32000 | 40000 | -2000 |
```

```
*********************************
*CALCULATION OF THE MAXIMUM*
*SUSTAINABLE RATE OF GROWTH*
*********************************
```

THE GROWTH RATE G IS DEFINED AS—

$$G = (D/E)*(R-I)*P+R*P$$

WHERE—
```
   D = AMOUNT OF COMPANY'S DEBT
   E = AMOUNT OF COMPANY'S EQUITY
   R = RATE OF RETURN ON ASSETS(%)
   I = AFTERTAX CURRENT COST OF DEBT(%)
   P = PROPORTION OF EARNINGS
       RETAINED BY COMPANY
 N.B.   P = (1-DIVIDEND PAYOUT RATIO)
GIVEN THE ABOVE PARAMETERS,FINA
WILL CALCULATE G

AMOUNT OF DEBT (D)            ?20
AMOUNT OF EQUITY (E)          ?80
RATE OF RETURN ON ASSETS (R)?15
AFTERTAX COST OF DEBT (I)    ?9
PROPTN EARNINGS RETAINED (P)?.8
```

```
         ********************
         * G =   13.20 % *
         ********************
```

Suite EXCU

Description

This suite of programs is called EXCU and it carries out the experience curve analyses considered in Chapter 3. For a set of input data comprising:

a series of data pairs giving the experience and the cost per unit, in real terms,

EXCU will carry out the following functions:

(1) It will compute: C_n, the cost of the nth unit, C_1, the cost of the first unit, λ, the elasticity coefficient, K, the slope of the experience function expressed as a percentage and ΔC, the rate of average cost decline, expressed as a percentage.

*(2) The future cost of the last unit produced during the current analysis.

*(3) A future mean cost per unit analysis.

*(4) A rate of mean cost decline analysis.

*(5) Future spending function parameters.

Print-out of EXCU

Below is given a print-out of the input data and also each of the five options in EXCU. Where appropriate, data is taken from Chapter 3.

---

*Options 2, 3, 4 and 5 were not considered in Chapter 3. Readers who are interested in pursuing these topics or in pursuing experience curve analysis to a greater depth should read Sallenave, J. P. Experience Curve Analysis for Industrial Planning, Lexington and Teakfield, Farnborough, 1976.

```
***********************
* OPTION 2 : EXCU *
***********************
THIS PROGRAM CARRIES OUT VARIOUS
EXPERIENCE CURVE CALCULATIONS AND
SHOULD BE USED IN CONJUNCTION WITH-

      CHAPTER 3
      EXPERIENCE CURVES


PRESS (RETURN) TO CONTINUE

THE EXPERIENCE FUNCTION IS

 CN = C1*N→(-LAMBDA)

WHERE:
 CN = COST OF NTH UNIT
 C1 = COST OF THE FIRST UNIT
 N = THE EXPERIENCE
 LAMBDA = ELASTICITY COEFFICIENT
 K = SLOPE OF THE LOG OF THE EXP. FUNC.
      EXPRESSED AS A PERCENTAGE
 DELTA C = RATE OF AVERAGE COST DECLINE
            EXPRESSED AS A PERCENTAGE

FOR A SERIES OF DATA PAIRS GIVING THE
EXPERIENCE AND THE UNIT COST EXCU WILL
COMPUTE THE ABOVE PARAMETERS, THEN YOU
WILL HAVE VARIOUS OPTIONS.


PRESS (RETURN) TO CONTINUE

**********************************************
* EXPERIENCE FUNCTION CALCULATION        *
**********************************************
INPUT 'N' AND 'CN' , BOTH VALUES
ON THE SAME LINE SEPARATED BY A
COMMA. TERMINATE YOU DATA SERIES
WITH THE SEQUENCE..
-1,-1

?2,100
?4,80
?8,64
?16,51
?32,41
?64,33
?128,26
?-1,-1
```

```
YOU HAVE INPUT
          EXPERIENCE        UNIT COST
          2                 100
          4                 80
          8                 64
          16                51
          32                41
          64                33
          128               26
ARE THESE CORRECT (Y/N)Y

     (1) C1                  =125.0975
     (2) LAMBDA              =-.3224
SLOPE. OF LOG EXP FUNC       =.7997
RATE OF COST DECLINE(%) =20.0273

PRESS (RETURN) TO CONTINUE


-------------------------------------------
SELECT AN OPTION BY TYPING IN THE
APPROPRIATE OPTION NO. AND THEN
THE APPROPRIATE DATA WHEN REQUESTED.
OPTION ?1

****************************************
*FUTURE COST OF LAST UNIT PRODUCED     *
****************************************

VOL. DURING LAST PERIOD OF OBSERVATION?
?128
 HOW MANY TIME PERIODS TO BE INCLUDED?
?4
GROWTH RATE,EXPRESSED AS DECIMAL
?.15
LAST COST OBSERVATION?
?26
VALUE FOR LAMBDA
?.3224
DO YOU KNOW TOTAL EXPERIENCE TO DATE?
ANSWER (Y/N)
?256
WRONG REPLY - RETYPE
?Y
PLEASE GIVE VALUE
?256
     PERIOD      COST
     1           30.1007
     2           30.6226
     3           31.2005
     4           31.8384

LIKE TO VARY SOME PARAMETERS
ANSWER (Y/N)
?N
```

```
-------------------------------------------
SELECT AN OPTION BY TYPING IN THE
APPROPRIATE OPTION NO. AND THEN
THE APPROPRIATE DATA WHEN REQUESTED.
OPTION ?2

*:*:*:*:*:*:*:*:*:*:*:*:*:*:*:*:*:*:*:*:*:*:*:*:*:*:*:*:*:*:*:*:*
*FUTURE AVERAGE COST PER UNIT ANALYSIS*
*:*:*:*:*:*:*:*:*:*:*:*:*:*:*:*:*:*:*:*:*:*:*:*:*:*:*:*:*:*:*:*:*

THIS YEARS AVERAGE COST PER UNIT
?26
GROWTH RATE,EXPRESSED AS DECIMAL
?.15
VALUE FOR LAMBDA
?.3224
FUTURE AVERAGE COST PER UNIT IS24.8545

LIKE TO VARY SOME PARAMETERS
ANSWER (Y/N)
?N


-------------------------------------------
SELECT AN OPTION BY TYPING IN THE
APPROPRIATE OPTION NO. AND THEN
THE APPROPRIATE DATA WHEN REQUESTED.
OPTION ?3

*:*:*:*:*:*:*:*:*:*:*:*:*:*:*:*:*:*:*:*:*:*:*:*:*:*:*:*:*:*:*:*:*
*RATE OF AVERAGE COST DECLINE ANALYSIS*
*:*:*:*:*:*:*:*:*:*:*:*:*:*:*:*:*:*:*:*:*:*:*:*:*:*:*:*:*:*:*:*:*

VALUE FOR LAMBDA
?.3224
GROWTH RATE,EXPRESSED AS DECIMAL
?.15
RATE OF AVERAGE COST DECLINE = 4.4059

LIKE TO VARY SOME PARAMETERS
ANSWER (Y/N)
?N
```

```
------------------------------------------
SELECT AN OPTION BY TYPING IN THE
APPROPRIATE OPTION NO. AND THEN
THE APPROPRIATE DATA WHEN REQUESTED.
OPTION ?4

*************************************************
*FUTURE SPENDING FUNCTION PARAMETERS   *
*************************************************

   THE FUTURE SPENDING FUNCTION IS:

     S(T+1) = S(T) * (1+GAMMA)+(1-LAMBDA)

   WHERE:
     (1) S(T) IS INVESTMENT IN PERIOD T
     (2) S(T+1) IS INVESTMENT IN PERIOD T+1
     (3) GAMMA IS RATE OF MARKET GROWTH
     (4) LAMBDA IS ELASTICITY COEFFICIENT
         OF EXPERIENCE FUNCTION

GROWTH RATE, EXPRESSED AS DECIMAL
?.15
SUPPLY A VALUE FOR LAMBDA
?.3224
HOW MANY TIME PERIODS DO YOU WISH
FUTURE SPENDING TO BE EVALUATED ?
SUPPLY VALUE IN RANGE 1 TO 40
?3
WHAT IS CURRENT INVESTMENT?
?2300

     PERIOD      FUTURE INVESTMENT
     1           2528.4635
     2           2779.6208
     3           3055.726

LIKE TO VARY SOME PARAMETERS
ANSWER (Y/N)
?N


------------------------------------------
SELECT AN OPTION BY TYPING IN THE
APPROPRIATE OPTION NO. AND THEN
THE APPROPRIATE DATA WHEN REQUESTED.
OPTION ?0
```

Suite PROM

Description

This suite of programs is called PROM and it carries out the product market portfolio analysis considered in Chapter 4. Given a set of input data comprising the following:

(1) The year (or period under analysis).
(2) The company name (companies should be delineated by a number).
(3) The sales values of the products per year (or period under analysis).
(4) The sales volume of the products per year (or period under analysis).
(5) The rate of growth of the markets for the products.

PROM will calculate the following:

(1) the coordinates (market growth rate and relative market share) to fix a product in the matrix,
(2) the radius of a circle proportional to the value of the annual sales of the product. For this calculation it is assumed that the product with the lowest annual sales can be a circle with a radius of 1.0 units and all other products will be represented by circles whose radii are scaled relative to this product (i.e. the one with the lowest annual sales). Thus, if there are just two products with annual sales of 100 and 185, they can be represented by circles whose radii are 1.0 and 1.85 units respectively, out the following functions.

These calculations are offered in two options.

(1) A Multi-company Growth-Gain Matrix for a single-product option. In the example given in the print-out on pages 263 to 265 the data is taken from page 106 of Chapter 4.
(2) A Multi-product Growth-Gain Matrix for a single company. In the example given in the print-out on pages 265 to 267 the data is taken from page 113 to Chapter 4.
(3) The maximum sustainable rate of growth. (Note this option is also available in the FINA suite.)

Note that PROM does not have a Growth-Gain Matrix option. This option has not been included because no calculations are required to fix the products on this matrix (the rate of market growth and the rate of product growth normally will be given) and also the relative areas of the circles can be obtained from the Growth Share Matrices in Option 1 or Option 2.

Print-out of PROM

Below is given a print-out of the input data and also each of the three options in PROM. Where appropriate, data is taken from Chapter 4.

```
*:*:*:*:*:*:*:*:*:*:*:*:*:*:*:*:
*OPTION 3: PROM*
*:*:*:*:*:*:*:*:*:*:*:*:*:*:*:*:

THIS PROGRAM CARRIES OUT VARIOUS
PRODUCT MARKET PORTFOLIO CALCULATIONS
AND SHOULD BE USED IN CONJUNCTION
WITH...
            CHAPTER 4
   THE PRODUCT MARKET PORTFOLIO

PRESS (RETURN) TO CONTINUE


THE OPTIONS AVAILIBLE ARE-

    0      TERMINATE CURRENT RUN
    1      MULTI-COMPANY GROWTH SHARE
           MATRIX(SINGLE PRODUCT)
    2      MULTI-PRODUCT GROWTH SHARE
           MATRIX(SINGLE COMPANY)
    3      CALCULATION OF MAXIMUM
           SUSTAINABLE RATE OF GROWTH
    4      DISPLAY OPTION MENU


-------------------------------------------
SELECT AN OPTION BY TYPING IN THE
APPROPRIATE OPTION NO. AND THEN
THE APPROPRIATE DATA WHEN REQUESTED.
OPTION ?1
*:*:*:*:*:*:*:*:*:*:*:*:*:*:*:*:*:*:*:*:*:*:*:*:*:*:*:*:*:*:*:
*   MULTI-COMPANY GROWTH SHARE MATRIX   *
*           FOR A SINGLE PRODUCT        *
*:*:*:*:*:*:*:*:*:*:*:*:*:*:*:*:*:*:*:*:*:*:*:*:*:*:*:*:*:*:*:
FOR A SERIES OF INPUT DATA COMPRISING-
         1) YEAR
         2) COMPANY(NUMERIC REPRESENTATION)
         3) SALES VALUE
         4) SALES VOLUME
         5) MARKET GROWTH RATE
PROM WILL CALCULATE THE RELATIVE MARKET
SHARE AND THE RELATIVE RAD. OF A CIRCLE
WHOSE AREA IS PROPORTIONAL TO THE SALES
VALUE FOR EACH CASE.
THE INPUT DATA IS REQUIRED IN THE
FOLLOWING FORMAT.
FIRST THE NUMBER OF CASES(OR LINES)
THEN FOR EACH CASE ENTER A LINE OF
DATA VALUES 1) TO 5) AS ABOVE, EACH
VALUE BEING SEPARATED FROM THE NEXT BY
A COMMA . THE DATA VALUES MUST BE IN
ORDER GIVEN ABOVE.
```

```
PLEASE INPUT NUMBER OF CASES NOW?6
PLEASE INPUT FOR CASE 1
YR,CO,SALES VAL,SALES VOL,MKT GR RATE
?1979,1,500,100,12
FOR CASE 1YOU HAVE INPUT
YEAR                    1979
COMPANY                 1
SALES VALUE             500
SALES VOLUME            100
MARKET GROWTH RATE 12
ARE THESE CORRECT (Y/N)Y
PLEASE INPUT FOR CASE 2
YR,CO,SALES VAL,SALES VOL,MKT GR RATE
?1979,2,400,80,12
FOR CASE 2YOU HAVE INPUT
YEAR                    1979
COMPANY                 2
SALES VALUE             400
SALES VOLUME            80
MARKET GROWTH RATE 12
ARE THESE CORRECT (Y/N)Y
PLEASE INPUT FOR CASE 3
YR,CO,SALES VAL,SALES VOL,MKT GR RATE
?1979,3,100,10,12
FOR CASE 3YOU HAVE INPUT
YEAR                    1979
COMPANY                 3
SALES VALUE             100
SALES VOLUME            10
MARKET GROWTH RATE 12
ARE THESE CORRECT (Y/N)Y
PLEASE INPUT FOR CASE 4
YR,CO,SALES VAL,SALES VOL,MKT GR RATE
?1980,1}750,150,15,
FOR CASE 4YOU HAVE INPUT
YEAR                    1980
COMPANY                 1
SALES VALUE             750
SALES VOLUME            150
MARKET GROWTH RATE 15
ARE THESE CORRECT (Y/N)Y
PLEASE INPUT FOR CASE 5
YR,CO,SALES VAL,SALES VOL,MKT GR RATE
?1980,2,500,100,15
FOR CASE 5YOU HAVE INPUT
YEAR                    1980
COMPANY                 2
SALES VALUE             500
SALES VOLUME            100
MARKET GROWTH RATE 15
ARE THESE CORRECT (Y/N)Y
PLEASE INPUT FOR CASE 6
YR,CO,SALES VAL,SALES VOL,MKT GR RATE
?1980,3,220,22,15
FOR CASE 6YOU HAVE INPUT
YEAR                    1980
COMPANY                 3
SALES VALUE             220
SALES VOLUME            22
MARKET GROWTH RATE 15
ARE THESE CORRECT (Y/N)Y
```

```
************************************************
*YEAR *COMP* REL. RAD. *REL.MRKT. *GROWTH*
*      *-ANY*OF CIRCLE*  SHARE   * RATE *
************************************************
*1979 *  1 *  2.2361 *  1.2500 *12.00 *
*1979 *  2 *  2.0000 *   .8000 *12.00 *
*1979 *  3 *  1.0000 *   .1000 *12.00 *
*1980 *  1 *  2.7386 *  1.5000 *15.00 *
*1980 *  2 *  2.2361 *   .6667 *15.00 *
*1980 *  3 *  1.4832 *   .1467 *15.00 *
************************************************
```

LIKE TO VARY SOME PARAMETERS (Y/N)N

SELECT AN OPTION BY TYPING IN THE
APPROPRIATE OPTION NO. AND THEN
THE APPROPRIATE DATA WHEN REQUESTED.
OPTION ?2
```
***********************************************
*    MULTI-PRODUCT GROWTH SHARE MATRIX    *
*          FOR A SINGLE COMPANY           *
***********************************************
```
FOR A SERIES OF INPUT DATA COMPRISING-
        1) YEAR
        2) PRODUCT(NUMERIC REPRESENTATION)
        3) SALES VALUE
        4) REL. MARKET SHARE
        5) MARKET GROWTH RATE
PROM WILL CALCULATE THE REL. RAD. OF A
CIRCLE WHOSE AREA IS PROP. TO THE SALES
VALUE FOR EACH CASE.
THE INPUT DATA IS REQUIRED IN THE
FOLLOWING FORMAT.
FIRST THE NUMBER OF CASES(OR LINES)
THEN FOR EACH CASE ENTER A LINE OF
DATA VALUES 1) TO 5) AS ABOVE,EACH
VALUE BEING SEPARATED FROM THE NEXT BY
A COMMA . THE DATA VALUES MUST BE IN
ORDER GIVEN ABOVE.
PLEASE INPUT NUMBER OF CASES NOW?11
PLEASE INPUT FOR CASE 1
YR,PROD,SALES VAL,REL MKT SHR,MKT GR RTE
?1983,1,1,.2,1
FOR CASE 1 YOU HAVE INPUT
YEAR   1983
PRODUCT   1
SALES VALUE   1
RELATIVE MKT SHARE .2
MKT GROWTH RATE   1
ARE THESE CORRECT (Y/N)Y
PLEASE INPUT FOR CASE 2
YR,PROD,SALES VAL,REL MKT SHR,MKT GR RTE
?1983,2,1,.3,2
FOR CASE 2 YOU HAVE INPUT
YEAR   1983
PRODUCT   2
SALES VALUE   1
RELATIVE MKT SHARE .3
MKT GROWTH RATE   2
ARE THESE CORRECT (Y/N)Y
```
```

```
PLEASE INPUT FOR CASE 3
YR, PROD, SALES VAL, REL MKT SHR, MKT GR RTE
?1983, 3, 1.8, .5, 8
FOR CASE 3 YOU HAVE INPUT
YEAR              1983
PRODUCT           3
SALES VALUE       1.8
RELATIVE MKT SHARE .5
MKT GROWTH RATE    8
ARE THESE CORRECT (Y/N) Y
PLEASE INPUT FOR CASE 4
YR, PROD, SALES VAL, REL MKT SHR, MKT GR RTE
?1983, 4, 1.8, .15, 15
FOR CASE 4 YOU HAVE INPUT
YEAR              1983
PRODUCT           4
SALES VALUE       1.8
RELATIVE MKT SHARE .15
MKT GROWTH RATE    15
ARE THESE CORRECT (Y/N) Y
PLEASE INPUT FOR CASE 5
YR, PROD, SALES VAL, REL MKT SHR, MKT GR RTE
?1983, 5, 4, .6, 15
FOR CASE 5 YOU HAVE INPUT
YEAR              1983
PRODUCT           5
SALES VALUE       4
RELATIVE MKT SHARE .6
MKT GROWTH RATE    15
ARE THESE CORRECT (Y/N) Y
PLEASE INPUT FOR CASE 6
YR, PROD, SALES VAL, REL MKT SHR, MKT GR RTE
?1983, 6, 4, .67, 19
FOR CASE 6 YOU HAVE INPUT
YEAR              1983
PRODUCT           6
SALES VALUE       4
RELATIVE MKT SHARE .67
MKT GROWTH RATE    19
ARE THESE CORRECT (Y/N) Y
PLEASE INPUT FOR CASE 7
YR, PROD, SALES VAL, REL MKT SHR, MKT GR RTE
?1983, 7, 5.4, 1.0, 17
FOR CASE 7 YOU HAVE INPUT
YEAR              1983
PRODUCT           7
SALES VALUE       5.4
RELATIVE MKT SHARE 1
MKT GROWTH RATE    17
ARE THESE CORRECT (Y/N) Y
PLEASE INPUT FOR CASE 8
YR, PROD, SALES VAL, REL MKT SHR, MKT GR RTE
?1983, 8, 7.1, 2.0, 14
FOR CASE 8 YOU HAVE INPUT
YEAR              1983
PRODUCT           8
SALES VALUE       7.1
RELATIVE MKT SHARE 2
MKT GROWTH RATE    14
ARE THESE CORRECT (Y/N) Y
```

```
PLEASE INPUT FOR CASE 9
YR,PROD,SALES VAL,REL MKT SHR,MKT GR RTE
?1983,9,116,5,12
FOR CASE 9 YOU HAVE INPUT
YEAR                    1983
PRODUCT                 9
SALES VALUE             116
RELATIVE MKT SHARE 5
MKT GROWTH RATE         12
ARE THESE CORRECT (Y/N)Y
PLEASE INPUT FOR CASE 10
YR,PROD,SALES VAL,REL MKT SHR,MKT GR RTE
?1983,10,115,5,6
FOR CASE 10 YOU HAVE INPUT
YEAR                    1983
PRODUCT                 10
SALES VALUE             115
RELATIVE MKT SHARE 5
MKT GROWTH RATE         6
ARE THESE CORRECT (Y/N)Y
PLEASE INPUT FOR CASE 11
YR,PROD,SALES VAL,REL MKT SHR,MKT GR RTE
?1983,11,94,2,3
FOR CASE 11 YOU HAVE INPUT
YEAR                    1983
PRODUCT                 11
SALES VALUE             94
RELATIVE MKT SHARE 2
MKT GROWTH RATE         3
ARE THESE CORRECT (Y/N)Y


************************************************
*YEAR *PROD* REL. RAD. *REL.MRKT. *GROWTH*
*      *-UCT*OF CIRCLE*  SHARE    * RATE *
************************************************
*1983 *  1 *  1.0000 *   .2000 * 1.00 *
*1983 *  2 *  1.0000 *   .3000 * 2.00 *
*1983 *  3 *  1.3416 *   .5000 * 8.00 *
*1983 *  4 *  1.3416 *   .1500 *15.00 *
*1983 *  5 *  2.0000 *   .6000 *15.00 *
*1983 *  6 *  2.0000 *   .6700 *19.00 *
*1983 *  7 *  2.3238 *  1.0000 *17.00 *
*1983 *  8 *  2.6646 *  2.0000 *14.00 *
*1983 *  9 * 10.7703 *  5.0000 *12.00 *
*1983 * 10 * 10.7238 *  5.0000 * 6.00 *
*1983 * 11 *  9.6954 *  2.0000 * 3.00 *
************************************************

LIKE TO VARY SOME PARAMETERS (Y/N)N
```

Suite SCEN

Description

This suite of programs is called SCEN and it may be useful in carrying out calculations to assist scenario planning. Given a set of input data comprising pairs of values (X being the independent variable — usually time — and Y being the dependent variable), SCEN will carry out the following functions:

(1) *Linear Regression*
Using the model
$$Y = a + bX$$
It will
　(a)　compute the regression equation, and
　(b)　on request, make forecasts.

(2) *Non-linear Regression*
Using the model
$$\log Y = \log a + \log b\, X$$
It will
　(a)　compute the regression equation, and
　(b)　on request, make forecasts.

(3) *Time Series Analysis of Monthly Data*
Using the multiplicative time series model
$$Y = T \times S \times C \times I$$
where　T is the linear trend, calculated by ordinary least squares,
　　　　S is the seasonal index, calculated by using an average of the ratio to twelve-month centred moving method,
　　　　C is the cyclical index, calculated by dividing the original data, $TSCI$ by TS and then obtaining a 3-month moving average of the remaining CI series. This last step also automatically yields I.
It will
　(a)　decompose the series into its constituent elements: T, S, C and I,
　(b)　on request, make forecasts,
　(c)　on request, print-out a table of deseasonalised data.

(4) *Time Series Analysis of Quarterly Data*
Using the multiplicative model
$$Y = T \times S$$
where　T is the linear trend, calculated by ordinary least squares, and

S is the quarterly seasonal index, obtained by using an average of a ratio to 4 quarter moving average method.

It will

(a) decompose the series into its constituent elements, i.e. T and S,

(b) on request, make forecasts.

(5) *Time Series Analysis Using Annual Data*
Using the multiplicative model

$$Y = T \times C$$

where T is the trend, calculated by ordinary least squares and C is the cyclical index obtained by dividing the original series, TC by T

It will decompose the series into its constituent elements T and C.

(6) *Exponential Smoothing*

This type of forecast is a one-period ahead forecast using an exponentially weighted moving average. Note that this type of forecast can only be used in a stationary situation — i.e. where successive values fluctuate randomly about a reasonable steady average.

The model used is

$$U_{t+1} = A \cdot D_t + (1 - A) U_t$$

where U_{t+1} is the forecast for the next period ahead,

U_t is the forecast for the current period,

D is the actually observed value in the current period, and

A is the exponential smoothing constant.*

Given

a forecast for period t, U_t,

a smoothing constant between 0 and 1, A and

an observed value for period $t \cdot D_t$

It will make a forecast for the next period, $t+1$.

Note that the exponential smoothing constant always has a value in the range 0 to 1.0. For details see Ref. (4), p. 114. In the SCEN program the user selects the value.
Note on the Methodologies. This section has not dealt in any detail with forecasting methodologies. For further information on the methodologies supporting the programs given above see Refs. (1), (3), (4), (5) and (6).

```
*********************
* OPTION 5: SCEN *
*********************
```

THIS PROGRAM CARRIES OUT VARIOUS
FORECASTS AND SHOULD BE USED IN
CONJUNCTION WITH...

      CHAPTER 7
      SCENARIO PLANNING

OPTIONS AVAILABLE ARE...

    0   TERMINATE CURRENT RUN
    1   LINEAR REGRESSION
    2   NON-LINEAR REGRESSION
    3   TIME SERIES ANALYSIS (MONTHLY)
    4   TIME SERIES ANALYSIS (QUARTERLY)
    5   TIME SERIES ANALYSIS (YEARLY)
    6   EXPONENTIAL SMOOTHING

SELECT AN OPTION (0-6)1

```
************************
* LINEAR REGRESSION *
************************
```

THIS OPTION ALLOWS YOU TO MAKE
A LINEAR FORECAST USING THE MODEL

     Y = A + BX

WHERE:
     Y IS THE DEPENDENT VARIABLE
     X IS THE INDEPENDENT VARIABLE

FOR A GIVEN SET OF (X,Y) PAIRS
THIS OPTION WILL CALCULATE THE
REGRESSION COEFFICIENTS A & B

HOW MANY (X,Y) PAIRS TO BE INPUT5
 X,Y1,10373
 X,Y2,11144
 X,Y3,12086
 X,Y4,13904
 X,Y5,18879
YOU HAVE INPUT THE FOLLOWING

X	Y
1	10373
2	11144
3	12086
4	13904
5	18879

ARE THESE CORRECT (Y/N) ·Y

ARE THESE CORRECT (Y/N)Y

PLEASE WAIT, CALCULATING REGRESSION

FOR THE DATA YOU HAVE INPUT THE
REGRESSION EQUATION IS...

   Y = 7345.6+1977.2X

PRESS (RETURN) TO CONTINUE
DO YOU WISH TO MAKE A FORECAST (Y/N)Y
INDEPENDENT VARIABLE (X) VALUE6

FOR X = 6 FORECAST VALUE=19208.8

DO YOU WISH TO MAKE A FORECAST (Y/N)Y
INDEPENDENT VARIABLE (X) VALUE7

FOR X = 7 FORECAST VALUE=21186

DO YOU WISH TO MAKE A FORECAST (Y/N)N

```
******************************
*NON-LINEAR REGRESSION*
******************************
```

THIS OPTION ALLOWS YOU TO MAKE A
FORECAST USING THE MODEL..

$$LOG(Y) = A + B.X$$

WHERE:
      Y IS THE DEPENDENT VARIABLE
      X IS THE INDEPENDENT VARIABLE

FOR A GIVEN SET OF (X,Y) PAIRS
THIS OPTION WILL CALCULATE THE
REGRESSION COEFFICIENTS A & B

HOW MANY (X,Y) PAIRS TO BE INPUT5
  X,Y1,10373
  X,Y2,11144
  X,Y3,12086
  X,Y4,13904
  X,Y5,18879
YOU HAVE INPUT THE FOLLOWING

X	Y
1	10373
2	11144
3	12086
4	13904
5	18879

ARE THESE CORRECT (Y/N)Y

PLEASE WAIT, CALCULATING REGRESSION

FOR THE DATA YOU HAVE INPUT THE
REGRESSION EQUATION IS...

$$LOG(Y) = 3.928+.0616X$$

PRESS (RETURN) TO CONTINUE
DO YOU WISH TO MAKE A FORECAST (Y/N)Y
INDEPENDENT VARIABLE (X) VALUE6

FOR X = 6 FORECAST VALUE=19842.6651

DO YOU WISH TO MAKE A FORECAST (Y/N)Y
INDEPENDENT VARIABLE (X) VALUE7

FOR X = 7 FORECAST VALUE=22866.5161

DO YOU WISH TO MAKE A FORECAST (Y/N)N

```
****************************************
*TIME SERIES ANALYSIS: MONTHLY DATA*
****************************************
```

THIS OPTION ALLOWS YOU TO MAKE A
FORECAST USING THE MODEL..

        $Y = T.S.C.I$

WHERE:
        Y IS THE DEPENDENT VARIABLE
        T IS THE LINEAR TREND
        S IS THE SEASONAL VARIATION
        C IS THE CYCLICAL FLUCTUATION
        I IS THE IRREGULAR COMPONENT

FOR THIS OPTION YOU MUST INPUT AT LEAST
24 CONSECUTIVE MONTHS OF DATA

PRESS (RETURN) TO CONTINUE

INPUT NUMBER OF MONTHS (24-48)25
INPUT OBSERVED VALUES FOR EACH MONTH
ONE VALUE ON EACH LINE
MONTH 1?3
MONTH 2?5
MONTH 3?7
MONTH 4?9
MONTH 5?9
MONTH 6?10
MONTH 7?11
MONTH 8?13
MONTH 9?15
MONTH 10?17
MONTH 11?20
MONTH 12?24
MONTH 13?21
MONTH 14?25
MONTH 15?36
MONTH 16?27
MONTH 17?27
MONTH 18?28
MONTH 19?29
MONTH 20?33
MONTH 21?36
MONTH 22?38
MONTH 23?39
MONTH 24?42
MONTH 25?45
```
```

```
YOU HAVE INPUT
                3          27
                5          28
                7          29
                9          33
                9          36
               10          38
               11          39
               13          42
               15          45
               17
               20
               24
               21
               25
               36
               27
ARE THESE CORRECT (Y/N)Y

PLEASE WAIT, COMPUTING TIME SERIES


    Y        T         S         C         I

    3       2.79     92.31
    5       4.46    102.74
    7       6.12    138.24    102.74    113.22
    9       7.79     97.15    103.63    105.35
    9       9.45     91.65    101.88     81.2
   10      11.11     90.32    107.51    110.68
   11      12.78     87.7     100.57    103.33
   13      14.44     91.23     98.83    100.81
   15      16.1      92.07     99.34     98.83
   17      17.77     93.15    100.85     97.85
   20      19.43    101.27    101.84     99.34
   24      21.1     112.94    101.69    101
   21      22.76     92.31    100.78    100.85
   25      24.42    102.74    100.11    100.62
   36      26.09    138.24     99.81    100.15
   27      27.75     97.15     99.87     99.76
   27      29.41     91.65    100.04     99.79
   28      31.08     90.32    100.01    100.13
   29      32.74     87.7     100.3      99.85
   33      34.41     91.23    101.96     97.83

PRESS (RETURN) TO CONTINUE

   36      36.07     92.07    104.84     96.33
   38      37.73     93.15    107.22     98.06
   39      39.4     101.27    104.76    103.48
   42      41.06    112.94     98.81    109.41
   45      42.73     92.31    100.81     96.97
DO YOU WISH TO MAKE A FORECAST(Y/N)Y
MONTH (NUMBER)29

FOR MONTH NUMBER 29 FORECAST IS 45.2569533

DO YOU WISH TO MAKE A FORECAST(Y/N)N
```

DO YOU WANT A TABLE OF DESEASONALISED
VALUES LISTED (Y/N)Y

DE-SEASONALISED VALUES

MONTH	ACTUAL	DE-SEASONALISED
1	3	3.25
2	5	4.87
3	7	5.06
4	9	9.26
5	9	9.82
6	10	11.07
7	11	12.54
8	13	14.25
9	15	16.29
10	17	18.25
11	20	19.75
12	24	21.25
13	21	22.75
14	25	24.33
15	36	26.04
16	27	27.79
17	27	29.46
18	28	31
19	29	33.07
20	33	36.17

PRESS (RETURN) TO CONTINUE

MONTH	ACTUAL	DE-SEASONALISED
21	36	39.1
22	38	40.79
23	39	38.51
24	42	37.19
25	45	48.75

```
************************************
*TIME SERIES ANALYSIS (QUARTERLY)*
************************************
```

THIS OPTION ALLOWS YOU TO MAKE A
FORECAST USING THE MODEL...

$$Y = T.S$$

WHERE:

Y IS THE DEPENDENT VARIABLE
T IS THE LINEAR TREND
S IS THE QUARTERLY SEASONAL INDEX

GIVEN THE QUARTERLY OBSERVED VALUES
FOR SEVERAL YEARS

```
NUMBER OF YEARS (2-12) 4
PLEASE INPUT QUARTERLY VALUES NOW
YEAR 1      QUARTER 1        ?5
YEAR 1      QUARTER 2        ?7
YEAR 1      QUARTER 3        ?9
YEAR 1      QUARTER 4        ?11
YEAR 2      QUARTER 1        ?7
YEAR 2      QUARTER 2        ?8
YEAR 2      QUARTER 3        ?12
YEAR 2      QUARTER 4        ?14
YEAR 3      QUARTER 1        ?20
YEAR 3      QUARTER 2        ?15
YEAR 3      QUARTER 3        ?19
YEAR 3      QUARTER 4        ?24
YEAR 4      QUARTER 1        ?27
YEAR 4      QUARTER 2        ?20
YEAR 4      QUARTER 3        ?25
YEAR 4      QUARTER 4        ?28
```

YOU HAVE INPUT..

YEAR	Q1	Q2	Q3	Q4
1	5	7	9	11
2	7	8	12	14
3	20	15	19	24
4	27	20	25	28

ARE THESE FIGURES CORRECT (Y/N)Y

```
PLEASE WAIT, COMPUTING TIME SERIES

  QUARTERLY SEASONAL INDEXES
  --------------------------

  QUARTER        INDEX
    1           105.62
    2            81.61
    3           101.13
    4           111.55


PRESS <RETURN> TO CONTINUE

YEAR    QUARTER ACTUAL   TREND    DESEASN

  1        1       5      4.29     4.73
  1        2       7      5.81     8.58
  1        3       9      7.33     8.9
  1        4      11      8.85     9.86
  2        1       7     10.37     6.63
  2        2       8     11.89     9.8
  2        3      12     13.41    11.87
  2        4      14     14.93    12.55
  3        1      20     16.45    18.94
  3        2      15     17.97    18.38
  3        3      19     19.49    18.79
  3        4      24     21       21.52
  4        1      27     22.52    25.56
  4        2      20     24.04    24.51
  4        3      25     25.56    24.72
  4        4      28     27.08    25.1




PRESS <RETURN> TO CONTINUE

WANT TO MAKE A FORECAST(Y/N)Y

YEAR NUMBER 7
FORECAST FOR YEAR 7

        QUARTER FORECAST
           1      43.04
           2      34.5
           3      44.29
           4      50.54

WANT TO MAKE A FORECAST(Y/N)N
```

```
**************************************
*TIME SERIES ANALYSIS (YEARLY)*
**************************************
```

THIS OPTION DECOMPOSES ANNUAL DATA INTO
TREND AND CYCLICAL ELEMENTS USING THE
MODEL...

$$Y = T.C$$

WHERE:

     Y IS THE DEPENDENT VARIABLE
     T IS THE LINEAR TREND
     C IS THE CYCLICAL FLUCTUATION

YOU MUST INPUT OBSERVED VALUES FOR
A CONSECUTIVE NUMBER OF YEARS.
NUMBER OF YEARS (2-20)5
INPUT OBSERVED VALUES FOR EACH YEAR NOW

```
YEAR 1          ?10373
YEAR 2          ?11144
YEAR 3          ?12086
YEAR 4          ?13904
YEAR 5          ?18879
```

YOU HAVE INPUT..

YEAR	VALUE
1	10373
2	11144
3	12086
4	13904
5	18879

ARE THESE CORRECT (Y/N)Y

PLEASE WAIT, COMPUTING TIME SERIES

YEAR	Y	T	C
1	10373	9322.8	111.26
2	11144	11300	98.62
3	12086	13277.2	91.03
4	13904	15254.4	91.15
5	18879	17231.6	109.56

PRESS (RETURN) TO CONTINUE

```
*********************************
*  EXPONENTIAL SMOOTHING*
*********************************

THIS OPTION ALLOWS YOU TO MAKE
A FORECAST USING THE EXPONENTIAL
SMOOTHING MODEL...

     U     =  A.D  +  (1-A).U
      T+1       T            T

WHERE:
  U     IS THE FORECAST FOR PERIOD T+1
   T+1
  U     IS THE FORECAST FOR PERIOD T
   T
  A     IS THE EXPONENTIAL SMOOTHING
        CONSTANT
  D     IS THE OBSERVED VALUE FOR
   T    PERIOD T

PRESS <RETURN> TO CONTINUE

FORECAST FOR PERIOD T (MAKE A GUESS)50
SMOOTHING CONSTANT (TRY 0.2)        .2
OBSERVED VALUE FOR PERIOD T         55

FORECAST VALUE FOR PERIOD T+1=51

WANT A FORECAST FOR NEXT PERIOD (Y/N)Y
OBSERVED VALUE FOR NEXT PERIOD      56
CHANGE SMOOTHING CONSTANT (Y/N)N
FORECAST VALUE FOR NEXT PERIOD IS 52
WANT A FORECAST FOR NEXT PERIOD (Y/N)N
```

Microcomputer Data Bases for Scenario Planning

With the advent of the very cheap software, data can now be stored cheaply, efficiently, flexibly and in an easily accessible fashion on a microcomputer. Two very well-known programs which could be used as the basis of a data base for scenario planning are now considered. The programs are PFS — a data base program — and VISICALC — a spreadsheet program.

Using PFS

PFS*, which stands for Personal Filing System, is a very flexible and easy to use data base which is used extensively on Apple computers. How

*PFS is an integrated set of packages — PFS FILE, PFS REPORT, PFS GRAPH and PFS WRITE — which is manufactured by the Software Publishing Corporation of California. Just one of the packages — PFS FILE — is used in this chapter.

PFS could be used as a data base for a hypothetical company is considered here. The company comprises a number of divisions, and data for each division for each year is held on the data base. The information held is similar to that which was suggested could be held in a "Data Base for the Organisation" on Page 221 in Chapter 7.

Because the display of this data base is restricted to 40 characters, horizontally, many of the elements of the data base have had their names abbreviated. The full names and, where appropriate, explanations are given in Table 86, Tables 87 and 88 display the information for divisions 2 and 3 for the year 1983. The data base set out below is meant to be indicative only of what can be achieved. Data bases such as PFS require absolutely no programming skills and they can be tailored, by untrained users, in all sorts of ways to meet the particular needs of the

Table 86. A Blank Page from the Data Base, with Explanations of the Item Names

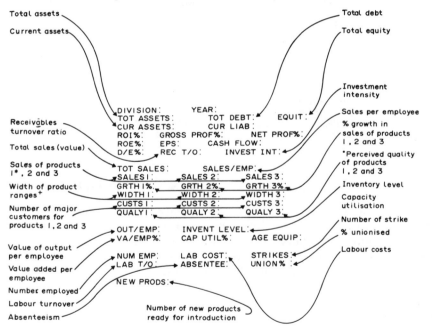

*Each product represents a range of products.
†Product range is defined as VW = very wide, W = wide, N = narrow
‵Perceived quality is "quality as perceived by customers" and is scaled A = above average, B = average, C = below average

organisation. Indeed, the scope of these programs is only limited by the imagination of the users. Such data bases offer a splendid method of efficient, up-to-date and inexpensive data storage.

Table 87. Information for Division 2 for 1983

```
DIVISION: 2    YEAR: 1983
TOT ASSETS: 100    TOT DEBT: 30 EQUIT: 70
CUR ASSETS: 20    CUR LIAB: 25
ROI%: 10GROSS PROF%: 15    NET PROF%: 8
ROE%: 9 EPS: 30    CASH FLOW: 5
D/E%: 30REC T/O: 4    INVEST INT: 1.3

TOT SALES: 258    SALES/EMP: 2.58
SALES1: 50    SALES2: 100 SALES3: 108
GRTH1%: 2    GRTH2%: 5    GRTH3%: 20
WIDTH1: VW    WIDTH2: N    WIDTH3: W
CUSTS1: 12    CUSTS2: 29    CUSTS3: 20
QUALY1: C    QUALY2: B    QUALY3: A

OUT/EMP: 2    INVENT LEVEL: 26
VA/EMP%: 1    CAP UTIL%: 60AGE EQUIP: 4

NUM EMP: 100LAB COST: B    STRIKES: 0
LAB T/O: 1    ABSENTEE: 2    UNION% : 20

NEW PRODS: 2
```

Using VISICALC

VISICALC* is an electronic worksheet which can be used to store and manipulate data, particularly quantitative data. Its manipulative powers are particularly useful for developing quantitative models of an organisation, or its environment, and are probably most useful for their ability to answer the "What if?" type of speculative question — a most useful facility for the uncertain area of scenario planning.

How VISICALC could be used as a data base for information on the "energy environment", as specified in Chapter 7, is now considered

---

VISICALC is one of a set of integrated packages manufactured by the Visicorp Corporation of California. The other packages are VISIFILE,VISISCHEDULE, VISITERM, DESKTOP/PLAN, VISIDEX, VISIPLOT, VISITREND/PLOT

Table 88. Information for Division 3 for 1983

```
DIVISION: 3    YEAR: 1982
TOT ASSETS: 140   TOT DEBT: 70 EQUIT: 70
CUR ASSETS: 40    CUR LIAB: 45
ROI%: 12GROSS PROF%: 27   NET PROF%: 10
ROE%: 11EPS: 35   CASH FLOW: 7
D/E%: 50REC T/O: 4   INVEST INT: 1.3


TOT SALES: 900   SALES/EMP: 3.0
SALES1: 300 SALES2: 200 SALES3: 400
GRTH1%: 10   GRTH2%: 12   GRTH3%: 15
WIDTH1: W    WIDTH2: W    WIDTH3: W
CUSTS1: 20   CUSTS2: 30   CUSTS3: 10
QUALY1: A    QUALY2: A    QUALY3: A


OUT/EMP: 2  INVENT LEVEL: 40
VA/EMP%: 1.3CAP UTIL%: 80AGE EQUIP: 3.4


NUM EMP: 200LAB COST: B  STRIKES: 1
LAB T/O: 1  ABSENTEE: 3  UNION% : 19


NEW PRODS: 0
```

briefly. Here it is assumed that the planner wishes to record, in a clear fashion, data on the world production of primary energy over the period 1970–1980, i.e. the data contained in Table 79 on page 227. This data has been loaded onto VISICALC and a print-out of the data is given in Table 89. While it is undoubtedly useful to be able to store information in this fashion, VISICALC has a powerful linked package — VISITREND — which can present graphic representations of the data. A selection of the type of graphs that VISITREND can create is shown in Figs. 75 to 80. The power of such graphs in depicting trends for, say, a group presentation, should be apparent. Finally, it should be emphasised that this short exposition is a very limited illustration of the power of spreadsheet packages such as VISICALC. For example, the package could be asked to *forecast* future world production of primary energy or to indicate the effects of "What if" questions of the type "If the production of oil increases at a rate of 5% per year for the next planning period while the production of coal increases at a rate of 7% per year over the next planning period, what will be the difference in the volumes at the end of the period and what are the implications for us?"

Table 89. VISICALC Printout of Data on World Production of Primary Energy

YEAR	TOTAL	COAL	OIL.	NAT GAS	HYD&NUC
1970	7350	2399	3473	1323	154
1971	7656	2395	3681	1415	165
1972	7980	2426	3888	1489	177
1973	8448	2470	4239	1554	185
1974	8537	2503	4251	1576	207
1975	8482	2633	4043	1585	222
1976	8951	2702	4359	1662	228
1977	9254	2763	4569	1671	250
1978	9332	2784	4557	1735	257
1979	9693	2844	4750	1836	263
1980	9635	2945	4527	1891	272

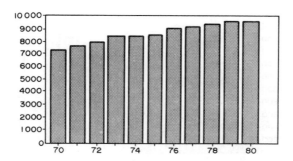

FIG. 75. *Total world production of primary energy 1970–1980 (millions of tonnes of coal equivalent)*

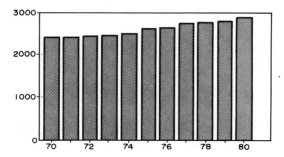

Fig. 76. *World production of primary energy, 1970–1980: coal (millions of tonnes of coal equivalent)*

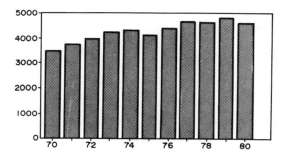

Fig. 77. *World production of primary energy, 1970–1980: crude oil (millions of tonnes of coal equivalent)*

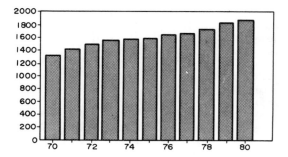

Fig. 78. *World production of primary energy, 1970–1980: natural gas (millions of tonnes of coal equivalent)*

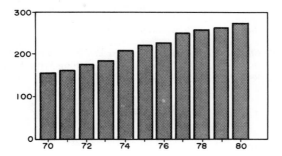

Fig. 79. *World production of primary energy, 1970–1980: hydro and nuclear electricity (millions of tonnes of coal equivalent)*

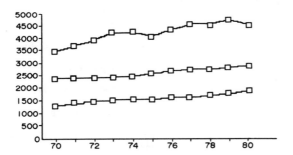

Fig. 80. *World production of primary energy, 1970–1980: coal, crude oil and natural gas (millions of tonnes of coal equivalent)*

Conclusion

The purpose of this chapter is to act as a catalyst to help accelerate the interaction of strategic management and microcomputers. Therefore, it should be viewed not as a finished manual on the topic, but rather, for those who have not yet integrated the two disciplines, as a foundation upon which they will be able to construct their own packages geared to their own particular needs.

Finally, by way of encouragement, this book was written on an Apple IIe computer.

References

1. Brown, R. G. *Smoothing Forecasting and Prediction of Discrete Time Series*, Prentice-Hall, 1962

2.   Harrison, F. L. "Microcomputers — The Breakthrough in Computer Modelling",
     Long Range Planning, Vol. 16, No. 5, Oct. 1983, pp. 94–99.
3.   *ICI, Short-term Forecasting*, ICI Monograph, No. 2, Oliver and Boyd, 1964.
4.   Littlechild, S. C. *Operational Research for Managers*, Philip Allan, 1978.
5.   Mason, R. D. *Statistical Techniques in Business and Economics*, R. D. Irwin, 1974.
6.   Trigg, D. W. and Leach, A. G. "Exponential Smoothing With Adaptive Response
     Rate", *Operational Research Quarterly*, Vol. 18, 1967.

Bibliography

Bhaskar, K. N. *Building Financial Models: A Simulation Approach*, Associated Business
     Programmes, 1978.
Bryant, J. W. (Ed.) *Financial Modelling in Corporate Management*, Wiley, Chichester, 1982.
"Business Information Systems", Financial Times Survey, *Financial Times*, 14 Dec. 1983.
Collins, A. C. "A Management Strategy for Information Processing", *Long Range Planning*,
     Vol. 16, No. 5, Oct. 1983, pp. 29–44.
"Computers", Financial Times Survey, *Financial Times*, 18 Jan. 1982.
"Computing Services and Software", Financial Times Survey, *Financial Times*, Nov. 5 1982.
Cripps, M. D. "In Tomorrow's Office — Networks and Microelectronics, *OR*, Vol. 34, No.
     4, Ap. 1983, pp. 385–387.
de Kluyver, C. A. and McNally, G. M "Developing a Corporate Planning Model", *Long
     Range Planning*, Vol. 15, No. 1, Feb. 1982, pp. 97–106.
Grinyer, P. H. "Financial Modelling in the U.K.", *Long Range Planning*, Vol. 16, No. 5, Oct.
     1983, pp. 58–72.
Hayen, R. L. "How to Design a Financial Planning Model", *Long Range Planning*, Vol. 16,
     No. 5, Oct. 1983, pp. 111–122.
Hirschheim, R. A. "Database — A Neglected Corporate Resource", *Long Range Planning*,
     Vol. 16, No. 5, Oct. 1983, pp. 79–88.
Holloway, C. and Pearce J. A. II, "Computer Assisted Strategic Planning," *Long Range
     Planning*, Vol. 15, No. 4, August 1982, pp. 56–63.
King, W. R. "Planning for Strategic Decision Support Systems", *Long Range Planning*, Vol.
     16, No. 5, Oct. 1983, pp. 73–78.
MacGregor, J. M. "What Users Think About Computer Models", *Long Range Planning*,
     Vol. 16, No. 5, Oct. 1983, pp. 45–57.
"Office Equipment", Financial Times Survey, *Financial Times*, 12 Oct. 1981.
"Personal Computers", Financial Times Survey, *Financial Times*, 8 Jan. 1983.
Reuber, G. L. "Bits, Bytes and Banking", *Business quarterly*, Vol. 48, No. 1, Spring 1983, pp.
     48–54.
Seiler, R. E. and Boockholdt, J. L. "Creative Development of Computerized Information
     Systems", *Long Range Planning*, Vol. 16, No. 5, Oct. 1983, pp. 100–106.
Shrivastava, P. "Strategic Planning for MIS", *Long Range Planning*, Vol. 16, No. 5, Oct.
     1983, pp. 19–28.
Sizer, R. "Key Issues in Managing Information", *Long Range Planning*, Vol. 16, No. 5, Oct.
     1983, pp. 19–28.
Tricker, R. I. *Effective Information Management: Developing Information Systems Strategies*,
     Beaumont Executive Press, Oxford, 1982.
Weidemann, P. "PINCO: Personal Information and Confidentiality Controls", *Long Range
     Planning*, Vol. 16, No. 5, Oct. 1983, pp. 107–111.

The Last Page

This book commenced with the phrase:

"How a challenge is perceived will determine how the challenge is met."

It concludes with the aspiration:

"Through the book, may readers have enhanced perceptions."

Source Listing of the Programs

```
80    HOME : CLEAR
90    ONERR  GOTO 25000
100   REM    THIS IS THE MAIN MENU PROGRAM OF THE SUITE..
110   REM
120   REM          TOOLS AND TECHNIQUES OF STRATEGIC MANAGEMENT
130   REM
140   REM    ...WRITTEN BY P.B. MC NAMEE AND L.J. ASQUITH
150   REM
160   REM  INSERT HERE A CLEAR SCREEN COMMAND FOR APPLE II
170   GOSUB 1000
180   PRINT "*"; TAB( 38);"*"
190   PRINT "*    TOOLS AND TECHNIQUES FOR"; TAB( 38);"*"
195   PRINT "*        STRATEGIC MANAGEMENT"; TAB( 38);"*"
200   PRINT "*"; TAB( 38);"*"
210   GOSUB 1000
220   PRINT : PRINT : PRINT
230   PRINT "    *****************************"
240   PRINT "    *  BASIC COMPUTER PROGRAMS  *"
250   PRINT "    *****************************"
260   PRINT : PRINT : PRINT
270   PRINT " THIS DISK CONTAINS A SET OF SMALL"
275   PRINT " COMPUTER PROGRAMS WRITTEN IN BASIC"
280   PRINT " WHICH SUPPORT THE BOOK.."
290   PRINT : PRINT " TOOLS AND TECHNIQUES FOR"
295   PRINT "    STRATEGIC MANAGEMENT"
300   PRINT "      BY P.B. MC NAMEE": PRINT
400   GOSUB 2000
405   PRINT  CHR$ (4);"NOMON,C,I,O"
410   PRINT " THERE ARE 4 SUITES ON THE DISK."
420   PRINT " THESE ARE...": PRINT
430   PRINT " 1 FINA: A SUITE OF PROGRAMS THAT CARRY"
440   PRINT "          OUT VARIOUS STRATEGIC FINANCIAL"
450   PRINT "          ANALYSIS"
460   PRINT " 2 EXCU: A SUITE OF PROGRAMS FOR"
470   PRINT "          EXPERIENCE CURVE CALCULATIONS"
480   PRINT " 3 PROM: A SUITE OF PROGRAMS THAT CARRY"
490   PRINT "          OUT VARIOUS PRODUCT MARKET"
500   PRINT "          PORTFOLIO CALCULATIONS"
510   PRINT " 4 SCEN: A SUITE OF PROGRAMS TO AID"
520   PRINT "          SCENARIO PLANNING"
530   PRINT : INPUT "SELECT OPTION (1-4)";IOPT%
540   IF (IOPT% > = 1 AND IOPT% < = 4) GOTO 560
550   PRINT " OPTION MUST BE IN RANGE 1 TO 4": GOTO 410
560   ON IOPT% GOTO 600,700,800,900
600   PRINT  CHR$ (4);"BRUN FINA"
700   PRINT  CHR$ (4);"BRUN EXCU"
800   PRINT  CHR$ (4);"BRUN PROM"
900   PRINT  CHR$ (4);"BRUN SCEN"
1000  FOR J = 1 TO 38: PRINT "*";: NEXT : PRINT : RETURN
2000  INPUT "PRESS <RETURN> TO CONTINUE";DUM$: RETURN
```

```
25000 IE =  PEEK (222)
25010  IF IE = 255 GOTO 25040
25020  IF IE = 254 GOTO 530
25030  PRINT "ERROR, STATUS=";IE
25040  PRINT "RE-STARTING YOU"
25050  FOR J = 1 TO 500:YN$ = "Y": NEXT J
25060  RUN
30000  END

90   ONERR  GOTO 20000
100  REM   WRITE PROGRAM TITLE AND TEXT
110  REM
115  DIM C1(25),N1(25)
150  GOSUB 12750
200  REM   EXPERIENCE FUNCTION EVALUATIONS
250  REM   ===============================
300  REM
350  REM   INPUT "ACCUMULATED VOLUME OF PRODUCTION FIGURES INTO N
400  REM   INPUT "COST OF N TH ITEM" FIGURES INTO C
450  REM
500  REM
510  PRINT : INPUT "PRESS <RETURN> TO CONTINUE";YN$: PRINT
550  GOSUB 15300
600  PRINT "* EXPERIENCE FUNCTION CALCULATION      *"
650  GOSUB 15300
700  PRINT "INPUT 'N' AND 'CN' , BOTH VALUES"
750  PRINT "ON THE SAME LINE SEPARATED BY A"
755  PRINT "COMMA. TERMINATE YOU DATA SERIES"
760  PRINT "WITH THE SEQUENCE.."
800  PRINT "-1,-1"
900  PRINT
950  X1 = 0.0
1000 X2 = 0.0
1050 N2 = 0.0
1100 C2 = 0.0
1150 S1 = 0
1200 S2 = 0
1250 S3 = 0
1255 NV = 0
1300 I = 0
1350  INPUT N1(I + 1),C1(I + 1)
1400  REM  N OR C CAN'T BE ZERO
1450  IF N1(I + 1) = 0 THEN 2200
1500  IF C1(I + 1) = 0 THEN 2200
1550  REM  LOOK FOR TERMINATOR LINE
1600  IF N1(I + 1) < 0 THEN 1620
1610  I = I + 1
1615  IF I < 25 GOTO 1350
1618  PRINT "MAX NUMBER OF VALUES INPUT"
1620  PRINT "YOU HAVE INPUT "
1625  PRINT  TAB( 10);"EXPERIENCE"; TAB( 25);"UNIT COST"
1630  FOR K = 1 TO I: PRINT  TAB( 10);N1(K); TAB( 25);C1(K): NEXT K
1635  INPUT "ARE THESE CORRECT (Y/N)";YN$
1640  IF YN$ = "N" GOTO 700
1645  IF YN$ < > "Y" GOTO 1635
1650  REM  EVALUATE LOGS FOR N &C
1660  FOR K = 1 TO I
1700 LN1 =  LOG (N1(K)) /  LOG (10)
1750 LC1 =  LOG (C1(K)) /  LOG (10)
1800 N2 = LN1 + N2
1850 C2 = LC1 + C2
1900 X1 = LN1 * LC1 + X1
1950 X2 = LN1 * LN1 + X2
2000  NEXT K
```

```
2010    GOTO 2350
2100    REM   ERRORS IN INPUT DATA
2150    REM   **********************
2200    PRINT " YOU HAVE GIVEN ZERO EITHER FOR N OR C"
2250    PRINT " CAN'T DO !! PLEASE RETYPE "
2300    GOTO 1350
2350    REM   ALL DATA HAS BEEN SUPPLIED - DO SUMS
2400    REM   SUM LOG(N) IN N2: SUM LOG(C) IN C2: SUM LOG(N)LOG(C) IN X1
2450    REM   SUM LOG(N)^2 IN X2
2500    REM   CALC LAMBDA
2550    I1 = I
2600    REM   EXPERIENCE FUNCTION CALCULATIONS
2650    REM   ********************************
2700    X3 = I1 * X1 - N2 * C2
2720    REM   T9=0 IMPLIES ONLY TERMINATOR INPUT !!
2730    T9 = I1 * X2 - N2 * N2
2740    IF T9 = 0 THEN   PRINT "TERMINATOR ONLY INPUT": GOTO 3500
2750    X3 = X3 / T9
2800    REM   CALCULATE LOG(C1), WHERE C1 IS COST OF FIRST UNIT
2850    C1 = C2 / I1 - X3 * N2 / I1
2900    REM   DETERMINE C1
2950    C1 = 10.0 ^ (C1): PRINT
3000    PRINT "   (1) C1                   ="; INT (10000 * C1 + .5) / 10000
3050    PRINT "   (2) LAMBDA               ="; INT (10000 * X3 + .5) / 10000
3100    REM    EVALUATE K AND DELTA C
3150    K = 2.0 ^ X3
3200    C = (1.0 - K) * 100.0
3250    PRINT "SLOPE OF LOG EXP FUNC   ="; INT (10000 * K + .5) / 10000
3300    PRINT "RATE OF COST DECLINE(%) ="; INT (10000 * C + .5) / 10000
3310    PRINT : INPUT "PRESS <RETURN> TO CONTINUE";YN$: PRINT
3320    GOSUB 18000
3350    REM   PRINT MENU AND _
3400    GOSUB 12100
3450    REM   PROMT FOR OPTION
3500    GOSUB 11450
3550    REM   OPTIONS 5,6,7,8 CAUSE REPROMPT
3600    REM   CHECK FOR OPTION 0 I. E. STOP RUN
3650    IF I = 0 THEN 15600
3700    REM   GO TO THE APPROPRIATE SECTION
3750    ON I GOTO 6250,8500,9500,3850,3500,3500,3500,3500,3400
3800    REM   ***THIS IS THE LOGICAL END OF THIS MODULE***
3850    REM   FUTURE SPENDING CALCULATIONS
3900    REM   ***************************
3950    PRINT
4000    GOSUB 15300
4050    PRINT "*FUTURE SPENDING FUNCTION PARAMETERS   *"
4100    GOSUB 15300
4150    PRINT
4200    PRINT " THE FUTURE SPENDING FUNCTION IS:"
4250    PRINT
4300    PRINT "    S(T+1) = S(T) * (1+GAMMA)^(1-LAMBDA)"
4350    PRINT
4400    PRINT " WHERE:"
4450    PRINT "    (1) S(T) IS INVESTMENT IN PERIOD T"
4500    PRINT "    (2) S(T+1) IS INVESTMENT IN PERIOD T+1"
4550    PRINT "    (3) GAMMA IS RATE OF MARKET GROWTH"
4600    PRINT "    (4) LAMBDA IS ELASTICITY COEFFICIENT"
4650    PRINT "        OF EXPERIENCE FUNCTION"
4700    PRINT
4750    REM   GET VALUE FOR GAMMA
4800    GOSUB 10950
4850    PRINT "SUPPLY A VALUE FOR LAMBDA"
4900    INPUT X3
4950    PRINT "HOW MANY TIME PERIODS DO YOU WISH"
```

```
5000    PRINT "FUTURE SPENDING TO BE EVALUATED ?"
5050    PRINT "SUPPLY VALUE IN RANGE 1 TO 40"
5100    INPUT P
5150    IF P < 1 THEN 5350
5200    IF P > 40 THEN 5350
5250    GOTO 5450
5300    REM     INVALID FUTURE SPENDING VALUE
5350    PRINT "VALUE OUT OF EXPECTED RANGE !!"
5400    GOTO 5100
5450    PRINT "WHAT IS CURRENT INVESTMENT?"
5500    INPUT ST
5550    IF ST < = 0.0 THEN 5650
5600    GOTO 5800
5650    REM     BAD INVESTMENT FIGURE
5700    PRINT "INVESTMENT MUST BE POSITIVE !!"
5750    GOTO 5100
5800    PRINT
5850    PRINT  TAB( 5);"PERIOD"; TAB( 15);"FUTURE INVESTMENT"
5900    FOR J = 1 TO P
5950 ST = ST * (1 + G) ^ (1 - X3)
6000    PRINT  TAB( 5);J; TAB( 15); INT (10000 * ST + .5) / 10000
6050    NEXT J
6100    GOSUB 10300
6150    IF I = 1 THEN 3500
6200    GOTO 4750
6250    REM  ** FUTURE COST OF LAST UNIT PRODUCED
6300    PRINT
6350    GOSUB 15300
6400    PRINT "*FUTURE COST OF LAST UNIT PRODUCED    * "
6450    GOSUB 15300
6500    PRINT
6550    REM  ** REQUEST PARAMETERS**
6600 S1 = 1
6650    PRINT "VOL. DURING LAST PERIOD OF OBSERVATION?"
6700    INPUT V
6750    IF V > = 0.0 THEN 6900
6800    PRINT "VOLUME CAN'T BE -VE - RETYPE"
6850    GOTO 6700
6900    PRINT " HOW MANY TIME PERIODS TO BE INCLUDED?"
6950    INPUT P
7000    IF P < 1 THEN 7150
7050    IF P > 40 THEN 7150
7100    GOTO 7250
7150    PRINT "VALUE OUT OF RANGE - RETYPE"
7200    GOTO 6950
7250    GOSUB 10950
7300    PRINT "LAST COST OBSERVATION?"
7350    INPUT C
7400    IF C > 0.0 THEN 7550
7450    PRINT "COST MUST BE +VE - RETYPE"
7500    GOTO 7350
7550    GOSUB 10750
7600    PRINT "DO YOU KNOW TOTAL EXPERIENCE TO DATE?"
7610    GOSUB 10400
7620    IF I = 0 THEN 7680
7630    PRINT "IT SHALL BE ASSUMED TOTAL EXPERIENCE IS"
7640    PRINT "APPOXIMATED BY VOL. DURING LAST PERIOD"
7650    PRINT "DIVIDED BY GROWTH RATE"
7660 W = G
7670    GOTO 8000
7680    PRINT "PLEASE GIVE VALUE"
7690    INPUT W
7700    IF W > 0.0 THEN 7730
7710    PRINT "TOTAL EXPERIENCE MUST BE +VE,RETYPE"
```

```
7720    GOTO 7690
7730 W = V / W
8000 G = 1.0 + G
8050    PRINT  TAB( 5);"PERIOD"; TAB( 15);"COST"
8100    FOR I = 1 TO P
8150 C1 = C * (1.0 + W * G ^ I) ^ L
8200    PRINT  TAB( 5);I; TAB( 15); INT (10000 * C1 + .5) / 10000
8250    NEXT I
8300    REM   * ANOTHER ANALYSIS?"
8350    GOSUB 10300
8400    IF I = 1 THEN 3500
8450    GOTO 6250
8500    REM   ** FUTURE AVERAGE COST PER UNIT
8550    PRINT
8600    GOSUB 15300
8650    PRINT "*FUTURE AVERAGE COST PER UNIT ANALYSIS*"
8700    GOSUB 15300
8750    PRINT
8800    PRINT "THIS YEARS AVERAGE COST PER UNIT"
8850    INPUT C
8900    IF C > 0.0 THEN 9050
8950    PRINT "COST MUST BE +VE - RETYPE"
9000    GOTO 8850
9050    GOSUB 10950
9100    GOSUB 10750
9150 G = 1.0 + G
9200 C = C * G ^ ( - L)
9250    PRINT "FUTURE AVERAGE COST PER UNIT IS";
9300    PRINT  INT (10000 * C + .5) / 10000
9350    GOSUB 10300
9400    IF I = 1 THEN 3500
9450    GOTO 8800
9500    PRINT
9550    GOSUB 15300
9600    PRINT "*RATE OF AVERAGE COST DECLINE ANALYSIS*"
9650    GOSUB 15300
9700    PRINT
9750    GOSUB 10750
9800    GOSUB 10950
9850 G = 1.0 + G
9900 G = 1.0 - G ^ ( - L)
9950 G = 100.0 * G
10000   PRINT "RATE OF AVERAGE COST DECLINE = ";
10050   PRINT  INT (10000 * G + .5) / 10000
10100   GOSUB 10300
10150   IF I = 1 THEN 3500
10200   GOTO 9750
10250   REM   ** SUBROUTINE FOR VARY PARAMETERS REPLY
10300   PRINT
10350   PRINT "LIKE TO VARY SOME PARAMETERS "
10400   PRINT "ANSWER (Y/N)"
10450   INPUT YN$
10500   IF YN$ = "Y" THEN I = 0: GOTO 10700
10550   IF YN$ = "N" THEN I = 1: GOTO 10700
10600   PRINT "WRONG REPLY - RETYPE"
10650   GOTO 10450
10700   RETURN
10750   REM   GET VALUE FOR LAMBDA
10800   PRINT "VALUE FOR LAMBDA"
10850   INPUT L
10900   RETURN
10950   REM   ** GROWTH RATE SUBROUTINE
11000   PRINT "GROWTH RATE,EXPRESSED AS DECIMAL"
11050   INPUT G
```

```
11100   IF G < 0.0 THEN 11250
11150   IF G > 1.0 THEN 11250
11200   GOTO 11350
11250   PRINT "INVALID GROWTH RATE - RETYPE"
11300   GOTO 11050
11350   RETURN
11400   REM   GET OPTION
11450   PRINT
11500   PRINT "---------------------------------------"
11550   PRINT "SELECT AN OPTION BY TYPING IN THE"
11600   PRINT "APPROPRIATE OPTION NO. AND THEN"
11650   PRINT "THE APPROPRIATE DATA WHEN REQUESTED."
11700   PRINT "OPTION ";
11750   INPUT I
11800   IF I < 0 THEN 11950
11850   IF I > 9 THEN 11950
11900   GOTO 12050
11950   PRINT "OPTION SHOULD BE IN RANGE 0-9,RETYPE"
12000   GOTO 11750
12050   RETURN
12100   REM   MENU SELECTION
12150   PRINT
12200   PRINT "THE OPTIONS AVAILIBLE ARE"
12250   PRINT
12300   PRINT " 0    TERMINATE CURRENT RUN"
12350   PRINT " 1    FUTURE COST OF LAST UNIT PRODUCED"
12400   PRINT "      DURING CURRENT ANALYSIS"
12450   PRINT " 2    FUTURE MEAN UNIT COST ANALYSIS"
12500   PRINT " 3    RATE OF MEAN COST DECLINE ANALYSIS"
12550   PRINT " 4    FUTURE SPENDING FUNCTION PARAMETERS"
12600   PRINT " 9    DISPLAY MENU"
12650   PRINT
12700   RETURN
12750   PRINT
12760   PRINT "    *******************"
12770   PRINT "    * OPTION 2 : EXCU *"
12780   PRINT "    *******************"
13700   PRINT "THIS PROGRAM CARRIES OUT VARIOUS "
13750   PRINT "EXPERIENCE CURVE CALCULATIONS AND "
13800   PRINT "SHOULD BE USED IN CONJUNCTION WITH-"
13850   PRINT
13860   PRINT "       CHAPTER 3"
13870   PRINT "    EXPERIENCE CURVES"
14250   PRINT
14260   PRINT : INPUT "PRESS <RETURN> TO CONTINUE";YN$: PRINT
14300   PRINT "THE EXPERIENCE FUNCTION IS"
14350   PRINT
14400   PRINT " CN = C1*N^(-LAMBDA)"
14450   PRINT
14500   PRINT "WHERE:"
14550   PRINT " CN = COST OF NTH UNIT"
14600   PRINT " C1 = COST OF THE FIRST UNIT"
14650   PRINT " N = THE EXPERIENCE"
14700   PRINT " LAMBDA = ELASTICITY COEFFICIENT"
14750   PRINT " K = SLOPE OF THE LOG OF THE EXP. FUNC."
14800   PRINT "       EXPRESSED AS A PERCENTAGE"
14850   PRINT " DELTA C = RATE OF AVERAGE COST DECLINE"
14900   PRINT "          EXPRESSED AS A PERCENTAGE"
14950   PRINT
15000   PRINT "FOR A SERIES OF DATA PAIRS GIVING THE"
15050   PRINT "EXPERIENCE AND THE UNIT COST EXCU WILL"
15100   PRINT "COMPUTE THE ABOVE PARAMETERS,THEN YOU"
15150   PRINT "WILL HAVE VARIOUS OPTIONS."
15200   PRINT
```

```
15250    RETURN
15300    REM   PRINT A LINE OF ASTERISKS
15350    FOR J = 1 TO 39
15400    PRINT "*";
15450    NEXT J
15500    PRINT
15550    RETURN
15600    PRINT
15650    PRINT "        ***END OF RUN***"
15700    PRINT   CHR$ (4);"BRUN MASTER"
18000    FOR J = 1 TO I
18010    N1(J) =  LOG (N1(J)) /  LOG (10)
18020    C1(J) =  LOG (C1(J)) /  LOG (10)
18030    NEXT J
18040    X1 = N1(1):X2 = N1(I):Y1 = C1(1):Y2 = C1(I)
18050    FOR J = 1 TO I
18060    IF X1 > N1(J) THEN X1 = N1(J)
18070    IF X2 < N1(J) THEN X2 = N1(J)
18080    IF Y1 > C1(J) THEN Y1 = C1(J)
18090    IF Y2 < C1(J) THEN Y2 = C1(J)
18100    NEXT J
18110    SX = (X2 - X1) / 279:SY = (Y2 - Y1) / 159
18120    POKE 34,20: HGR : HOME
18130    HPLOT 0,0 TO 0,159 TO 279,159
18140    FOR J = 1 TO I - 1
18150    XX =  INT ((N1(J) - X1) / SX):YY = 159 -  INT ((C1(J) - Y1) / SY)
18160    GOSUB 18500
18170    HPLOT XX,YY TO  INT ((N1(J + 1) - X1) / SX),159 -
INT ((C1(J + 1) - Y1) / SY)
18180    NEXT J
18190    PRINT "     EXPERIENCE CURVE"
18200    PRINT "  LOG (COSTS) VS. LOG (VOLUME)"
18210    INPUT "PRESS <RETURN> TO CONTINUE";YN$
18220    TEXT : RETURN
18500    DX = 2:DY = 2
18510    IF XX + DX > 279 THEN DX = 279 - XX
18520    IF YY + DY > 159 THEN DY = 159 - YY
18530    HPLOT  ABS (XX - 2), ABS (YY - 2) TO XX,YY TO  ABS (XX - 2),YY +
18540    HPLOT XX + DX, ABS (YY - 2) TO XX,YY TO XX + DX,YY + DY
18550    RETURN
20000    IE =  PEEK (222)
20010    IF IE = 255 GOTO 15700
20020    PRINT "ERROR, STATUS";IE
20030    GOTO 15700

90  ONERR  GOTO 25000
100   REM           **************
105   REM           *PROGRAM PROM*
110   REM           **************
115   REM   SET UP VARIABLE ARRAYS
120.  DIM Y1(20),C1(20),R1(20),M1(20),V1(20),S1(20),G1(20)
125   REM   SET UP GLOBAL CONSTANT P = 1/PI
130 P = 1 / 3.14159
135   REM   PRINT TITLE
140   PRINT
150   PRINT "      ****************"
160   PRINT "      *OPTION 3: PROM*"
170   PRINT "      ****************"
180   PRINT : PRINT "THIS PROGRAM CARRIES OUT VARIOUS"
190   PRINT "PRODUCT MARKET PORTFOLIO CALCULATIONS"
200   PRINT "AND SHOULD BE USED IN CONJUNCTION"
210   PRINT "WITH..."
220   PRINT "             CHAPTER 4"
```

```
230   PRINT "  THE PRODUCT MARKET PORTFOLIO"
240   PRINT : INPUT "PRESS <RETURN> TO CONTINUE";YN$: PRINT
295   REM   PRINT MENU
300   GOSUB 14000
305   REM   GET OPTION
310   GOSUB 11000
315   REM   CHECK FOR OPTION ZERO,I.E. END RUN
320   IF I = 0 THEN  GOTO 30000
325   REM   OTHERWISE SELECT OPTION
330   ON I GOSUB 1000,2000,3000,14000
335   GOTO 305
340   REM
345   REM    ***THIS IS THE LOGICAL END OF THIS MODULE***
350   REM
1000  REM
1005  REM              ***OPTION 1***
1010  REM
1015  GOSUB 10000
1020  PRINT "*  MULTI-COMPANY GROWTH SHARE MATRIX  *"
1025  PRINT "*          FOR A SINGLE PRODUCT         *"
1030  GOSUB 10000
1040  PRINT "FOR A SERIES OF INPUT DATA COMPRISING-"
1045  PRINT "     1) YEAR"
1050  PRINT "     2) COMPANY(NUMERIC REPRESENTATION)"
1055  PRINT "     3) SALES VALUE"
1060  PRINT "     4) SALES VOLUME"
1065  PRINT "     5) MARKET GROWTH RATE"
1070  PRINT "PROM WILL CALCULATE THE RELATIVE MARKET"
1075  PRINT "SHARE AND THE RELATIVE RAD. OF A CIRCLE"
1080  PRINT "WHOSE AREA IS PROPORTIONAL TO THE SALES"
1085  PRINT "VALUE FOR EACH CASE."
1090  PRINT "THE INPUT DATA IS REQUIRED IN THE "
1095  PRINT "FOLLOWING FORMAT."
1100  PRINT "FIRST THE NUMBER OF CASES(OR LINES)"
1105  PRINT "THEN FOR EACH CASE ENTER A LINE OF"
1110  PRINT "DATA VALUES 1) TO 5) AS ABOVE,EACH"
1115  PRINT "VALUE BEING SEPARATED FROM THE NEXT BY"
1120  PRINT "A COMMA . THE DATA VALUES MUST BE IN "
1125  PRINT "ORDER GIVEN ABOVE."
1135  PRINT "PLEASE INPUT NUMBER OF CASES NOW";
1140  INPUT N1
1145  REM  CHECK N1 IS +VE INTEGER IN RANGE 1 TO 20
1150  X =  INT (N1)
1155  IF X <  > N1 THEN  GOTO 1165
1160  IF (N1 > 0) AND (N1 < 21) THEN  GOTO 1185
1165  PRINT "NUMBER OF CASES SHOULD BE A +VE INTEGER"
1170  PRINT "IN THE RANGE OF 1 TO 20."
1175  PRINT "PLEASE RETYPE"
1180  GOTO 1140
1185  REM  N1 O.K. SO GET REST OF DATA
1195  FOR J = 1 TO N1
1196  PRINT "PLEASE INPUT FOR CASE ";J
1197  PRINT "YR,CO,SALES VAL,SALES VOL,MKT GR RATE"
1200  INPUT Y1(J),C1(J),S1(J),V1(J),G1(J)
1202  PRINT "FOR CASE ";J;"YOU HAVE INPUT"
1204  PRINT "YEAR"; TAB( 20);Y1(J)
1206  PRINT "COMPANY"; TAB( 20);C1(J)
1208  PRINT "SALES VALUE"; TAB( 20);S1(J)
1210  PRINT "SALES VOLUME"; TAB( 20);V1(J)
1211  PRINT "MARKET GROWTH RATE"; TAB( 20);G1(J)
1212  INPUT "ARE THESE CORRECT (Y/N)";YN$
1213  IF YN$ = "N" THEN  PRINT "RE-INPUT VALUES FOR CASE ";J: GOTO 1200
1214  IF YN$ <  > "Y" GOTO 1212
1216  NEXT J
```

```
1218   REM   CALCULATE RADIUS OF CIRCLE,AREA OF WHICH
1219   REM   IS PROPORTIONAL TO SALES VALUE
1220   GOSUB 15000
1275   REM   NOW CALCULATE RELATIVE MARKET SHARE
1280   REM   FOR EACH CASE
1285   FOR K = 1 TO N1
1290 X =  - 999
1295   FOR J = 1 TO N1
1300   REM   CHECK FOR CASE OF SAME CO.,DIFFERENT YEARS
1305   IF C1(J) = C1(K) THEN   GOTO 1345
1310   REM   CHECK FOR CASE OF SAME CO.,SAME YEAR
1315   IF J = K THEN   GOTO 1345
1320   REM   CHECK FOR CASE OF DIFFERENT CO.,SAME YEAR
1325   IF Y1(J) < > Y1(K) THEN   GOTO 1345
1330   REM   CHECK FOR NEXT LARGEST RIVAL
1335   IF X > V1(J) THEN   GOTO 1345
1340 X = V1(J)
1345   NEXT J
1347   IF X < 0 THEN X = V1(K)
1350 M1(K) = V1(K) / X
1355   NEXT K
1360   REM       PRINT RESULTS TABLE
1365   PRINT
1370   GOSUB 10000
1375   PRINT "*YEAR *COMP* REL.RAD.*REL.MRKT.*GROWTH*"
1380   PRINT "*     *-ANY*OF CIRCLE*  SHARE  * RATE *"
1385   GOSUB 10000
1390   REM   SUBROUTINE 16000 FORMATS OUTPUT FOR PRETTY PRINT
1395   GOSUB 16000
1565   GOSUB 10000
1570   REM   ASK USER IF PARAMETERS TO BE VARIED
1575   GOSUB 12000
1580   IF I = 0 THEN 1090
1585   RETURN
2000   REM
2005   REM               ***OPTION 2***
2010   REM
2015   GOSUB 10000
2020   PRINT "*  MULTI-PRODUCT GROWTH SHARE MATRIX   *"
2025   PRINT "*          FOR A SINGLE COMPANY        *"
2030   GOSUB 10000
2040   PRINT "FOR A SERIES OF INPUT DATA COMPRISING-"
2045   PRINT "     1) YEAR"
2050   PRINT "     2) PRODUCT(NUMERIC REPRESENTATION)"
2055   PRINT "     3) SALES VALUE"
2060   PRINT "     4) REL. MARKET SHARE"
2065   PRINT "     5) MARKET GROWTH RATE"
2070   PRINT "PROM WILL CALCULATE THE REL. RAD. OF A"
2075   PRINT "CIRCLE WHOSE AREA IS PROP. TO THE SALES"
2080   PRINT "VALUE FOR EACH CASE."
2085   PRINT "THE INPUT DATA IS REQUIRED IN THE "
2090   PRINT "FOLLOWING FORMAT."
2095   PRINT "FIRST THE NUMBER OF CASES(OR LINES)"
2100   PRINT "THEN FOR EACH CASE ENTER A LINE OF"
2105   PRINT "DATA VALUES 1) TO 5) AS ABOVE,EACH"
2110   PRINT "VALUE BEING SEPARATED FROM THE NEXT BY"
2115   PRINT "A COMMA . THE DATA VALUES MUST BE IN "
2120   PRINT "ORDER GIVEN ABOVE."
2130   PRINT "PLEASE INPUT NUMBER OF CASES NOW";
2135   INPUT N1
2140   REM   CHECK N1 IS +VE INTEGER IN RANGE 1 TO 20
2145 X =   INT (N1)
2150   IF X < > N1 THEN   GOTO 2160
2155   IF (N1 > 0) AND (N1 < 21) THEN   GOTO 2180
```

```
2160  PRINT "NUMBER OF CASES SHOULD BE A +VE INTEGER"
2165  PRINT "IN THE RANGE OF 1 TO 20."
2170  PRINT "PLEASE RETYPE"
2175  GOTO 2135
2180  REM   N1 O.K. SO GET REST OF DATA
2190  FOR J = 1 TO N1
2191  PRINT "PLEASE INPUT FOR CASE ";J
2192  PRINT "YR,PROD,SALES VAL,REL MKT SHR,MKT GR RTE"
2193  INPUT Y1(J),C1(J),S1(J),M1(J),G1(J)
2194  PRINT "FOR CASE ";J;" YOU HAVE INPUT"
2195  PRINT "YEAR"; TAB( 20);Y1(J)
2196  PRINT "PRODUCT"; TAB( 20);C1(J)
2197  PRINT "SALES VALUE"; TAB( 20);S1(J)
2198  PRINT "RELATIVE MKT SHARE"; TAB( 20);M1(J)
2199  PRINT "MKT GROWTH RATE"; TAB( 20);G1(J)
2200  INPUT "ARE THESE CORRECT (Y/N)";YN$
2201  IF YN$ = "N" THEN  PRINT "RE-INPUT VALUES FOR CASE ";J: GOTO 2193
2202  IF YN$ <  > "Y" GOTO 2200
2204  NEXT J
2205  REM   CALCULATE RADIUS OF CIRCLE,AREA OF WHICH
2210  REM   IS PROPORTIONAL TO SALES VALUE
2215  GOSUB 15000
2270  REM      PRINT RESULTS TABLE
2275  PRINT
2280  GOSUB 10000
2285  PRINT "*YEAR *PROD* REL.RAD.*REL.MRKT.*GROWTH*"
2290  PRINT "*      *-UCT*OF CIRCLE*  SHARE  * RATE *"
2295  GOSUB 10000
2300  REM   SUBROUTINE 16000 FORMATS OUTPUT FOR PRETTY PRINTING
2305  GOSUB 16000
2475  GOSUB 10000
2480  REM  ASK USER IF PARAMETERS TO BE VARIED
2485  GOSUB 12000
2490  IF I = 0 THEN 2085
2495  RETURN
3000  REM
3005  REM            ***OPTION 3***
3010  REM
3015  GOSUB 10000
3020  PRINT "*      CALCULATION OF THE MAXIMUM       *"
3025  PRINT "*      SUSTAINABLE RATE OF GROWTH       *"
3030  GOSUB 10000
3040  PRINT "THE GROWTH RATE G IS DEFINED AS-"
3045  PRINT
3050  PRINT "    G = (D/E)*(R-I)*P+R*P"
3055  PRINT
3060  PRINT "WHERE-"
3065  PRINT "  D = AMOUNT OF COMPANY'S DEBT"
3070  PRINT "  E = AMOUNT OF COMPANY'S EQUITY"
3075  PRINT "  R = RATE OF RETURN ON ASSETS(%)"
3080  PRINT "  I = AFTERTAX CURRENT COST OF DEBT(%)"
3085  PRINT "  P = PROPORTION OF EARNINGS"
3090  PRINT "      RETAINED BY COMPANY"
3095  PRINT
3100  PRINT " N.B.  P = (1-DIVIDEND PAYOUT RATIO)"
3105  PRINT
3110  PRINT "GIVEN THE ABOVE PARAMETERS,PROM"
3115  PRINT "WILL CALCULATE G"
3120  PRINT
3125  PRINT "AMOUNT OF DEBT (D)"; TAB( 30);
3130  INPUT D3
3135  PRINT "AMOUNT OF EQUITY (E)"; TAB( 30);
3140  INPUT E3
3145  PRINT "RATE OF RETURN ON ASSETS (R)"; TAB( 30);
```

```
3150   INPUT R3
3155   PRINT "AFTRTAX CRRNT CST OF DEBT (I)"; TAB( 30);
3160   INPUT I3
3165   PRINT "PRPRTN OF EARNINGS RTNED (P)"; TAB( 30);
3170   INPUT P3
3175   REM   CALCULATE GROWTH RATE
3180   G3 = ((D3 / E3) * (R3 - I3) + R3) * P3
3185   PRINT
3190   REM   G3 FORMATTED BY SUBROUTINE 13000
3195 X = G3
3200 DP = 2
3205 SL = 6
3210   GOSUB 13000
3215 S$ = "* G = " + S$ + " % *"
3220   PRINT "      ****************"
3225   PRINT "      ";S$
3230   PRINT "      ****************"
3235   PRINT
3240   REM   ASK USER IF PARAMETERS TO BE VARIED
3245   GOSUB 12000
3250   IF I = 0 THEN 3120
3255   RETURN
10000   REM   SUBROUTINE TO PRINT A LINE OF ASTERISKS
10010   FOR J = 1 TO 39
10020   PRINT "*";
10030   NEXT J
10040   PRINT
10050   RETURN
11000   REM   SUBROUTINE TO GET OPTION
11010   PRINT
11020   PRINT "----------------------------------------"
11030   PRINT "SELECT AN OPTION BY TYPING IN THE"
11040   PRINT "APPROPRIATE OPTION NO. AND THEN"
11050   PRINT "THE APPROPRIATE DATA WHEN REQUESTED."
11060   PRINT "OPTION ";
11070   INPUT I
11080   IF I < 0 THEN 11110
11090   IF I > 4 THEN 11110
11100   GOTO 11130
11110   PRINT "OPTION SHOULD BE IN RANGE 0-4,RETYPE"
11120   GOTO 11070
11130   RETURN
12000   REM   SUBROUTINE FOR VARY PARAMETERS REPLY
12010   PRINT
12020   INPUT "LIKE TO VARY SOME PARAMETERS (Y/N)";YN$
12030   IF YN$ = "Y" THEN I = 0: GOTO 12090
12035   IF YN$ <  > "N" GOTO 12020
12040 I = 1
12090   RETURN
13000   REM   FORMAT SUBROUTINE: THIS SUBROUTINE TAKES A NUMBER X
13005   REM   AND FORMATS IF ACCORDING TO THE ARGUMENTS PASSED
13010   REM   THE NUMBER IS ROUNDED TO DP DECIMAL PLACES
13015   REM   AND CONVERTED TO A STRING OF LENGTH SL AND
13020   REM   RIGHTMOST PADDED WITH ZEROS AND LEFTMOST
13025   REM   PADDED WITH BLANKS.IF THE VALUE OF DP
13030   REM   PASSED IS <=0 THE NUMERIC STRING IS JUST
13035   REM   LEFTMOST PADDED WITH BLANKS.MAX. VAL DP=6
13040 S$ =   STR$ (X)
13045   IF DP <  = 0 THEN   GOTO 13115
13050   IF DP > 6 THEN DP = 6
13055 X =   INT (X * (10 ^ DP) + 0.5) / (10 ^ DP)
13060 S$ =   STR$ (X)
13065 LX =   LEN (S$)
13070 DX = 0
```

```
13075   FOR J1 = 1 TO LX
13080   IF   MID$ (S$,J1,1) = "." THEN DX = LX - J1
13085   NEXT J1
13090   IF DX > 0 THEN   GOTO 13105
13095  S$ = S$ +   LEFT$ (".000000",DP + 1)
13100   GOTO 13115
13105   IF DX = DP THEN   GOTO 13115
13110  S$ = S$ +   LEFT$ ("000000",DP - DX)
13115  LX =   LEN (S$)
13120   IF LX < SL THEN   GOTO 13135
13125  S$ =   LEFT$ (S$,SL)
13130   GOTO 13150
13135   IF   LEN (S$) = SL THEN   GOTO 13150
13140  S$ = " " + S$
13145   GOTO 13135
13150   RETURN
14000   REM   SUBROUTINE TO PRINT MENU
14005   PRINT
14010   PRINT "THE OPTIONS AVAILIBLE ARE-"
14015   PRINT
14020   PRINT "   0     TERMINATE CURRENT RUN"
14025   PRINT "   1     MULTI-COMPANY GROWTH SHARE"
14030   PRINT "         MATRIX(SINGLE PRODUCT)"
14035   PRINT "   2     MULTI-PRODUCT GROWTH SHARE"
14040   PRINT "         MATRIX(SINGLE COMPANY)"
14045   PRINT "   3     CALCULATION OF MAXIMUM"
14050   PRINT "         SUSTAINABLE RATE OF GROWTH"
14055   PRINT "   4     DISPLAY OPTION MENU"
14060   PRINT
14065   RETURN
15000   REM   SUBROUTINE TO CALCULATE REL. RAD. OF
15005   REM      CIRCLE PROPORTIONAL TO SALES VOL.
15010  X = 1000
15015   FOR J = 1 TO N1
15020  R1(J) =   SQR (S1(J) * P)
15025   IF X < R1(J) THEN   GOTO 15035
15030  X = R1(J)
15035   NEXT J
15040   REM   X NOW CONTAINS MINIMUM VALUE OF R1(J)
15045   REM   USED TO CALCULATE RELATIVE RADIUS
15050   FOR J = 1 TO N1
15055  R1(J) = R1(J) / X
15060   NEXT J
15065   RETURN
16000   REM   SUB. TO ROUND RADIUS AND MARKET SHARE TO 4 DECIMAL
16005   REM   PLACES AND GROWTHR RATE TO 2 DECIMAL PLACES
16010   REM   THEN CONVERT TO STRINGS FOR PRETTY PRINTING
16015   FOR J = 1 TO N1
16020   REM   L$ IS OUTPUT LINE STRING,INITIALISED TO NULL
16025  L$ = ""
16030   REM   SUBROUTINE 13000 CONVERTS NUMBER TO STRING OF
16035   REM   LENGTH SL AND DP DEC. PLACES
16040  X = Y1(J)
16045  SL = 4
16050  DP = 0
16055   GOSUB 13000
16060  L$ = L$ + "*" + S$ + " "
16065  X = C1(J)
16070  SL = 3
16075  DP = 0
16080   GOSUB 13000
16085  L$ = L$ + "*" + S$ + " "
16090  X = R1(J)
16095  SL = 8
```

```
16100 DP = 4
16105  GOSUB 13000
16110 L$ = L$ + "*" + S$ + " "
16115 SL = 8
16120 X = M1(J)
16125 DP = 4
16130  GOSUB 13000
16135 L$ = L$ + "*" + S$ + " "
16140 SL = 5
16145 X = G1(J)
16150 DP = 2
16155  GOSUB 13000
16160 L$ = L$ + "*" + S$ + "*"
16165  PRINT L$
16170 NEXT J
16175  RETURN
25000 IE =  PEEK (222)
25010  IF IE = 255 GOTO 30015
25020  PRINT "ERROR, STATUS=";IE
25030  GOTO 30015
30000  PRINT
30005  PRINT "       ***END OF RUN***"
30010  PRINT
30015  PRINT  CHR$ (4);"BRUN MASTER"


90   ONERR  GOTO 25000
100  REM    ****************
110  REM    * PROGRAM FINA *
120  REM    ****************
130  REM
140  REM    WRITTEN BY L. ASQUITH AND P.B. MC NAMEE (MAR 1984)
150  REM
155  DIM D(39,2),R(14,2),Y(2)
156  C$ = "*NO-BALANCE*"
160  PRINT : PRINT " ********************"
170  PRINT " * OPTION 1 : FINA *"
180  PRINT " ********************"
190  PRINT "THIS PROGRAM CARRIES OUT VARIOUS"
200  PRINT "FINANCIAL ANALYSIS AND SHOULD BE"
210  PRINT "USED IN CONJUNCTION WITH..."
220  PRINT "         CHAPTER 2"
225  PRINT "         FINANCE FOR"
230  PRINT "   STRATEGIC MANAGEMENT": PRINT
250  PRINT "OPTIONS AVAILABLE ARE..."
260  PRINT " 0 TERMINATE CURRENT RUN"
270  PRINT " 1 RATIO ANALYSIS"
290  PRINT " 2 SOURCES AND USES OF"
300  PRINT "   FUNDS STATEMENTS"
310  PRINT " 3 FOR FUTURE DEVELOPMENT"
320  PRINT " 4 CALCULATION OF THE MAXIMUM"
330  PRINT "   SUSTAINABLE RATE OF GROWTH"
340  PRINT " 5 BREAK EVEN ANALYSIS"
345  PRINT " 6 INPUT NEW COMPANY BALANCE"
346  PRINT "   SHEET AND INCOME STATEMENT"
350  INPUT "SELECT AN OPTION (0-6)";IOP
360  IF IOP > = 0 AND IOP < = 6 GOTO 380
370  PRINT "ERROR, INVALID OPTION": GOTO 350
380  IF IOP = 0 GOTO 30000
390  IF IOP < > 6 GOTO 410
400  GOSUB 3000: GOSUB 4000: GOTO 250
410  ON IOP GOSUB 5000,7000,8000,9000,10000
420  GOTO 250
3000  REM
```

```
3001   REM     *******************************************
3002   REM     *SUBROUTINE 3000:INPUT COMPANY BALANCE SHEET*
3003   REM     *******************************************
3004   REM
3009   REM     THIS ROUTINE GETS ALL BALANCE SHEET INFORMATION
3010   REM     INTO ARRAY D WHICH MUST BE DIMENSIONED 36,2
3020   REM     THE COMPANY NAME IS RETURNED IN STRING C$ AND
3030   REM     THE YEAR(S) RETURNED IN Y(1) AND Y(2) (Y(1)<Y(2))
3040   REM     UP TO TWO YEARS MAY BE INPUT
3045   REM     NY IS SET TO THE NUMBER OF YEARS
3050   REM     *NOTE* ALL LOCAL VARS IN THIS ROUTINE TERMINATE WITH 3
3055   PRINT : PRINT "*********************************"
3060   PRINT "*BALANCE SHEET DATA INPUT SECTION*"
3070   PRINT "*********************************": PRINT
3080   PRINT "YOU ARE REQUIRED TO INPUT ANNUAL BALANCE"
3090   PRINT "SHEET FIGURES FOR THE COMPANY UNDER"
3100   PRINT "CONSIDERATION. YOU MAY INPUT FIGURES FOR"
3110   PRINT "UP TO TWO YEARS TRADING": PRINT
3120   INPUT "PLEASE GIVE COMPANY NAME:";C$: PRINT
3130   INPUT "NUMBER OF YEARS (1 OR 2):";NY: PRINT
3140   IF NY = 1 OR NY = 2 GOTO 3152
3150   PRINT "ERROR, NUMBER YEARS NOT VALID": PRINT : GOTO 3130
3152   FOR J3 = 1 TO NY: PRINT "YEAR ";J3;" IS";: INPUT Y(J3): NEXT J3
3154   IF NY = 1 GOTO 3190
3156   IF Y(1) < Y(2) GOTO 3190
3158   IF Y(1) = Y(2) THEN  PRINT "ERROR, YEARS THE SAME??": GOTO 3152
3160   ITMP = Y(1):Y(1) = Y(2):Y(2) = ITMP
3190   FOR J3 = 1 TO NY
3200   PRINT "FIXED ASSETS(COST) FOR YEAR   ";Y(J3): PRINT
3210   INPUT " LAND                         ";D(1,J3)
3220   INPUT " BUILDINGS                    ";D(2,J3)
3230   INPUT " EQUIPMENT                    ";D(3,J3)
3235   INPUT " DEPRECIATION                 ";D(4,J3)
3240   D(6,J3) = D(1,J3) + D(2,J3) + D(3,J3) - D(4,J3): PRINT
3250   PRINT "NET FIXED ASSETS             ";D(6,J3)
3260   PRINT : INPUT "IS THIS CORRECT (Y/N):";Y3$: PRINT
3270   IF Y3$ = "N" GOTO 3200
3280   IF Y3$ < > "Y" GOTO 3250
3285   INPUT "INVESTMENTS AND OTHER ASSETS  ";D(7,J3): PRINT
3290   PRINT "CURRENT ASSETS FOR YEAR       ";Y(J3): PRINT
3300   INPUT " INVENTORY                    ";D(8,J3)
3310   INPUT " ACCS RECEIVABLE              ";D(9,J3)
3320   INPUT " SHORT TERM INVESTMENTS       ";D(10,J3)
3330   INPUT " PREPAID EXPENSES             ";D(11,J3)
3340   INPUT " CASH                         ";D(12,J3)
3350   D(13,J3) = D(8,J3) + D(9,J3) + D(10,J3) + D(11,J3) + D(12,J3): PRINT

3360   PRINT "TOTAL CURRENT ASSETS          ";D(13,J3)
3370   PRINT : INPUT "IS THIS CORRECT (Y/N):";Y3$: PRINT
3380   IF Y3$ = "N" GOTO 3290
3390   IF Y3$ < > "Y" GOTO 3360
3400   D(14,J3) = D(6,J3) + D(7,J3) + D(13,J3): PRINT
3410   PRINT "TOTAL ASSETS                  ";D(14,J3)
3420   PRINT : PRINT "FINANCED BY:"
3430   PRINT " SHAREHOLDERS EQUITY"
3450   INPUT "     COMMON STOCK              ";D(16,J3)
3460   INPUT "     RETAINED EARNINGS         ";D(17,J3)
3470   D(18,J3) = D(16,J3) + D(17,J3): PRINT
3480   PRINT "     TOTAL EQUITY             ";D(18,J3)
3490   PRINT : INPUT "IS THIS CORRECT (Y/N):";Y3$: PRINT
3500   IF Y3$ = "N" GOTO 3420
3510   IF Y3$ < > "Y" GOTO 3480
3520   INPUT "LONG TERM DEBT                ";D(19,J3)
3530   INPUT "OTHER NONCURRENT LIABILITIES  ";D(20,J3)
```

```
3540  PRINT : PRINT "CURRENT LIABILITIES": PRINT
3550  INPUT " ACCOUNTS PAYABLE          ";D(21,J3)
3560  INPUT " NOTES PAYABLE             ";D(22,J3)
3570  INPUT " ACCRUED EXPENSES          ";D(23,J3)
3580  INPUT " TAXES                     ";D(24,J3)
3590 D(25,J3) = D(21,J3) + D(22,J3) + D(23,J3) + D(24,J3): PRINT
3600  PRINT "     TOTAL CURRENT LIABILITIES  ";D(25,J3)
3610  PRINT : INPUT "IS THIS CORRECT (Y/N):";Y3$: PRINT
3620  IF Y3$ = "N" GOTO 3540
3630  IF Y3$ < > "Y" GOTO 3600
3640 D(26,J3) = D(18,J3) + D(19,J3) + D(20,J3) + D(25,J3): PRINT
3650  PRINT "     TOTAL LIABILITIES        ";D(26,J3)
3660  IF  ABS (D(26,J3) - D(14,J3)) < 0.0001 GOTO 3745
3670  PRINT : PRINT "ERROR, FIGURES DO NOT BALANCE"
3680  PRINT "YOU MAY..."
3690  PRINT "         1) CONTINUE PROGRAM"
3700  PRINT "         2) RE-INPUT BALANCE SHEET"
3710  PRINT : INPUT "OPTION (1 OR 2) ";I3: PRINT
3720  IF I3 = 1 GOTO 3750
3730  IF I3 = 2 GOTO 3200
3740  GOTO 3710
3745  PRINT
3750  INPUT "AVG. NUM. SHARES OUTSTANDING  ";D(27,J3)
3760  NEXT J3
3870  RETURN
4000  REM
4001  REM    ***********************************************
4002  REM    *SUBROUTINE 4000:INPUT INCOME STATEMENT ROUTINE*
4003  REM    ***********************************************
4004  REM
4009  REM   THIS ROUTINE GETS THE INCOME STATEMENT FOR
4010  REM   COMPANY C$ INTO ARRAY D FOR THE NY YEARS
4020  REM   REFER TO SUBROUTINE 3000 FOR DEFINITIONS
4030  REM    OF ARRAYS AND VARIABLES
4040  REM
4050  PRINT : PRINT "********************************"
4060  PRINT "*INCOME STATEMENT INPUT SECTION*"
4070  PRINT "********************************": PRINT
4080  PRINT "YOU ARE REQUIRED TO INPUT THE INCOME"
4090  PRINT "STATEMENT FOR COMPANY ";C$
4100  PRINT " FOR THE YEAR(S) SPECIFIED PREVIOUSLY": PRINT
4120  FOR J4 = 1 TO NY
4125  PRINT "INCOME STATEMENT FOR YEAR    ";Y(J4): PRINT
4130  INPUT "NET SALES                ";D(28,J4)
4140  INPUT "COST OF SALES            ";D(29,J4)
4150 D(30,J4) = D(28,J4) - D(29,J4)
4160  PRINT "GROSS PROFIT               ";D(30,J4)
4170  PRINT : PRINT "EXPENSES": PRINT
4180  INPUT " SELLING GEN AND ADMIN     ";D(31,J4)
4190  INPUT " INTEREST                  ";D(32,J4)
4200  INPUT " DEPRECIATION              ";D(33,J4)
4210 D(34,J4) = D(31,J4) + D(32,J4) + D(33,J4)
4220  PRINT "TOTAL EXPENSES             ";D(34,J4)
4230 D(35,J4) = D(30,J4) - D(34,J4)
4240  PRINT "PROFIT BEFORE TAX          ";D(35,J4)
4250  INPUT "PROVISIONS FOR TAX        ";D(36,J4)
4260 D(37,J4) = D(35,J4) - D(36,J4)
4270  PRINT "NET EARNINGS               ";D(37,J4)
4280  INPUT "CASH DIVIDENDS            ";D(38,J4)
4290 D(39,J4) = D(37,J4) - D(38,J4)
4300  PRINT "RETAINED EARNINGS          ";D(39,J4)
4310  PRINT : INPUT "INCOME STATEMENT CORRECT (Y/N):";Y3$: PRINT
4320  IF Y3$ = "N" GOTO 4125
4330  IF Y3$ < > "Y" GOTO 4310
```

```
4340    NEXT J4
4350    RETURN
5000    REM
5001    REM     *********************************
5002    REM     *SUBROUTINE 5000:RATIO ANALYSIS*
5003    REM     *********************************
5004    REM
5009    REM     THIS ROUTINE CARRIES OUT RATIO ANALYSIS FOR THE
5010    REM     THE YEARS FOR WHICH A BALANCE SHEET HAS BEEN
5020    REM     INPUT. THE BALANCE SHEET LIVES IN ARRAY D AND
5030    REM     THE COMPANY NAME IN C$. THE YEAR COUNT (1 OR 2) IS
5040    REM     HELD IN NY AND THE ACTUAL YEARS IN ARRAY Y
5050    REM     NOTE THAT IF C$ = "*NO-BALANCE*" THEN NO BALANCE
5060    REM     SHEET HAS BEEN INPUT SO ROUTINES 3000 AND 4000
5070    REM     MUST BE CALLED TO INPUT THE RELEVENT INFO.
5075    REM     CALCULATED RATIOS ARE STORED IN ARRAY R WHICH
5076    REM     MUST BE DIMENSIONED 14,2 IN THE MAIN PROGRAM
5080    REM
5090    IF C$ <  > "*NO-BALANCE*" GOTO 5130
5100    GOSUB 3000: GOSUB 4000
5130    REM  P(1) & P(2) HOLD INVENTORIES OF PREVIOUS YEAR(S)
5140    P(1) = 0:P(2) = D(8,1)
5150    PRINT "PLEASE GIVE INVENTORY LEVEL OR AN"
5160    PRINT "ESTIMATE FOR YEAR ";Y(1) - 1: INPUT P(1)
5170    IF NY = 1 GOTO 5210
5180    IF Y(2) - Y(1) = 1 GOTO 5210
5190    PRINT "PLEASE GIVE INVENTORY LEVEL OR AN"
5200    PRINT "ESTIMATE FOR YEAR ";Y(2) - 1: INPUT P(2)
5210    FOR J = 1 TO NY
5220    R(1,J) = D(13,J) / D(25,J)
5230    R(2,J) = (D(13,J) - ((D(8,J) + P(J)) / 2)) / D(25,J)
5240    R(3,J) = 100 * (D(28,J) - D(29,J)) / D(28,J)
5250    R(4,J) = 100 * D(37,J) / D(28,J)
5260    R(5,J) = 100 * D(37,J) / D(14,J)
5270    R(6,J) = 100 * D(37,J) / D(18,J)
5280    R(7,J) = 100 * D(37,J) / D(27,J)
5290    R(8,J) = 100 * D(38,J) / D(37,J)
5300    R(9,J) = 100 * D(19,J) / D(18,J)
5310    R(10,J) = (D(35,J) + D(32,J)) / D(32,J)
5320    R(11,J) = D(28,J) / D(6,J)
5330    R(12,J) = D(28,J) / D(8,J)
5340    R(13,J) = D(28,J) / D(9,J)
5350    R(14,J) = 360 / R(13,J)
5352    NEXT J
5360    REM  ROUND ALL VALUES O NEAREST 0.05
5365    GOSUB 21000
5374    PRINT : PRINT "      ************************"
5376    PRINT "      * RATIO ANALYSIS RESULTS*"
5378    PRINT "      ************************"
5380    PRINT "COMPANY: ";C$
5390    PRINT  TAB( 20);Y(1);
5400    IF NY > 1 THEN  PRINT  TAB( 30);Y(2): GOTO 5405
5402    PRINT
5405    PRINT "*LIQUIDITY RATIOS*"
5410    PRINT "CURRENT RATIO        ";
5420    J = 1: GOSUB 20000
5430    PRINT "QUICK RATIO          ";
5440    J = 2: GOSUB 20000
5450    PRINT "*PROFITABILITY RATIOS*"
5460    PRINT "GROSS PROFIT MARGIN ";
5470    J = 3: GOSUB 20000
5480    PRINT "NET PROFIT MARGIN    ";
5490    J = 4: GOSUB 20000
5500    PRINT "RETURN ON INVSTMNTS ";
```

```
5510  J = 5: GOSUB 20000
5520   PRINT "RETURN ON EQUITY      ";
5530  J = 6: GOSUB 20000
5450   PRINT "*PROFITABILITY RATIOS*"
5460   PRINT "GROSS PROFIT MARGIN ";
5470  J = 3: GOSUB 20000
5480   PRINT "NET PROFIT MARGIN    ";
5490  J = 4: GOSUB 20000
5500   PRINT "RETURN ON INVSTMNTS ";
5510  J = 5: GOSUB 20000
5520   PRINT "RETURN ON EQUITY      ";
5530  J = 6: GOSUB 20000
5540   PRINT "EARNINGS PER SHARE   ";
5550  J = 7: GOSUB 20000
5560   PRINT "PAYOUT RATIO          ";
5570  J = 8: GOSUB 20000
5580   PRINT "*LEVERAGE RATIOS*"
5590   PRINT "DEBT - EQUITY         ";
5600  J = 9: GOSUB 20000
5610   PRINT "DEBT COVERAGE         ";
5620  J = 10: GOSUB 20000
5630   PRINT "*ACTIVITY RATIOS*"
5640   PRINT "FIXED ASSET TURNOVER";
5650  J = 11: GOSUB 20000
5660   PRINT "INVENTORY TURNOVER   ";
5670  J = 12: GOSUB 20000
5680   PRINT "ACCTS RECEV TURNOVER";
5690  J = 13: GOSUB 20000
5700   PRINT "AVG CLLCTN PRD(DAYS)";
5710  J = 14: GOSUB 20000
5720   PRINT : INPUT "PRESS <RETURN> TO CONTINUE";Y3$
5730   RETURN
7000   REM
7001   REM      *****************************************
7002   REM      *SUBROUTINE 7000:SOURCES AND USES OF FUNDS*
7003   REM      *****************************************
7004   REM
7010   IF C$ <  > "*NO-BALANCE*" GOTO 7030
7020   GOSUB 3000: GOSUB 4000
7030   IF NY > 1 GOTO 7050
7040   PRINT : PRINT "REQUIRE 2 CONSECUTIVE YEARS FIGURES"
7042   PRINT "TO COMPUTE USE OF FUNDS STATEMENT": RETURN
7050   IF Y(1) + 1 <  > Y(2) GOTO 7040
7060   PRINT : PRINT  TAB( 15);"COMPANY: ";C$
7080   PRINT "         SOURCES AND USES OF FUNDS": PRINT
7090   PRINT "SOURCES OF FUNDS"; TAB( 30);Y(2)
7100   PRINT "PROFIT BEFORE TAX"; TAB( 30);D(35,2)
7105   PRINT "ADJMTS FOR ITEMS NOT INVOLVING"
7110   PRINT "FUND MOVEMENTS:"
7115  R(1,1) = D(4,2) - D(4,1):R(2,1) = D(35,2) + R(1,1)
7120   PRINT "  DEPRECIATION"; TAB( 30);R(1,1)
7130   PRINT "TOTAL GENERATED"; TAB( 30);R(2,1)
7140   PRINT "FUNDS FROM OTHER SOURCES:"
7145  R(3,1) = D(16,2) - D(16,1)
7150   PRINT "  ISSUE OF SHARES FOR CASH"; TAB( 30);R(3,1)
7155   PRINT  TAB( 30);R(2,1) + R(3,1)
7160   PRINT "APPLICATION OF FUNDS:"
7165  R(4,1) =   - 1 * ((D(1,2) + D(2,2) + D(3,2)) - (D(1,1) + D(2,1) + D(3,1)))
7170   PRINT "  PURCHASE OF FIXED ASSETS"; TAB( 30);R(4,1)
7180  R(5,1) = D(19,2) - D(19,1)
7190   PRINT "  REDEMPTN OF LONG TERM DEBT   "; TAB( 30);R(5,1)
7200   PRINT "  DIVIDENDS PAID"; TAB( 30);  - 1 * D(38,2)
7205  R(6,1) =   - 1 * (D(24,1) + D(36,2) - D(24,2))
```

```
7210  PRINT "    TAX PAID"; TAB( 30);R(6,1)
7215  X1 = R(4,1) + R(5,1) - D(38,2) + R(6,1)
7216  PRINT   TAB( 30);X1
7217  PRINT   TAB( 30);R(2,1) + R(3,1) + X1
7218  PRINT : INPUT "PRESS <RETURN> TO CONTINUE";A$: PRINT
7220  PRINT "INCREASE IN WORKING CAPITAL:"
7225  R(7,1) = D(8,2) - D(8,1)
7230  PRINT "   INVENTORY"; TAB( 30);R(7,1)
7232  R(9,1) = D(9,2) - D(9,1)
7234  PRINT "  ACCOUNTS RECEIVABLE"; TAB( 30);R(9,1)
7235  R(8,1) = D(11,2) - D(11,1)
7240  PRINT "   PREPAYMENTS"; TAB( 30);R(8,1)
7255  R(10,1) =  - 1 * (D(21,2) - D(21,1))
7260  PRINT "  ACCOUNTS PAYABLE"; TAB( 30);R(10,1)
7265  R(11,1) =  - 1 * (D(22,2) - D(22,1))
7270  PRINT "  NOTES PAYABLE"; TAB( 30);R(11,1)
7275  R(12,1) =  - 1 * (D(23,2) - D(23,1))
7280  PRINT "  ACCRUED EXPENSES"; TAB( 30);R(12,1)
7290  PRINT "MOVEMENT IN NET LIQUID FUNDS:"
7295  R(13,1) = D(12,2) - D(12,1):R(14,1) = D(10,2) - D(10,1)
7300  PRINT "   INCREASE IN CASH"; TAB( 30);R(13,1)
7310  PRINT "   SHORT TERM INVSTMNT INCREASE"; TAB( 30);R(14,1)
7315  X2 = 0.0: FOR J = 7 TO 14:X2 = X2 + R(J,1): NEXT J: PRINT  TAB( 30);X
      2
7320  PRINT : INPUT "PRESS <RETURN> TO CONTINUE";Y3$: PRINT
7330  RETURN
8000  REM
8001  REM     *****************************************
8002  REM     *SUBROUTINE 8000:PROJECTED BALANCE SHEETS*
8003  REM     *****************************************
8004  REM
8010  PRINT "YET TO BE WRITTEN"
8020  RETURN
9000  REM
9001  REM     ***********************************************
9002  REM     *SUBROUTINE 9000:MAX SUSTAINABLE RATE OF GROWTH*
9003  REM     ***********************************************
9004  REM
9006  PRINT "      ***************************"
9008  PRINT "      *CALCULATION OF THE MAXIMUM*"
9010  PRINT "      *SUSTAINABLE RATE OF GROWTH*"
9020  PRINT "      ***************************"
9030  PRINT "THE GROWTH RATE G IS DEFINED AS-"
9040  PRINT
9050  PRINT "    G = (D/E)*(R-I)*P+R*P"
9060  PRINT
9070  PRINT "WHERE-"
9080  PRINT "   D = AMOUNT OF COMPANY'S DEBT"
9090  PRINT "   E = AMOUNT OF COMPANY'S EQUITY"
9100  PRINT "   R = RATE OF RETURN ON ASSETS(%)"
9110  PRINT "   I = AFTERTAX CURRENT COST OF DEBT(%)"
9120  PRINT "   P = PROPORTION OF EARNINGS"
9130  PRINT "       RETAINED BY COMPANY"
9150  PRINT " N.B.   P = (1-DIVIDEND PAYOUT RATIO)"
9170  PRINT "GIVEN THE ABOVE PARAMETERS,FINA"
9180  PRINT "WILL CALCULATE G"
9190  PRINT
9200  PRINT "AMOUNT OF DEBT (D)         ";
9210  INPUT D3
9220  PRINT "AMOUNT OF EQUITY (E)        ";
9240  INPUT E3
9250  PRINT "RATE OF RETURN ON ASSETS (R)";
9270  INPUT R3
9290  PRINT "AFTERTAX COST OF DEBT (I)    ";
9300  INPUT I3
```

```
9320    PRINT "PROPTN EARNINGS RETAINED (P)";
9330    INPUT P3
9350    REM   CALCULATE GROWTH RATE
9360    G3 = ((D3 / E3) * (R3 - I3) + R3) * P3
9370    PRINT
9380    REM   G3 FORMATTED BY SUBROUTINE 22000
9390    X = G3
9400    DP = 2
9410    SL = 6
9420    GOSUB 22000
9430    S$ = "* G = " + S$ + " % *"
9440    PRINT "     ****************"
9450    PRINT "          ";S$
9460    PRINT "     ****************"
9470    PRINT
9480    RETURN
10000   REM
10001   REM   ***************************************
10002   REM   *SUBROUTINE 10000:BREAK EVEN ANALYSIS*
10003   REM   ***************************************
10004   REM
10010   PRINT : PRINT "    :*****************:*"
10020   PRINT "    *BREAK-EVEN ANALYSIS*"
10030   PRINT "    ********************": PRINT
10032   PRINT "THIS OPTION CALCULATES THE LINEAR"
10034   PRINT "BREAKEVEN POINT AND OPTIONALLY "
10036   PRINT "ALLOWS YOU TO LINK THIS TO SALES"
10038   PRINT "FORECASTS FOR VARIOUS PRICES ": PRINT
10040   INPUT "COMPANY NAME       ";B1$
10050   INPUT "PRODUCT NAME       ";B2$
10060   INPUT "DATE (YEAR)        ";Y
10070   INPUT "FIXED COSTS        ";F
10080   INPUT "VARIABLE UNIT COSTS  ";X1
10090   INPUT "UNIT SELLING PRICE   ";X2
10100   IF X2 > X1 GOTO 10130
10110   PRINT : PRINT "ERROR, VARIABLE UNIT COST GREATER "
10120   PRINT "THAN SELLING PRICE": GOTO 10080
10130   BP = F / (X2 - X1)
10135   PRINT : PRINT "COMPANY: ";B1$
10140   PRINT "BREAKEVEN POINT FOR PRODUCT: ";B2$
10150   PRINT "FOR ";Y;" AT A PRICE OF ";X2;" IS"
10160   PRINT : PRINT TAB( 15);"****************"
10170   PRINT  TAB( 15);BP;" UNITS"
10180   PRINT  TAB( 15);"****************"
10190   PRINT : INPUT "PRESS <RETURN> TO CONTINUE";Y3$
10195   GOSUB 24000
10200   PRINT : PRINT "DO YOU WISH TO LINK THIS TO "
10210   PRINT "SALES FORECASTS TO CALCULATE THE"
10220   PRINT "OPTIMAL INTEREST BEFORE TAX (BIT)"
10230   INPUT "(Y/N)";Y3$
10240   IF Y3$ = "N" THEN   RETURN
10250   IF Y3$ <  > "Y" GOTO 10190
10260   INPUT "HOW MANY SALES FORECASTS ";NF
10270   IF NF > 1 AND NF < 15 GOTO 10290
10280   PRINT "YOU MAY ONLY HAVE 1 TO 14 FORECASTS": GOTO 10260
10290   FOR J = 1 TO NF
10300   PRINT J;" FORECAST PRICE";: INPUT R(J,1)
10302   IF R(J,1) > X1 GOTO 10310
10304   PRINT "ERROR, FORECAST PRICE LESS THAN OR"
10306   PRINT "EQUAL COST PRICE. PLEASE RE-INPUT": GOTO 10300
10310   PRINT J;" FORECAST SALES";: INPUT R(J,2)
10420   NEXT J
10430   PRINT : PRINT "PRICE"; TAB( 10);"SALES"; TAB( 20);"BREAKEVEN"; TAB(
    30);"PROFIT"
```

```
10440   PRINT  TAB( 10);"FORECAST"; TAB( 20`,"POINT"; TAB( 30);"B.I.T.": PRINT

10450   FOR J = 1 TO NF
10455 X2 = R(J,1) - X1:BP =  INT (F / X2 + .5)
10460   PRINT R(J,1); TAB( 10);R(J,2); TAB( 20);BP; TAB( 30);X2 * (R(J,2) -
   BP)
10470   NEXT J
10480   PRINT : INPUT "PRESS <RETURN> TO CONTINUE";Y3$
10485   FOR J = 1 TO NF
10486 R(J,1) = R(J,1) * R(J,2)
10487 R(J,2) = F + X1 * R(J,2)
10488   NEXT J
10489   GOSUB 24500
10490   RETURN
20000   REM
20010   REM      *****************************
20020   REM      *SUBROUTINE 20000:SEE SUB 5000*
20030   REM      *****************************
20040   REM
20050   PRINT  TAB( 20);R(J,1);
20060   IF NY > 1 THEN  PRINT  TAB( 30);R(J,2): GOTO 20070
20065   PRINT
20070   RETURN
21000   REM
21010   REM      ***************************************************
21020   REM      *SUBROUTINE 21000:ROUNDS ARRAY R TO NEAREST .05*
21030   REM      ***************************************************
21040   REM
21050   FOR J = 1 TO 14
21060   FOR K = 1 TO NY
21070 R(J,K) = ( INT (R(J,K) * 100 + .5)) / 100.0
21080   NEXT K
21090   NEXT J
21100   RETURN
22000   REM  FORMAT SUBROUTINE: THIS SUBROUTINE TAKES A NUMBER X
22010   REM  AND FORMATS IF ACCORDING TO THE ARGUMENTS PASSED
22020   REM  THE NUMBER IS ROUNDED TO DP DECIMAL PLACES
22030   REM  AND CONVERTED TO A STRING OF LENGTH SL AND
22040   REM  RIGHTMOST PADDED WITH ZEROS AND LEFTMOST
22050   REM  PADDED WITH BLANKS.IF THE VALUE OF DP
22060   REM  PASSED IS <=0 THE NUMERIC STRING IS JUST
22070   REM  LEFTMOST PADDED WITH BLANKS.MAX. VAL DP=6
22080 S$ =  STR$ (X)
22090   IF DP <  = 0 THEN  GOTO 22230
22100   IF DP > 6 THEN DP = 6
22110 X =  INT (X * (10 ^ DP) + 0.5) / (10 ^ DP)
22120 S$ =  STR$ (X)
22130 LX =  LEN (S$)
22140 DX = 0
22150   FOR J1 = 1 TO LX
22160   IF  MID$ (S$,J1,1) = "." THEN DX = LX - J1
22170   NEXT J1
22180   IF DX > 0 THEN  GOTO 22210
22190 S$ = S$ +  LEFT$ (".000000",DP + 1)
22200   GOTO 22230
22210   IF DX = DP THEN  GOTO 22230
22220 S$ = S$ +  LEFT$ ("000000",DP - DX)
22230 LX =  LEN (S$)
22240   IF LX < SL THEN  GOTO 22270
22250 S$ =  LEFT$ (S$,SL)
22260   GOTO 22300
22270   IF  LEN (S$) = SL THEN  GOTO 22300
22280 S$ = " " + S$
22290   GOTO 22270
```

```
22300    RETURN
23000    POKE 34,20: HGR : HOME
23010    HPLOT 0,0 TO 0,159 TO 279,159
23020    RETURN
23100    HPLOT  ABS (XX - 2),YY TO XX,YY TO XX, ABS (YY - 2)
23110 DX = 2:DY = 2
23120    IF XX + DX > 279 THEN DX = 279 - XX
23130    IF YY + DY > 159 THEN DY = 159 - YY
23140    HPLOT XX + DX,YY TO XX,YY TO XX,YY + DY
23150    RETURN
23200 DX = 2:DY = 2
23210    IF XX + DX > 279 THEN DX = 279 - XX
23220    IF YY + DY > 159 THEN DY = 159 - YY
23230    HPLOT  ABS (XX - 2), ABS (YY - 2) TO XX,YY TO  ABS (XX - 2),YY +

23240    HPLOT XX + DX, ABS (YY - 2) TO XX,YY TO XX + DX,YY + DY
23250    RETURN
24000    GOSUB 23000
24010 X3 = 2 * BP:Y1 = 2 * BP * X1:Y2 = 2 * BP * X2
24020 SX = X3 / 279:SY = Y2 / 159
24030 YY = 159 -  INT (F / SY)
24040    HPLOT 0,YY TO  INT (X3 / SX),YY
24060    HPLOT 0,YY TO  INT (X3 / SX),159 -  INT (Y1 / SY)
24070    HPLOT 0,159 TO  INT (X3 / SX),159 -  INT (Y2 / SY)
24080    FOR J = 0 TO X3 STEP  INT (X3 / 10.0)
24090 XX =  INT (J / SX):YY = 159 -  INT ((Y2 * J) / (X3 * SY))
24100    GOSUB 23100
24110 YY = 159 -  INT (((Y1 - F) * J / X3 + F) / SY)
24120    GOSUB 23200
24130    NEXT J
24140    PRINT "    +   REVENUE"
24150    PRINT "    X  VARIABLE COSTS"
24160    PRINT "    -   FIXED COSTS"
24170    INPUT "PRESS <RETURN> TO CONTINUE";Y3$
24180    TEXT : RETURN
24500    GOSUB 23000
24510 X1 = 1:X2 = NF:Y1 = R(1,1):Y2 = R(1,1)
24520    FOR J = 1 TO NF
24530    IF Y1 > R(J,1) THEN Y1 = R(J,1)
24540    IF Y1 > R(J,2) THEN Y1 = R(J,2)
24550    IF Y2 < R(J,1) THEN Y2 = R(J,1)
24560    IF Y2 < R(J,2) THEN Y2 = R(J,2)
24570    NEXT J
24580 SX = (X2 - X1) / 279:SY = (Y2 - Y1) / 159
24590    FOR J = 1 TO NF - 1
24600 XX =  INT ((J - 1) / SX):YY = 159 -  INT ((R(J,1) - Y1) / SY)
24610    GOSUB 23100
24620    HPLOT XX,YY TO  INT (J / SX),159 -  INT ((R(J + 1,1) - Y1) / SY)
24630 YY = 159 -  INT ((R(J,2) - Y1) / SY)
24640    GOSUB 23200
24650    HPLOT XX,YY TO  INT (J / SX),159 -  INT ((R(J + 1,2) - Y1) / SY)
24660    NEXT J
24670    PRINT "      +   REVENUE"
24680    PRINT "      X  TOTAL COSTS"
24690    INPUT "PRESS <RETURN> TO CONTINUE";Y3$
24700    TEXT : RETURN
25000 IE =  PEEK (222)
25010    IF IE = 255 GOTO 30000
25020    PRINT "ERROR, STATUS=";IE
30000    PRINT  CHR$ (4);"BRUN MASTER"


90   ONERR  GOTO 30000
100    REM
```

```
110   REM        ****************
120   REM        * PROGRAM SCEN *
130   REM        ****************
140   REM
145   DIM X(48),Y(48),YT(48),YS(48),YC(48),YI(48)
148 LL =  LOG (10)
150   PRINT : PRINT "      ******************"
160   PRINT "      * OPTION 5: SCEN *"
170   PRINT "      ******************": PRINT
180   PRINT "THIS PROGRAM CARRIES OUT VARIOUS"
190   PRINT "FORECASTS AND SHOULD BE USED IN"
200   PRINT "CONJUNCTION WITH..."
210   PRINT : PRINT "       CHAPTER 7"
220   PRINT "    SCENARIO PLANNING": PRINT
240   PRINT "OPTIONS AVAILABLE ARE...": PRINT
250   PRINT "    0    TERMINATE CURRENT RUN"
260   PRINT "    1    LINEAR REGRESSION"
265   PRINT "    2    NON-LINEAR REGRESSION"
270   PRINT "    3    TIME SERIES ANALYSIS (MONTHLY)"
272   PRINT "    4    TIME SERIES ANALYSIS (QUARTERLY)"
276   PRINT "    5    TIME SERIES ANALYSIS (YEARLY)"
280   PRINT "    6    EXPONENTIAL SMOOTHING": PRINT
290   INPUT "SELECT AN OPTION (0-6)";I
300   IF I < 0 OR I > 6 THEN  PRINT "INVALID OPTION": GOTO 290
310   IF I < 1 GOTO 30000
320   ON I GOSUB 1000,6000,2000,7000,8000,4000
330   PRINT : GOTO 240
1000   REM
1010   REM          LINEAR REGRESSION
1020   REM
1021   NL$ = "F"
1022   PRINT : PRINT "    ********************"
1024   PRINT "    * LINEAR REGRESSION *"
1026   PRINT "    ********************": PRINT
1030   PRINT "THIS OPTION ALLOWS YOU TO MAKE"
1040   PRINT "A LINEAR FORECAST USING THE MODEL": PRINT
1060   PRINT "      Y = A + BX": PRINT
1070   PRINT "WHERE:"
1080   PRINT "      Y IS THE DEPENDENT VARIABLE"
1090   PRINT "      X IS THE INDEPENDENT VARIABLE"
1100   PRINT : PRINT "FOR A GIVEN SET OF (X,Y) PAIRS"
1110   PRINT "THIS OPTION WILL CALCULATE THE "
1120   PRINT "REGRESSION COEFFICIENTS A & B": PRINT
1130   INPUT "HOW MANY (X,Y) PAIRS TO BE INPUT";N
1140   IF N > 2 AND N < 21 THEN  GOTO 1170
1150   PRINT "NUMBER OF PAIRS MUST BE IN RANGE 2-20"
1160   GOTO 1130
1170   FOR J = 1 TO N
1180   INPUT "  X,Y";X(J),Y(J)
1190   NEXT J
1200   PRINT "YOU HAVE INPUT THE FOLLOWING": PRINT
1210   PRINT  TAB( 11);"X"; TAB( 21);"Y"
1220   FOR J = 1 TO N
1230   PRINT  TAB( 10);X(J); TAB( 20);Y(J)
1240   NEXT J
1250   PRINT : INPUT "ARE THESE CORRECT (Y/N)";YN$: PRINT
1260   IF YN$ = "N" GOTO 1130
1270   IF YN$ <  > "Y" GOTO 1250
1280   PRINT "PLEASE WAIT, CALCULATING REGRESSION"
1285   IF NL$ = "T" GOTO 6100
1290   GOSUB 5000
1300   PRINT : PRINT "FOR THE DATA YOU HAVE INPUT THE"
1360   PRINT "REGRESSION EQUATION IS...": PRINT
1362 YL$ = "   Y = "
```

```
1364   IF NL$ = "T" THEN YL$ = " LOG(Y) = "
1365   IF B < 0 GOTO 1375
1370   PRINT YL$;A;"+";B;"X": PRINT : GOTO 1376
1375   PRINT YL$;A;"-"; ABS (B);"X"
1376   INPUT "GRAPH THIS (Y/N)?";YN$
1377   IF YN$ = "Y" THEN   GOSUB 26000
1380   INPUT "DO YOU WISH TO MAKE A FORECAST (Y/N)";YN$
1390   IF YN$ = "N" GOTO 1450
1400   IF YN$ < > "Y" GOTO 1380
1410   INPUT "INDEPENDENT VARIABLE (X) VALUE";XF
1420 YF = A + B * XF
1425   IF NL$ = "T" THEN YF =   EXP (LL * YF)
1430   PRINT : PRINT "FOR X = ";XF;" FORECAST VALUE=";YF: PRINT
1440   GOTO 1380
1450   RETURN
2000   REM
2010   REM         TIME SERIES ANALYSIS (MONTHLY)
2020   REM
2030   PRINT : PRINT "  ************************************"
2040   PRINT "  *TIME SERIES ANALYSIS: MONTHLY DATA*"
2050   PRINT "  ************************************": PRINT
2060   PRINT "THIS OPTION ALLOWS YOU TO MAKE A "
2070   PRINT "FORECAST USING THE MODEL..": PRINT
2080   PRINT "      Y = T.S.C.I": PRINT
2090   PRINT "WHERE:"
2100   PRINT "       Y IS THE DEPENDENT VARIABLE"
2110   PRINT "       T IS THE LINEAR TREND"
2120   PRINT "       S IS THE SEASONAL VARIATION"
2130   PRINT "       C IS THE CYCLICAL FLUCTUATION"
2140   PRINT "       I IS THE IRREGULAR COMPONENT"
2150   PRINT : PRINT "FOR THIS OPTION YOU MUST INPUT AT LEAST"
2160   PRINT "24 CONSECUTIVE MONTHS OF DATA"
2170   PRINT : INPUT "PRESS <RETURN> TO CONTINUE";YN$: PRINT
2180   INPUT "INPUT NUMBER OF MONTHS (24-48)";N
2182   IF N > = 24 AND N < 49 THEN   GOTO 2190
2184   PRINT "INVALID INPUT": GOTO 2180
2190   PRINT "INPUT OBSERVED VALUES FOR EACH MONTH"
2200   PRINT "ONE VALUE ON EACH LINE"
2210   FOR J = 1 TO N
2220   PRINT "MONTH ";J;: INPUT Y(J):X(J) = J
2230   NEXT J
2240   PRINT "YOU HAVE INPUT"
2250   FOR J = 1 TO 16
2260   PRINT  TAB( 10);Y(J);
2270   IF 16 + J < = N THEN   PRINT  TAB( 20);Y(16 + J);
2280   IF 32 + J < = N THEN   PRINT  TAB( 30);Y(32 + J);
2290   PRINT : NEXT J
2300   INPUT "ARE THESE CORRECT (Y/N)";YN$
2310   IF YN$ = "N" GOTO 2190
2320   IF YN$ < > "Y" GOTO 2300
2325   PRINT : PRINT "PLEASE WAIT, COMPUTING TIME SERIES": PRINT
2330   REM   COMPUTE TREND EQUATION (COEFFS RETURNED IN A & B)
2340   GOSUB 5000
2350   FOR J = 1 TO N:YT(J) = A + B * X(J): NEXT J
2360   REM   COMPUTE SEASONAL VARIATION
2370   KS = 1
2375 SY = 0.0
2380   FOR J = KS TO KS + 11:SY = SY + Y(J): NEXT J
2390   YS(KS) = SY / 12.0:KS = KS + 1
2400   IF KS + 11 < = N GOTO 2375
2410   KS = KS - 1:K = 1
2420   SY = 0.0
2430   FOR J = K TO K + 1:SY = SY + YS(J): NEXT J
2440   YS(K) = SY / 2.0:K = K + 1
```

```
2450   IF K + 1 <  = KS GOTO 2420
2460   KS = KS - 1
2470   FOR J = 1 TO KS
2480   YS(J) = Y(J + 6) * 100.0 / YS(J)
2490   NEXT J
2500   FOR J = 1 TO 12
2510   K = 1
2520   IF J + 12 <  = KS THEN YS(J) = YS(J) + YS(J + 12):K = K + 1
2530   IF J + 24 <  = KS THEN YS(J) = YS(J) + YS(J + 24):K = K + 1
2540   IF J + 32 <  = KS THEN YS(J) = YS(J) + YS(J + 32):K = K + 1
2550   YS(J) = YS(J) / K
2560   NEXT J
2570   FOR J = 1 TO 6:YC(J) = YS(J + 6): NEXT J
2580   FOR J = 7 TO 12:YC(J) = YS(J - 6): NEXT J
2585   K = 1
2590   FOR J = 1 TO 48
2600   YS(J) = YC(K):K = K + 1
2610   IF K > 12 THEN K = 1
2620   NEXT J
2630   REM   CALCULATE CYCLICAL AND IRREGULAR COMPONENTS
2640   FOR J = 1 TO N:YI(J) = Y(J) / (YS(J) * YT(J)): NEXT J
2650   K = 1
2660   SY = 0.0
2670   FOR J = K TO K + 2:SY = SY + YI(J): NEXT J
2680   YC(K) = SY / 3.0:K = K + 1
2690   IF K + 2 <  = N GOTO 2660
2700   FOR J = 1 TO N - 2:YI(J) = YI(J) / YC(J): NEXT J
2701   FOR J = N TO 3 STEP  - 1
2702   YC(J) = 10000.0 * YC(J - 2):YI(J) = 100.0 * YI(J - 2): NEXT J
2704   PRINT : PRINT " Y "; TAB( 8);" T"; TAB( 16);" S"; TAB( 24);" C";; TAB(
       32);" I": PRINT
2710   FOR J = 1 TO N
2720   YT(J) =   INT (100.0 * YT(J) + .5) / 100.0
2730   YS(J) =   INT (100.0 * YS(J) + .5) / 100.0
2740   YC(J) =   INT (100.0 * YC(J) + .5) / 100.0
2750   YI(J) =   INT (100.0 * YI(J) + .5) / 100.0
2760   PRINT Y(J); TAB( 8);YT(J); TAB( 16);YS(J); TAB( 24);
2770   IF J > 2 THEN   PRINT YC(J); TAB( 32);YI(J): GOTO 2772
2771   PRINT
2772   IF 20 *   INT (J / 20) <  > J GOTO 2780
2774   PRINT : INPUT "PRESS <RETURN> TO CONTINUE ";YN$: PRINT
2780   NEXT J
2790   INPUT "DO YOU WISH TO MAKE A FORECAST(Y/N)";YN$
2800   IF YN$ = "N" GOTO 2890
2810   IF YN$ <  > "Y" GOTO 2790
2820   INPUT "MONTH (NUMBER)";MN
2830   IF MN > 1 AND MN < 100 GOTO 2845
2840   PRINT "MONTH MUST BE IN RANGE 1 TO 100": GOTO 2790
2845   MN = MN - 1
2850   J =   ABS (MN - 12 *   INT (MN / 12)) + 1
2855   MN = MN + 1
2860   YF = (A + B * MN) * YS(J) / 100.0
2870   PRINT : PRINT "FOR MONTH NUMBER ";MN;" FORECAST IS ";YF: PRINT
2880   GOTO 2790
2890   PRINT : PRINT "DO YOU WANT A TABLE OF DESEASONALISED"
2990   INPUT "VALUES LISTED (Y/N)";YN$: PRINT
3000   IF YN$ = "N" GOTO 3110
3010   IF YN$ <  > "Y" GOTO 2890
3020   PRINT : PRINT "  DE-SEASONALISED VALUES"
3030   PRINT "_____": PRINT
3040   PRINT  TAB( 5);"MONTH"; TAB( 15);"ACTUAL"; TAB( 25);"DE-SEASONALISED
       "
3050   FOR J = 1 TO N
3055   YC(J) =   INT (100 * ((100 * Y(J)) / YS(J)) + .5) / 100
```

```
3060   PRINT   TAB( 5);X(J); TAB( 15);Y(J); TAB( 25);YC(J)
3070   IF J < > 20 *  INT (J / 20) GOTO 3090
3080   INPUT "PRESS <RETURN> TO CONTINUE";YN$
3090   NEXT J
3091   INPUT "GRAPH THIS (Y/N)?";YN$
3092   IF YN$ = "Y" THEN  GOSUB 28000
3110   RETURN
4000   REM
4010   REM        EXPONENTIAL SMOOTHING
4020   REM
4030   PRINT : PRINT "    ************************"
4040   PRINT "   * EXPONENTIAL SMOOTHING*"
4050   PRINT "    ************************": PRINT
4060   PRINT "THIS OPTION ALLOWS YOU TO MAKE"
4070   PRINT "A FORECAST USING THE EXPONENTIAL"
4080   PRINT "SMOOTHING MODEL...": PRINT
4090   PRINT "    U    = A.D  + (1-A).U"
4100   PRINT "     T+1     T          T": PRINT
4110   PRINT "WHERE:"
4120   PRINT "   U    IS THE FORECAST FOR PERIOD T+1"
4130   PRINT "    T+1"
4140   PRINT "   U    IS THE FORECAST FOR PERIOD T"
4150   PRINT "    T"
4160   PRINT "   A    IS THE EXPONENTIAL SMOOTHING"
4170   PRINT "        CONSTANT"
4180   PRINT "   D    IS THE OBSERVED VALUE FOR"
4190   PRINT "    T   PERIOD T"
4200   PRINT : INPUT "PRESS <RETURN> TO CONTINUE";YN$: PRINT
4210   INPUT "FORECAST FOR PERIOD T (MAKE A GUESS)";U1
4220   INPUT "SMOOTHING CONSTANT (TRY 0.2)       ";A
4230   INPUT "OBSERVED VALUE FOR PERIOD T        ";D
4240 U2 = A * D + (1 - A) * U1
4250   PRINT : PRINT "FORECAST VALUE FOR PERIOD T+1=";U2: PRINT
4260   INPUT "WANT A FORECAST FOR NEXT PERIOD (Y/N)";YN$
4270   IF YN$ = "N" GOTO 4370
4280   IF YN$ < > "Y" GOTO 4260
4290   INPUT "OBSERVED VALUE FOR NEXT PERIOD     ";D
4300   INPUT "CHANGE SMOOTHING CONSTANT (Y/N)";YN$
4310   IF YN$ = "N" GOTO 4340
4320   IF YN$ < > "Y" GOTO 4300
4330   INPUT "NEW SMOOTHING CONSTANT            ";A
4340 U1 = U2:U2 = A * D + (1 - A) * U1
4350   PRINT "FORECAST VALUE FOR NEXT PERIOD IS ";U2
4360   GOTO 4260
4370   RETURN
5000 SY = 0.0:SX = 0.0:XY = 0.0:XX = 0.0
5010   FOR J = 1 TO N
5020 SY = SY + Y(J):SX = SX + X(J):XY = XY + X(J) * Y(J):XX = XX + X(J)
     X(J)
5030   NEXT J
5040 B = (N * XY - SX * SY) / (N * XX - SX * SX)
5050 A = (XY * SX - SY * XX) / (SX * SX - N * XX)
5055 A =  INT (10000 * A + .5) / 10000
5056 B =  INT (10000 * B + .5) / 10000
5060   RETURN
6000   REM
6010   REM        NON-LINEAR REGRESSION
6020   REM
6025 NL$ = "T"
6030   PRINT : PRINT "    **********************"
6040   PRINT "   *NON-LINEAR REGRESSION*"
6050   PRINT "    **********************": PRINT
6060   PRINT "THIS OPTION ALLOWS YOU TO MAKE A"
6070   PRINT "FORECAST USING THE MODEL..": PRINT
```

```
6080   PRINT "      LOG(Y) = A + B.X": PRINT
6090   GOTO 1070
6100   FOR J = 1 TO N:Y(J) =  LOG (Y(J)) / LL: NEXT J
6110   GOTO 1290
7000   REM
7010   REM            TIME SERIES ANALYSIS (QUARTERLY)
7020   REM
7030   PRINT : PRINT "     ********************************"
7040   PRINT "     *TIME SERIES ANALYSIS (QUARTERLY)*"
7050   PRINT "     ********************************": PRINT
7060   PRINT "THIS OPTION ALLOWS YOU TO MAKE A"
7061   PRINT "FORECAST USING THE MODEL...": PRINT
7062   PRINT "     Y = T.S": PRINT : PRINT "WHERE:"
7063   PRINT "     Y IS THE DEPENDENT VARIABLE"
7064   PRINT "     T IS THE LINEAR TREND"
7065   PRINT "     S IS THE QUARTERLY SEASONAL INDEX": PRINT
7070   PRINT "GIVEN THE QUARTERLY OBSERVED VALUES"
7080   PRINT "FOR SEVERAL YEARS": PRINT
7090   INPUT "NUMBER OF YEARS (2-12) ";N
7100   IF N > 2 AND N < 12 GOTO 7130
7120   PRINT "ERROR, NUMBER OF YEARS NOT VALID"
7130   PRINT "PLEASE INPUT QUARTERLY VALUES NOW":KS = 1
7140   FOR J = 1 TO N: FOR K = 1 TO 4
7150   PRINT "YEAR ";J; TAB( 12);"QUARTER"; TAB( 20);K; TAB( 30);: INPUT Y(
       KS)
7160   X(KS) = KS:KS = KS + 1: NEXT K: NEXT J: PRINT
7170   N = KS - 1: PRINT "YOU HAVE INPUT..": PRINT
7180   PRINT "YEAR"; TAB( 8);" Q1"; TAB( 16);" Q2"; TAB( 24);" Q3"; TAB( 32
       );" Q4"
7185   KS = 1
7190   FOR J = 1 TO N STEP 4
7200   PRINT KS; TAB( 8);Y(J); TAB( 16);Y(J + 1); TAB( 24);Y(J + 2); TAB( 3
       2);Y(J + 3)
7210   KS = KS + 1: NEXT J: PRINT
7220   INPUT "ARE THESE FIGURES CORRECT (Y/N)";YN$
7230   IF YN$ = "N" GOTO 7090
7240   IF YN$ < > "Y" GOTO 7220
7250   PRINT : PRINT "PLEASE WAIT, COMPUTING TIME SERIES"
7260   KS = 1
7270   SY = 0.0
7280   FOR J = KS TO KS + 3:SY = SY + Y(J): NEXT J
7290   YS(KS) = SY / 4.0:KS = KS + 1
7300   IF KS + 3 < = N GOTO 7270
7310   KS = KS - 1:K = 1
7320   SY = 0.0
7322   FOR J = K TO K + 1:SY = SY + YS(J): NEXT J
7324   YS(K) = SY / 2.0:K = K + 1
7326   IF K + 1 < = KS GOTO 7320
7328   KS = K - 1
7330   FOR J = 1 TO KS:YS(J) = Y(J + 2) / YS(J): NEXT J
7336   FOR J = 1 TO 4
7338   L = 1
7340   FOR K = 2 TO 12
7350   IF J + (K - 1) * 4 < = KS THEN YS(J) = YS(J) + YS(J + (K - 1) * 4):
       L = L + 1
7360   NEXT K
7370   YS(J) = 100.0 * YS(J) / L: NEXT J
7375   YI(1) = YS(3):YI(2) = YS(4):YI(3) = YS(1):YI(4) = YS(2)
7380   PRINT : PRINT "  QUARTERLY SEASONAL INDEXES "
7390   PRINT "  ------------------------": PRINT
7400   PRINT " QUARTER"; TAB( 15);" INDEX"
7410   FOR J = 1 TO 4
7420   PRINT  TAB( 3);J; TAB( 15); INT (100. * YI(J) + .5) / 100.0: NEXT J:
       PRINT
```

```
7422  GOSUB 5000
7425  FOR J = 1 TO N:YT(J) =   INT ((A + B * X(J)) * 100. + .5) / 100: N
      J
7430  PRINT : INPUT "PRESS <RETURN> TO CONTINUE";YN$: PRINT
7435  PRINT "YEAR"; TAB( 8);"QUARTER"; TAB( 16);"ACTUAL"; TAB( 24);"TREI
      ; TAB( 32);
7436  PRINT  TAB( 32);"DESEASN": PRINT :K = 0:I = 0
7440  FOR J = 1 TO N
7445  I = I + 1
7446  IF I > 4 THEN I = 1
7450  IF (J - 1) = 4 *  INT ((J - 1) / 4) THEN K = K + 1
7455  YC(J) =   INT (100. * (100. * Y(J) / YI(I)) + .5) / 100.
7460  PRINT  TAB( 2);K; TAB( 10);I; TAB( 16);Y(J); TAB( 24);YT(J); TAB(
      );YC(J)
7470  IF J <  > 20 *  INT (J / 20) GOTO 7490
7480  INPUT "PRESS <RETURN> TO CONTINUE";YN$
7490  NEXT J
7492  N = KS
7495  INPUT "GRAPH THIS (Y/N)?";YN$
7496  IF YN$ = "Y" THEN  GOSUB 28000
7500  PRINT : INPUT "WANT TO MAKE A FORECAST(Y/N)";YN$: PRINT
7510  IF YN$ = "N" GOTO 7620
7520  IF YN$ <  > "Y" GOTO 7500
7530  INPUT "YEAR NUMBER ";YF
7540  IF YF < 1 OR YF > 12 THEN  PRINT "INVALID, YEAR MUST BE 2 TO 12":
      7530
7550  PRINT "FORECAST FOR YEAR ";YF: PRINT :YF = (YF - 1) * 4 + 1
7560  PRINT  TAB( 8);"QUARTER"; TAB( 16);"FORECAST"
7570  FOR J = 1 TO 4
7575  X = ((A + B * YF) * YI(J)) / 100.0
7580  PRINT  TAB( 10);J; TAB( 17);  INT (100. * X + .5) / 100.:YF = YF +
7590  NEXT J
7600  GOTO 7500
7610  PRINT : INPUT "PRESS <RETURN> TO CONTINUE";YN$: PRINT
7620  RETURN
8000  REM
8010  REM      TIME SERIES ANALYSIS (YEARLY)
8020  REM
8030  PRINT : PRINT "    *********************************"
8040  PRINT "    *TIME SERIES ANALYSIS (YEARLY)*"
8050  PRINT "    *********************************": PRINT
8060  PRINT "THIS OPTION DECOMPOSES ANNUAL DATA INTO"
8070  PRINT "TREND AND CYCLICAL ELEMENTS USING THE"
8075  PRINT "MODEL...": PRINT
8080  PRINT "     Y = T.C": PRINT
8090  PRINT "WHERE:"
8100  PRINT "     Y IS THE DEPENDENT VARIABLE"
8110  PRINT "     T IS THE LINEAR TREND"
8120  PRINT "     C IS THE CYCLICAL FLUCTUATION": PRINT
8130  PRINT "YOU MUST INPUT OBSERVED VALUES FOR "
8140  PRINT "A CONSECUTIVE NUMBER OF YEARS."
8150  INPUT "NUMBER OF YEARS (2-20)";N
8160  IF N > = 2 AND N < = 20 GOTO 8180
8170  PRINT "INVALID NUMBER OF YEARS ": GOTO 8150
8180  PRINT "INPUT OBSERVED VALUES FOR EACH YEAR NOW"
8190  FOR J = 1 TO N
8200  PRINT "YEAR ";J; TAB( 15);: INPUT Y(J):X(J) = J
8210  NEXT J
8220  PRINT : PRINT "YOU HAVE INPUT.."
8230  PRINT  TAB( 5);"YEAR"; TAB( 15);"VALUE"
8240  FOR J = 1 TO N: PRINT  TAB( 5);J; TAB( 15);Y(J): NEXT J
8250  PRINT : INPUT "ARE THESE CORRECT (Y/N)";YN$: PRINT
8260  IF YN$ = "N" GOTO 8130
8270  IF YN$ <  > "Y" GOTO 8250
```

```
8280    PRINT "PLEASE WAIT, COMPUTING TIME SERIES"
8290    GOSUB 5000
8300    FOR J = 1 TO N:YT(J) = A + B * X(J):YC(J) = 100.0 * Y(J) / YT(J): NEXT
        J
8310    PRINT : PRINT " YEAR"; TAB( 10);" Y"; TAB( 20);" T"; TAB( 30);" C"
8320    FOR J = 1 TO N
8330    YT(J) =   INT (YT(J) * 100.0 + .5) / 100.0:YC(J) =   INT (YC(J) * 100.0
        + .5) / 100.0
8340    PRINT  TAB( 2);J; TAB( 10);Y(J); TAB( 20);YT(J); TAB( 30);YC(J)
8350    NEXT J
8360    PRINT : INPUT "PRESS <RETURN> TO CONTINUE";YN$: PRINT
8370    RETURN
25000   IE =   PEEK (222)
25010    IF IE = 255 GOTO 30000
25020    PRINT "ERROR, STATUS=";IE
25030    GOTO 30000
26000    PRINT "PLEASE WAIT.."
26010   X1 = X(1):X2 = X(2):Y1 = Y(1):Y2 = Y(2)
26020    FOR J = 1 TO N
26030    IF X1 > X(J) THEN X1 = X(J)
26040    IF X2 < X(J) THEN X2 = X(J)
26070    IF Y1 > Y(J) THEN Y1 = Y(J)
26080    IF Y2 < Y(J) THEN Y2 = Y(J)
26085    NEXT J
26100    POKE 34,20: HGR : HOME
26110    HPLOT 0,0 TO 0,159 TO 279,159
26120   Y3 = A + B * X1:Y4 = A + B * X2
26121   SX = (X2 - X1) / 279
26122    IF Y4 > Y2 THEN Y2 = Y4
26123    IF Y3 < Y1 THEN Y1 = Y3
26124   SY = (Y2 - Y1) / 159
26130    HPLOT   INT ((X1 - X1) / SX), INT (159 - (Y3 - Y1) / SY) TO   INT ((X
        2 - X1) / SX), INT (159 - (Y4 - Y1) / SY)
26140    FOR J = 1 TO N
26150   XX =   INT ((X(J) - X1) / SX):YY =   INT (159 - (Y(J) - Y1) / SY)
26160    GOSUB 27000
26170    NEXT J
26190    PRINT "REGRESSION PLOT"
26195    PRINT "NOTE ORIGIN AT XMIN,YMIN"
26200    INPUT "PRESS <RETURN> TO CONTINUE";YN$
26210    TEXT : RETURN
27000    HPLOT  ABS (XX - 2),YY TO XX,YY TO XX, ABS (YY - 2)
27010   DX = 2:DY = 2
27020    IF XX + DX > 279 THEN DX = 279 - XX
27030    IF YY + DY > 159 THEN DY = 159 - YY
27040    HPLOT XX + DX,YY TO XX,YY TO XX,YY + DY
27050    RETURN
27100   DX = 2:DY = 2
27110    IF XX + DX > 279 THEN DX = 279 - XX
27120    IF YY + DX > 159 THEN DY = 159 - YY
27130    HPLOT  ABS (XX - 2), ABS (YY - 2) TO XX,YY TO  ABS (XX - 2),YY + DY
27140    HPLOT XX + DX, ABS (YY - 2) TO XX,YY TO XX + DX,YY + DY
27150    RETURN
28000    PRINT "PLEASE WAIT"
28010   X1 = X(1):X2 = X(N):Y1 = Y(1):Y2 = Y(N)
28015   SX = (X2 - X1) / 279
28020    FOR J = 1 TO N
28030   X(J) =   INT ((X(J) - X1) / SX)
28040    IF Y1 > Y(J) THEN Y1 = Y(J)
28050    IF Y1 > YT(J) THEN Y1 = YT(J)
28060    IF Y1 > YC(J) THEN Y1 = YC(J)
28070    IF Y2 < Y(J) THEN Y2 = Y(J)
28080    IF Y2 < YT(J) THEN Y2 = YT(J)
```

```
28090   IF Y2 < YC(J) THEN Y2 = YC(J)
28100   NEXT J
28110   SY = (Y2 - Y1) / 159
28130   POKE 34,20: HGR : HOME
28135   HPLOT 0,0 TO 0,159 TO 279,159
28140   HPLOT 0,159 -  INT ((YT(1) - Y1) / SY) TO 279,159 -  INT ((YT(N)
        Y1) / SY)
28150   FOR J = 1 TO N - 1
28160   XX = X(J):YY = 159 -  INT ((Y(J) - Y1) / SY): GOSUB 27000
28170   HPLOT XX,YY TO X(J + 1),159 -  INT ((Y(J + 1) - Y1) / SY)
28180   YY = 159 -  INT ((YC(J) - Y1) / SY): GOSUB 27100
28190   HPLOT XX,YY TO X(J + 1),159 -  INT ((YC(J + 1) - Y1) / SY)
28200   NEXT J
28210   PRINT "   + ACTUAL VALUES": PRINT "   X DE-SEASONALISED VALUES"
            PRINT     "   - LINEAR TREND"
28220   INPUT "PRESS <RETURN> TO CONTINUE";YN$
28230   TEXT : RETURN
30000   PRINT  CHR$ (4);"NOMON,C,I,O"
30001   PRINT  CHR$ (4);"BRUN MASTER"
```

Index

317